STUDY GUIDE

To accompany James T. McClave
and P. George Benson
STATISTICS FOR BUSINESS AND ECONOMICS
Fifth Edition

Susan L. Reiland

DELLEN PUBLISHING COMPANY, San Francisco
an imprint of
MACMILLAN PUBLISHING COMPANY, New York

MAXWELL MACMILLAN CANADA, Toronto

Printed in the United States of America.

Permissions: Dellen Publishing Company
400 Pacific Avenue
San Francisco, California 94133

Orders: Dellen Publishing Company
c/o Macmillan Publishing Company
Front and Brown Streets
Riverside, New Jersey 08075

Macmillan Publishing Company
866 Third Avenue
New York, New York 10022

Macmillan Publishing Company
is part of the
Maxwell Communication Group of Companies.

Maxwell Macmillan Canada, Inc.
1200 Eglinton Avenue East
Suite 200
Don Mills, Ontario M3C 3N1

ISBN: 0-02-399226-3

Printing: 1 2 3 4 5 6 Year: 1 2 3 4 5

PREFACE

This study guide is designed to accompany the textbook *Statistics for Business and Economics*, Fifth Edition, by McClave and Benson (Dellen Publishing Company, 1991). It is intended for use as a supplement to, and not a replacement for, the textbook. Thus, it is expected that the student will read the expository material in the textbook before referring to the corresponding sections of the study guide for reinforcement.

The following items are included for all chapters, which are titled and ordered as in the textbook:

1. A brief *summary* highlights the concepts and terms that were introduced and explained in the textbook material.

2. Section-by-section *examples* provide the student with relevant business applications of the statistical concepts; detailed *solutions* are given.

3. *Exercises* allow the student to check his or her mastery of the material in each section; *answers* for most exercises are included at the end of the study guide.

S. L. R.

CONTENTS

1
WHAT IS STATISTICS?

SUMMARY

Every statistical problem is composed of four elements: a population, a sample, an inference, and a measure of the reliability of the inference. It is the goal of statistics to use the information available in a *sample* to make an *inference* (that is, a decision, prediction, estimate, or generalization) about the *population* of measurements from which the sample was selected. With each inference is associated a measure of its *reliability*; each estimate or prediction will be accompanied by a bound on the estimation or prediction error, and each decision by a statement reflecting our confidence in the decision.

Examples

1.1 The New York Stock Exchange (NYSE) consists of a listing of approximately 1500 companies that offer shares of company stock to the public. Stock brokers are interested not only in the individual stocks, but also in general trends established by the market as a whole. They often base inferences upon the daily closing prices of the group of 30 NYSE stocks that comprise the Dow Jones Industrial Index.

a. Identify the population, the sample, and the variable in the context of this problem.

b. What are some inferences of possible interest to a stock broker? How would the reliability of the inferences be assessed?

Solution

a. *Population:* the set of all 1500 companies on the New York Stock Exchange.

Sample: the set of the 30 Dow Jones Industrial stocks. (Note that the sample is a subset of the population about which inferences are to be made.)

Variable: the daily closing price of a company's stock.

b. The broker may be interested in estimating the average closing price of a share of stock on the NYSE, or the percentage of stocks whose closing prices were less than $75 per share on a particular day. Each estimate would be accompanied by a bound on the prediction error, i.e., by a numerical value that the error of the prediction is unlikely to exceed.

1.2 The Environmental Protection Agency (EPA) performs gasoline mileage tests on new automobiles. In one recent test, the EPA reported that results of testing on 20 new automobiles of a particular model indicated an average mileage per gallon rating of 36.3.

a. Specify the sample, the variable, and the population of interest.

b. How might a potential automobile buyer use the information provided by the EPA?

Solution

a. *Sample:* the set of 20 autos used in this test.

Variable: the miles per gallon of each auto.

Population: the set of all new autos of this particular model.

b. The buyer would be interested in predicting the average gasoline mileage that would be achieved by the auto he or she purchases.

Exercises

1.1 A recent survey concluded that among all 1990 college graduates with degrees in Business, accounting majors had the highest average starting salary, at $2086 per month.

a. Identify the population about which the inference was made.

b. What is needed to complete the inferential statement?

1.2 The Nielsen ratings are used to rank the major network programs. A recent game on Monday Night Football was being watched in 223 of the 972 homes contacted by the Nielsen pollsters. Make an inference about the popularity of Monday Night Football.

1.3 At ticket gates at many airports across the country is posted the following notice: "Due to deliberate overbooking of flights, there may not be a seat available for everyone who has a ticket. . . ." Because of the loss of revenue due to "no-shows" (those who hold a reservation but fail to appear for the flight and do not notify the airline in advance), it is a common practice among airlines to overbook certain flights intentionally. To determine how many reservations should be taken for a particular flight, the airline must develop a reliable estimate of the percentage of no-shows.

a. How might the goal of the airline be accomplished?

b. Specify the population of interest in this problem.

c. If you were in charge of customer relations for the airline, what information do you think would be useful in evaluating the reliability of the estimate? (This notion will be treated formally in subsequent chapters.)

1.4 Refer to Example 1.1. What is the *largest* possible sample of NYSE stocks that could be selected on a given day? What would you say about the reliability of inferences made from this particular sample?

1.5 Examine some recent issues of *Business Week*, *Forbes*, *Wall Street Journal*, or other business magazines. Look for applications of statistics in articles or advertisements in which decisions, estimates, or predictions are being made. Are the population, variable, and sample clearly identified? Do the inferences always contain an associated measure of reliability?

2
GRAPHICAL DESCRIPTIONS OF DATA

SUMMARY

Since the objective of statistics is to use sample data to make inferences about a population, we must be able to summarize and describe the sample measurements. Graphical methods are useful techniques for describing qualitative (nominal and ordinal) data and quantitative (interval and ratio) data. The *bar chart* and *pie chart* are graphical tools used to describe qualitative data sets. The *stem and leaf display*, *relative frequency histogram*, and *time series plot* are important graphical techniques for describing quantitative data sets.

Although graphical methods easily convey a visual description of a data set, it is difficult to obtain measures of reliability for inferences made from graphical summaries. Thus, the techniques discussed in this chapter will be supplemented by numerical methods of data description, to be presented in Chapter 3.

2.1 TYPES OF DATA

Examples

2.1 Consumer preference studies are often conducted by specialists in market research. Consider a questionnaire designed to be administered to customers at a local shopping center. The following information may be requested from each customer interviewed:

a. Sex
b. Age
c. Marital status
d. Type of store visited most frequently at the shopping center
e. Number of visits per month customer makes to shopping center
f. Annual income of household
g. Time of day it is most convenient for customer to shop

Classify the data generated in response to the questionnaire items as one of four types: nominal, ordinal, interval, or ratio.

Solution

a. nominal
b. ratio
c. nominal
d. nominal
e. ratio
f. ratio
g. interval

2.2 Classify the following examples of business data as either nominal, ordinal, interval, or ratio.

a. The interest rate charged on all home mortgages by a savings and loan association during the past 6 months.

b. The cash value of inventory on hand for each of the country's publishers of college textbooks.

c. The day of the week indicated by each of a sample of 200 newspaper publishers as the day for which most advertising is sold.

d. The brand of the best-selling lawn mower at each of the 10 largest discount store chains in the Southeast.

e. The percent increase in arrests for traffic violations by the Highway Patrol departments of the 48 contiguous United States after enactment of the 55 miles per hour speed limit.

Solution

a. ratio
b. ratio
c. nominal
d. nominal
e. ratio

2.3 When one applies for a major credit card, standard biographical information is requested. Classify the responses to the following items as nominal, ordinal, interval, or ratio.

a. City of residence
b. Length of time at current residence
c. Bank reference
d. Type of job
e. Monthly salary
f. Number of dependents
g. Maximum amount of credit for which application is being made

Solution

a. nominal
b. ratio
c. nominal
d. nominal
e. ratio
f. ratio
g. ratio

Exercises

2.1 Futures (commodities) markets are often used in forecasting business activity. Classify each of the examples of market data given below as nominal, ordinal, interval, or ratio.

a. The level of yield on interest rate futures.

b. The price of a bushel of wheat, deliverable in May.

c. The month during which gold futures were most actively traded.

2.2 Classify the following examples of business data as nominal, ordinal, interval, or ratio.

a. The amount paid in federal taxes last year by each of the country's 500 largest industrial corporations.

b. The highest educational degree attained by each employee of a scientific research corporation.

c. The political party affiliation of a sample of mayors from cities with populations of at least 500,000.

d. The number of claims filed with an automobile insurance company on Tuesdays following three-day holiday weekends during the past year.

e. The largest selling brand of soft contact lenses in each of the states where advertising by optometrists is permitted by law.

f. The cost of a routine examination by each of a sample of 40 dentists engaged in private practice in the Northeast.

2.3 Give some examples of nominal, ordinal, interval, and ratio data which may arise from a survey in a field of particular interest to you.

2.2 GRAPHICAL METHODS FOR DESCRIBING QUALITATIVE DATA: THE BAR CHART (Optional)

Examples

2.4 A questionnaire administered recently to the subordinate staff at a large electronics firm indicated that 23 individuals thought they were overpaid, 76 thought they were adequately paid, and 63 thought they were underpaid. Compute the relative frequency for each response category.

Solution

It is first required to compute $n = 23 + 76 + 63 = 162$. Then the relative frequencies are calculated as shown in the table.

CATEGORY	FREQUENCY f_i	RELATIVE FREQUENCY f_i/n
Overpaid	23	23/162 = .14
Adequately paid	76	76/162 = .47
Underpaid	63	63/162 = .39
	n = 162	162/162 = 1.00

Note that the sum of the frequencies will equal n, the number of measurements in the sample, and the sum of the relative frequencies will equal 1.

2.5 Construct a frequency bar chart and a relative frequency bar chart for the qualitative data of Example 2.4.

Solution

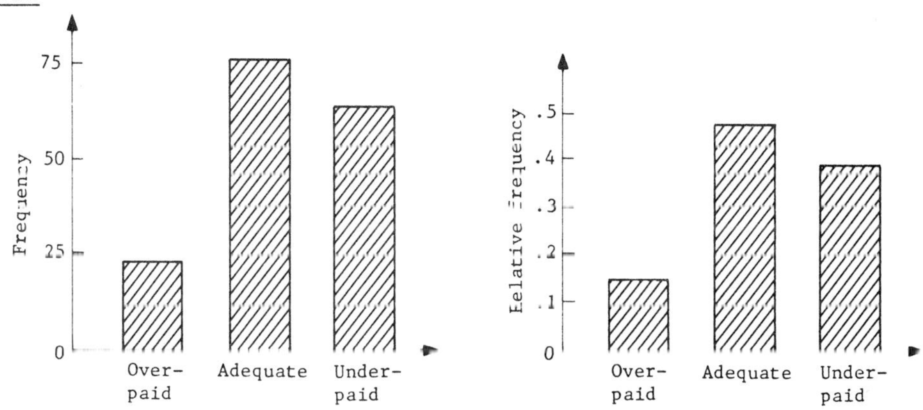

FREQUENCY BAR CHART   RELATIVE FREQUENCY BAR CHART

Note that for a given category, the height of the bar is proportional to the category frequency (or relative frequency).

Exercises

2.4 A survey of 200 homes in a major metropolitan area indicated that 90 subscribe to the morning newspaper, 72 subscribe to the evening paper, 14 receive both papers, and the remainder subscribe to neither. Construct a relative frequency bar chart for the data.

2.5 A restaurant in financial trouble conducted a survey to help determine why it was not attracting more customers. Each respondent was asked to state the primary reason why he or she does not eat at the restaurant. The results were classified as follows:

Too expensive	48
Quality of food	19
Inconvenient location	17
Unfamiliar with the restaurant	31
Other reason	35

a. Construct a relative frequency bar chart for the data.

b. Based on this sample, in which area(s) would you advise the restaurant to concentrate its effort to attract customers?

2.6 Fifty customers in the housewares section of a department store were asked to state their primary reason for visiting the store today. Construct a relative frequency bar chart to describe the following results:

Return an item purchased previously	8
Make a new purchase	24
Browse	14
Other	4

2.3 GRAPHICAL METHODS FOR DESCRIBING QUALITATIVE DATA: THE PIE CHART (Optional)

Example

2.6 A sample of 300 mortgage applications yielded the following information on the applicant's current residence:

Own home	130
Own condominium	35
Rent apartment	110
Rent house	15
Other	10

Construct a pie chart to depict this qualitative data.

Solution

The size of the pie slice allocated to a particular category is proportional to the relative frequency of the category. Thus, the relative frequencies and corresponding slices assigned are computed in the table.

CATEGORY	RELATIVE FREQUENCY	SIZE OF PIE SLICE
Own home	130/300 = .433	.433 × 360° = 156°
Own condominium	35/300 = .117	.117 × 360° = 42°
Rent apartment	110/300 = .367	.367 × 360° = 132°
Rent house	15/300 = .050	.050 × 360° = 18°
Other	10/300 = .033	.033 × 360° = 12°

The resulting pie chart is:

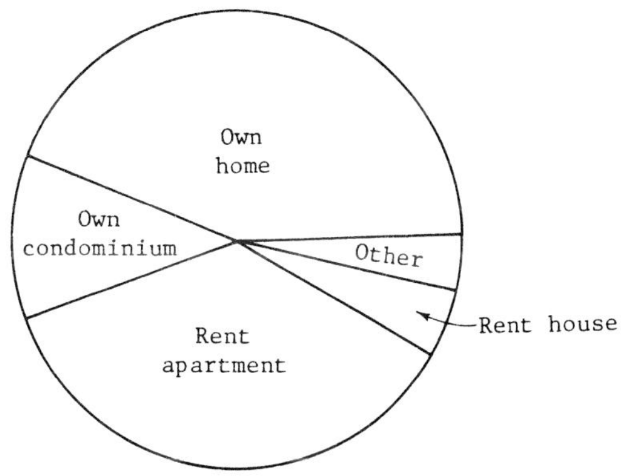

Exercises

2.7 To gain insight on how well the law works to compensate the victims of automobile accidents, a study into auto accidents was undertaken by a citizen's lobby group. The resulting distribution of reparations is as follows:

SOURCE OF REPARATION TO INJURED PARTY	PERCENT OF TOTAL DOLLARS
Liability of third parties who had negligently caused the accident	55
Injured's own insurance:	
Accident	22
Hospital and medical	11
Life and burial	5
Social Security	2
Employer and Workmen's Compensation	1
Other	4

Illustrate the distribution of reparations with a pie chart.

2.8 The following pie chart represents the distribution of working capital for a major advertising firm:

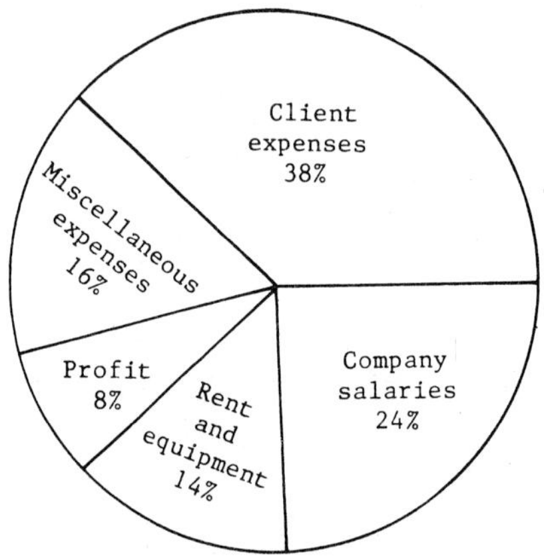

a. How many degrees of the circle does each slice of the pie occupy?

b. If last month's working capital was \$200,000, how much was allocated to each of the separate categories?

2.4 GRAPHICAL METHODS FOR DESCRIBING QUANTITATIVE DATA: STEM AND LEAF DISPLAYS

Example

2.7 The following data set represents a sample of the amount spent on textbooks in one semester by accounting majors at a large state university:

153	198	179	248	148
181	253	258	203	180
209	181	204	216	176
169	195	132	233	195
152	127	277	169	209

Construct a stem and leaf display for the textbook cost data.

Solution

The first number in the data set is 153. We will designate the first two digits (15) of this number as its stem; we will call the last digit (3) its leaf, as illustrated here:

Stem	Leaf
15	3

The stem and leaf of the number 181 are 18 and 1, respectively. Similarly, the stem and leaf of the number 209 are 20 and 9, respectively.

The first step in forming a stem and leaf display for this data set is to list all stem possibilities in a column starting with the smallest stem (12, corresponding to the number 127) and ending with the largest (27, corresponding to the number 277), as shown in the figure. The next step is to place the leaf of each number in the data set in the row of the display corresponding to the number's stem. For example, for the number 153, the leaf 3 is placed in the stem row 15. Similarly, for the number 181, the leaf 1 is placed in the stem row 18.

After the leaves of the twenty-five numbers are placed in the appropriate stem rows, the completed stem and leaf display will appear as shown in the figure at the right. You can see that the stem and leaf display partitions the data set into sixteen categories corresponding to the sixteen stems.

Stems	Leaves
12	7
13	2
14	8
15	32
16	99
17	96
18	110
19	855
20	9439
21	6
22	
23	3
24	8
25	38
26	
27	7

Exercises

2.9 Consider the following sample data:

213	228	241	268	234	303
274	316	319	320	227	226
224	267	303	266	265	237
288	291	285	270	254	215

a. Using the first two digits of each number as a stem, list the stem possibilities in order.

b. Place the leaf for each observation in the appropriate stem row to form a stem and leaf display.

2.10 Hospitals are required to file a yearly cost report in order to obtain reimbursement from the state for patient bills paid through the Medicare, Medicaid, and Blue Cross programs. Many factors contribute to the amount of reimbursement that the hospital receives. One important factor is bed size (i.e., the total number of beds available for patient use). The data below represent the bed sizes for fifty-four hospitals that were satisfied with their cost report reimbursements last year. Construct a stem and leaf display for the bed size data.

303	550	243	282	195	310
288	188	190	335	473	169
292	492	200	478	182	172
231	375	171	262	198	313
600	264	311	371	145	242
278	183	215	719	519	382
249	350	99	218	300	450
337	330	252	400	514	427
533	930	319	210	550	488

2.5 GRAPHICAL METHODS FOR DESCRIBING QUANTITATIVE DATA: HISTOGRAMS

Example

2.8 The following data constitute a sample of closing prices of 50 stocks from the New York Stock Exchange. (Prices have been rounded off to the first decimal.)

31.4	23.6	11.8	24.9	83.8	40.0	16.6	10.4	4.9	19.0
77.0	34.9	23.3	35.5	40.1	11.9	15.5	24.1	10.1	19.3
19.6	15.3	28.9	6.6	38.8	4.0	2.4	8.5	7.6	22.3
48.9	47.1	16.8	17.8	32.3	8.9	21.3	16.9	31.5	21.5
16.8	29.0	29.6	12.1	11.8	23.4	30.3	15.6	49.3	18.4

Construct a relative frequency histogram to summarize this quantitative data set.

Solution

We will construct eight measurement classes for the data on closing prices. The smallest measurement is 2.4, so we begin the first class at 2.35. To determine the length of each measurement class, we observe that the data span a range of 83.8 - 2.4 = 81.4; thus, each measurement class should have a length of 81.4/8, or approximately 10.2. The measurement classes, frequencies, and relative frequencies are shown below.

MEASUREMENT CLASS	FREQUENCY	RELATIVE FREQUENCY
2.35-12.55	13	13/50 = .26
12.55-22.75	15	.30
22.75-32.95	12	.24
32.95-43.15	5	.10
43.15-53.35	3	.06
53.35-63.55	0	.00
63.55-73.75	0	.00
73.75-83.95	2	.04

The relative frequencies are plotted as rectangles over the corresponding measurement classes in the histogram below.

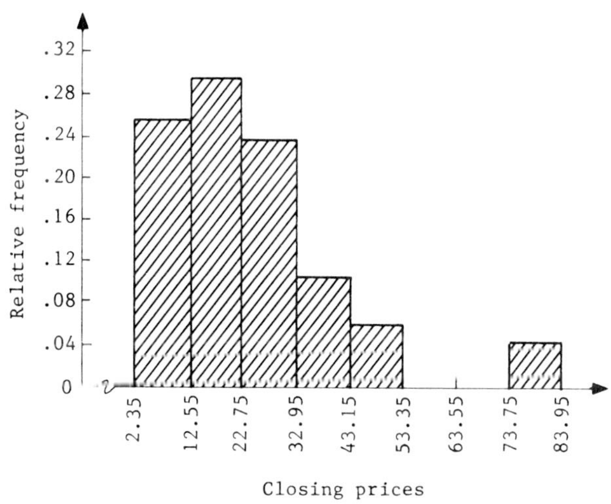

Exercises

2.11 Forty drivers from Southern California reported the following amounts (in dollars) spent on annual automobile insurance premiums:

320	297	423	193	403	203	443	179
276	223	163	208	198	278	303	199
195	185	297	297	241	236	270	287
403	190	248	253	250	323	285	236
383	238	220	347	291	410	230	263

Construct a relative frequency histogram for these data, using six measurement classes.

2.12 a. Repeat Exercise 2.11, using four measurement classes.

b. Repeat Exercise 2.11, using eight measurement classes.

c. How do the graphical representations of the data differ as the number of measurement classes is changed?

2.13 A real estate broker wishes to describe the price distribution of single-family homes in a particular area. The following data show the sales prices (in thousands of dollars) of the last 20 homes sold in the area.

157.0	149.2	162.8	166.7
159.5	156.0	188.0	178.2
148.7	164.3	170.9	155.6
197.5	172.1	166.2	158.0
183.1	159.4	159.9	163.0

Construct a relative frequency histogram for the data.

2.14 The following histogram summarizes the distribution of 1990 total deposits for a sample of 200 members of the Association of Bank Holding Companies.

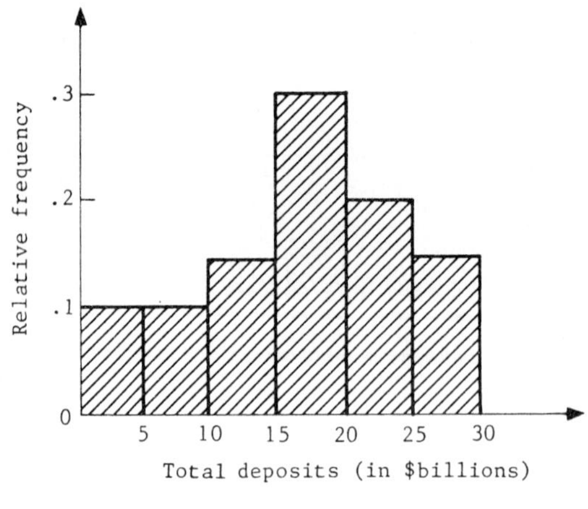

a. How many of the sampled holding companies had 1990 total deposits of at least $20 billion?

b. From the information provided by the histogram, how might you numerically describe the distribution of 1987 total deposits for this sample of holding companies?

2.6 GRAPHICAL METHODS FOR DESCRIBING QUANTITATIVE DATA: CUMULATIVE RELATIVE FREQUENCY DISTRIBUTIONS (Optional)

Example

2.9 Refer to Example 2.8. Construct a cumulative relative frequency distribution for the data on closing prices.

Solution

We will first calculate the cumulative frequency and the cumulative relative frequency for each class:

MEASUREMENT CLASS	FREQUENCY	CUMULATIVE FREQUENCY	RELATIVE FREQUENCY	CUMULATIVE RELATIVE FREQUENCY
2.35–12.55	13	13	.26	.26
12.55–22.75	15	28	.30	.56
22.75–32.95	12	40	.24	.80
32.95–43.15	5	45	.10	.90
43.15–53.35	3	48	.06	.96
53.35–63.55	0	48	.00	.96
63.55–73.75	0	48	.00	.96
73.75–83.95	2	50	.04	1.00

The cumulative relative frequency distribution is now graphed by plotting the class cumulative relative frequency as a rectangle over the corresponding measurement class.

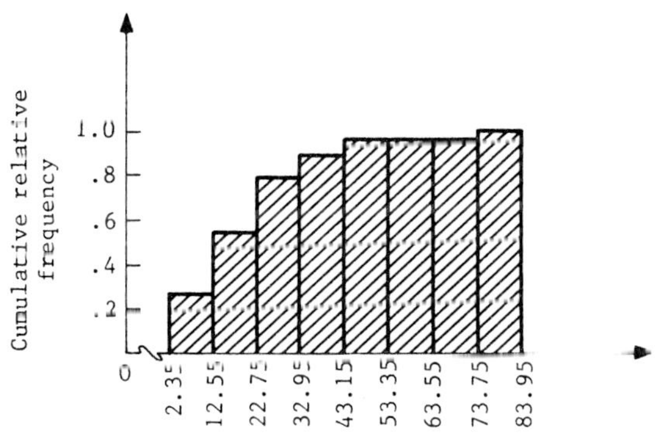

Exercises

2.15 Refer to Exercise 2.11. Construct a cumulative relative frequency distribution for the automobile insurance premium data.

2.16 Refer to Exercise 2.13. Construct a cumulative relative frequency distribution for the sale price data.

3
NUMERICAL DESCRIPTIVE MEASURES

SUMMARY

In this chapter, several numerical measures for describing the central tendency and variability of a data set were presented.

The *mode* is the measurement that is observed most frequently in the data set. The *mean* is the arithmetic average of a set of quantitative data; it is the most preferred measure for making inferences about the central tendency of the population. The *median* of a data set is a number such that half the measurements fall below the median and half fall above. The relative positions of the mean and median provide information about the *skewness* of the frequency distribution.

The simplest measure of the variability of a quantitative data set is the *range*. However, the *variance* and *standard deviation* are the preferred measures for purposes of making inferences about a population.

We may use the mean and standard deviation to make statements about the fraction of measurements within a specified interval. One rule, based on Chebyshev's theorem, applies to any sample of measurements, regardless of the shape of the frequency distribution. The Empirical Rule is applicable when the frequency distribution for the sample is mound-shaped.

To describe the location of a specific measurement relative to the rest of the data set, a measure of *relative standing*, such as a *percentile* or *quartile* or *z score*, is used. A *box plot* may be used to detect *outliers* in a data set.

The *rare event* approach to inference making was illustrated in this chapter. The principle of this method is the following: The more unlikely it is that a particular sample came from a hypothesized population, the more strongly we tend to believe that the hypothesized population is not the one from which the sample was selected.

3.1 THE MODE: A MEASURE OF CENTRAL TENDENCY

Examples

3.1 The following data show the number of hospitalizations required during the past two years by the vice presidents of a privately owned state bank:

0, 3, 0, 0, 1, 0, 2, 1

Calculate the mode for these data.

Solution

The measurement 0 is observed four times, more frequently than any other value. Thus, the mode for this data set is 0.

3.2 The following relative frequency distribution shows the ages at purchase of the first home in a metropolitan area. Find the mode for these data.

CLASS	RELATIVE FREQUENCY	CLASS	RELATIVE FREQUENCY
27.5-32.5	.05	47.5-52.5	.10
32.5-37.5	.10	52.5-57.5	.06
37.5-42.5	.35	57.5-62.5	.04
42.5-47.5	.30		

Solution

The modal class, the interval containing the most measurements, is 37.5-42.5. Thus, the mode is equal to the midpoint of this class interval, or $(37.5 + 42.5)/2 = 40.0$.

3.3 An electronics company reported the following sales figures (in thousands) for televisions last year:

TYPE OF TELEVISION	NUMBER OF TELEVISIONS SOLD
Portable (color)	41
Portable (black/white)	16
Console (color)	25
Console (black/white)	19

How might the proprietor of a retail sales outlet for the company use this information when ordering the inventory for next year?

Solution

The proprietor may observe that the modal type of television sold last year was the portable color variety. It would be advisable to have an adequate supply of portable color sets on hand for the upcoming year.

Exercises

3.1 The numbers of automobile insurance claims received at a district office were recorded for 10 consecutive business days as follows:

0, 2, 3, 1, 3, 2, 4, 3, 2, 3

Compute the mode for this set of data.

3.2 The following is the relative frequency distribution of 500 Civil Service examination scores achieved by recent job applicants with the United States Postal Service. Determine the modal examination score for this group of applicants.

CLASS	RELATIVE FREQUENCY	CLASS	RELATIVE FREQUENCY
19.5-39.5	.12	59.5-79.5	.36
39.5-59.5	.28	79.5-99.5	.24

3.3 Why is the mode of particular interest as a measure of central tendency to a production manager in a shoe factory?

3.2 THE ARITHMETIC MEAN: A MEASURE OF CENTRAL TENDENCY

Examples

3.4 Compute $\sum_{i=1}^{4} x_i$, where $x_1 = 2$, $x_2 = 4$, $x_3 = 7$, and $x_4 = 5$.

Solution

The summation notation tells us to sum the measurements beginning with x_1 and ending with x_4. Thus,

$$\sum_{i=1}^{4} x_i = x_1 + x_2 + x_3 + x_4 = 2 + 4 + 7 + 5 = 18.$$

3.5 Eight employees of a university administration were asked to report the number of miles traveled using mass transportation during a typical week. The responses were as follows:

$$50,\ 0,\ 100,\ 65,\ 420,\ 70,\ 0,\ 100$$

Compute the mean for this sample of measurements.

Solution

$$\bar{x} = \frac{\sum_{i=1}^{n} x_i}{n} = \frac{\sum_{i=1}^{8} x_i}{8} = \frac{50 + 0 + 100 + 65 + 420 + 70 + 0 + 100}{8}$$

$$= \frac{805}{8} = 100.6$$

The employees travel, on the average, 100.6 miles per week using mass transportation.

3.6 The following data represent the daily profits on 15 randomly chosen business days for a boutique specializing in leather gift items:

\$70.11	\$71.46	\$69.96	\$81.70	\$69.25
78.12	79.47	61.73	51.35	64.37
88.37	80.37	81.00	71.29	78.83

Compute the mean profit for these 15 business days.

Solution

$$\bar{x} = \frac{\sum_{i=1}^{15} x_i}{15} = \frac{70.11 + 78.12 + 88.37 + \cdots + 64.37 + 78.83}{15} = \$73.16$$

The average profit realized was \$73.16.

Exercises

3.4 Compute $\sum_{i=1}^{5} x_i$, where $x_1 = 3$, $x_2 = 4$, $x_3 = 5$, $x_4 = 2$, and $x_5 = 1$.

3.5 The unemployment rates (in percent) for the six largest cities of a southern state during the third quarter of 1989 were reported as follows:

6.8 7.3 7.8 5.9 8.2 6.5

Compute the mean unemployment rate for this group of cities.

3.6 Refer to Example 2.8. Calculate the mean closing price for the sample of 50 stocks.

3.7 The following data show the Graduate Management Aptitude Test (GMAT) scores for a group of eight mathematics majors who are applying for admission to a graduate business school. Compute the mean GMAT score for this sample of applicants:

540, 480, 520, 690, 630, 450, 640, 580

3.8 The number of hours of "down-time" for a university computing system was recorded for six consecutive days, during which time new tape drive equipment was being installed and tested. Compute the average "down-time" for the following results:

10.2, 6.3, 4.0, 2.1, 8.5, 4.6

3.3 THE MEDIAN: ANOTHER MEASURE OF CENTRAL TENDENCY

Examples

3.7 Many companies have a majority of young employees who receive lower salaries than more experienced people. Thus, there is often an imbalance between the bottom and top levels of a company's salary structure. Consider the following salaries (in thousands of dollars) for seven employees of an advertising agency:

25.1, 24.9, 20.9, 21.4, 72.2, 22.3, 21.8

Compute the median salary for these employees.

Solution

It is first required to arrange the seven measurements in ascending order:

20.9, 21.4, 21.8, 22.3, 24.9, 25.1, 72.2

Since the number of measurements is odd, the median is the middle observation. Thus, the median salary for this sample of employees is $22,300.

3.8 Refer to Example 3.7. Suppose the agency hires an additional junior executive at a salary of $48,000. Determine the median salary for the eight employees.

Solution

The new salary is recorded in thousands of dollars as 48.0. Then the sample is ordered as follows:

20.9, 21.4, 21.8, 22.3, 24.9, 25.1, 48.0, 72.2

The number of measurements is even, so the median is the average of the middle two observations:

$$\text{Median} = \frac{22.3 + 24.9}{2} = 23.6$$

The median salary is increased to $23,600 with the hiring of the new employee.

Exercises

3.9 The following data represent the number of days beyond the estimated completion date required to finish six building construction projects. (Negative values indicate the construction was completed before the target date.)

4, 23, -6, 12, -20, 31

Calculate the median for this sample.

3.10 Refer to Exercise 3.9. Eliminate the smallest measurement (-20) and compute the median of the remaining five measurements.

Supplementary Exercises

3.11 Refer to Example 3.7.

a. Compute the mean salary for the seven employees of the advertising agency.

b. Which measure (mean or median) is more appropriate for describing the central tendency of this data set?

3.12 Give an example of a situation in which the mode would be a more appropriate measure of central tendency than the mean.

3.13 Suppose you are interviewed for a job and are offered a starting salary of $27,500 per year. What would be your reaction to this offer if you had the additional information that:

a. The mean starting salary for all jobs of this type is $29,000.

b. The mean starting salary for all jobs of this type is $27,000.

c. The modal starting salary is $27,500.

d. The median starting salary is $27,000.

e. The mean starting salary is $29,000, the median is $27,000, and the mode is $26,000.

f. The mean starting salary is $27,000 and the median is $28,000.

3.4 THE RANGE: A MEASURE OF VARIABILITY

Examples

3.9 The following two data sets show the salaries (in thousands of dollars) for five industrial salesmen from each of two different companies. Compute the range in salaries for each sample.

COMPANY A	COMPANY B
37	66
61	58
79	51
76	63
47	62

Solution

For Company A: Range = largest salary - smallest salary
= 79 - 37
= 42

The salaries for these salesmen in Company A have a range of $42,000.

Similarly, for Company B: Range = 66 - 51 = 15

The sample salaries from Company A are more variable than those from Company B.

3.10 The following histograms show the relative frequencies of years of experience for the managers of two companies. Compute the range in years of experience for the two companies and comment on why the range is often an inadequate measure of the variability of a set of data.

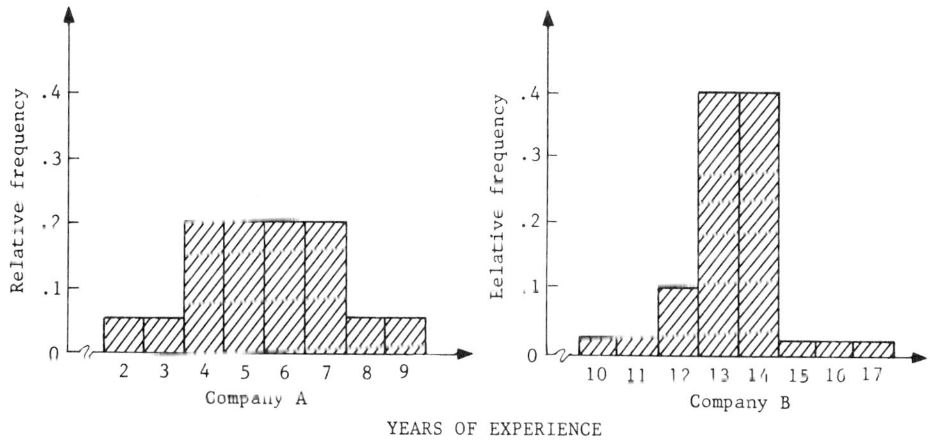

Solution

For Company A: Range = 9 - 2 = 7 years
For Company B: Range = 17 - 10 = 7 years

Although the ranges of the two data sets are equal, the measurements for Company A are more spread out than are those for Company B. A more informative numerical measure of variability is necessary for these data sets.

Exercises

3.14 The net operating incomes (in millions of dollars) of 12 leading banks in the United States last year are given below:

257	182	180	81	105	56
313	127	91	96	85	38

Find the range in operating incomes for these banks.

3.15 The Chamber of Commerce of a large city is interested in monthly rental rates of three-bedroom, two-bath apartments in the area. Managers of seven apartment complexes submitted the following rental rates for their three-bedroom, two-bath units:

$350, $415, $285, $245, $510, $360, $390

Compute the range in rental rates for this sample.

3.5 VARIANCE AND STANDARD DEVIATION

Examples

3.11 Compute the variance and standard deviation for the sample of Company A salaries in Example 3.9.

Solution

It is necessary first to compute the sample mean salary:

$$\bar{x} = \frac{\Sigma x_i}{n} = \frac{37 + 61 + 79 + 76 + 47}{5} = \frac{300}{5} = 60$$

The calculations required for s^2 are shown in the following table.

DATA: x_i	$x_i - \bar{x}$	$(x_i - \bar{x})^2$
27	$37 - 60 = -23$	$(-23)^2 = 529$
51	$61 - 60 = 1$	$(1)^2 = 1$
69	$79 - 60 = 19$	$(19)^2 = 361$
66	$76 - 60 = 16$	$(16)^2 = 256$
37	$47 - 60 = -13$	$(-13)^2 = 169$
$\Sigma x_i = 300$		$\Sigma(x_i - \bar{x})^2 = 1316$

Now, $s^2 = \dfrac{\Sigma(x_i - \bar{x})^2}{n - 1} = \dfrac{1316}{5 - 1} = \dfrac{1316}{4} = 329$, and $s = \sqrt{329} = 18.14$.

For these data, the sample variance is 329 and the standard deviation is 18.14.

3.12 Records for eight multinational corporations indicated the following percentages of total company assets held in the United States:

80 46 76 54 55 44 58 51

Compute the mean and variance for this sample of measurements.

Solution

For this set of data

$$\bar{x} = \frac{\Sigma x_i}{n} = \frac{80 + 46 + 76 + 54 + 55 + 44 + 58 + 51}{8} = \frac{464}{8} = 58.$$

Then

$$s^2 = \frac{\Sigma(x_i - \bar{x})^2}{n - 1}$$

$$= \frac{1}{7}[(80 - 58)^2 + (46 - 58)^2 + (76 - 58)^2 + (54 - 58)^2 + (55 - 58)^2 + 44 - 58)^2 + (58 - 58)^2 + (51 - 58)^2]$$

$$= \frac{1}{7}(484 + 144 + 324 + 16 + 9 + 196 + 0 + 49)$$

$$= \frac{1}{7}(1222) = 174.57.$$

Exercises

3.16 Calculate the variance and standard deviation for the sample of Company B salaries in Example 3.9.

3.17 The following measurements represent the number of hours of petty leave taken during the past month by seven employees of a large department store:

5, 8, 0, 3, 10, 4, 2

Calculate s^2 and s for these data.

3.6 CALCULATION FORMULAS FOR VARIANCE AND STANDARD DEVIATION

Examples

3.13 For the following data set, compute

$$\sum_{i=1}^{n} x_i, \quad \sum_{i=1}^{n} x_i^2, \text{ and } \left(\sum_{i=1}^{n} x_i\right)^2: \quad -2, 1, 4, 0, 8, 1.$$

Solution

$$\sum_{i=1}^{n} x_i = \sum_{i=1}^{6} x_i = -2 + 1 + 4 + 0 + 8 + 1 = 12$$

$$\sum_{i=1}^{6} x_i^2 = (-2)^2 + (1)^2 + (4)^2 + (0)^2 + (8)^2 + (1)^2 = 86$$

$$\left(\sum_{i=1}^{6} x_i\right)^2 = (12)^2 = 144$$

3.14 For a particular data set, the following information is known:

$$n = 6, \quad \sum_{i=1}^{n} x_i^2 = 176, \quad \sum_{i=1}^{n} x_i = 18$$

Compute the sample variance and standard deviation.

Solution

The shortcut formula for sample variance will be applied:

$$s^2 = \frac{\Sigma x_i^2 - \dfrac{(\Sigma x_i)^2}{n}}{n - 1} = \frac{176 - \dfrac{(18)^2}{6}}{6 - 1} = \frac{176 - \dfrac{324}{6}}{5} = \frac{176 - 54}{5} = \frac{122}{5} = 24.4$$

Thus, the sample variance is 24.4 and the standard deviation is

$s = \sqrt{s^2} = \sqrt{24.4} = 4.94.$

3.15 Five senior employees of an aerospace corporation received the following percentage increases in their salaries during the last fiscal year:

14, 9, 16, 13, 15

Use the shortcut formula to compute s^2 for this data set.

Solution

For these $n = 5$ measurements,

$\Sigma x_i = 14 + 9 + 16 + 13 + 15 = 67$

and

$\Sigma x_i^2 = (14)^2 + (9)^2 + (16)^2 + (13)^2 + (15)^2 = 927.$

Then

$$s^2 = \frac{\Sigma x_i^2 - \dfrac{(\Sigma x_i)^2}{n}}{n - 1} = \frac{927 - \dfrac{(67)^2}{5}}{4} = \frac{927 - 897.8}{4} = 7.3.$$

Exercises

3.18 Compute $\sum_{i=1}^{n} x_i$, $\sum_{i=1}^{n} x_i^2$, and $\left(\sum_{i=1}^{n} x_i\right)^2$ for the following data sets.

a. -1, 0, 4, 2, 6, -3

b. 42, 51, 38, 34, 48

3.19 Given the following information about a data set of interest, calculate the sample variance and standard deviation:

$$\sum_{i=1}^{12} x_i = 435, \quad \sum_{i=1}^{12} x_i^2 = 19{,}840$$

3.20 Use the shortcut formula to compute s^2 for the data given in Exercise 3.17.

3.21 Drivers for an interstate trucking company reported the following number of miles driven during the past 24 hours:

420, 360, 380, 290, 450, 360

Compute the sample variance and standard deviation of the mileages, using the shortcut formula.

3.7 INTERPRETING THE STANDARD DEVIATION

Examples

3.16 Recent real estate figures have shown that the average length of residency in a given home is 13 years, and the standard deviation is 4 years. If we make no assumptions about the frequency distribution of lengths of residency, what can be said about the fraction of homeowners who live in their houses between 9 and 17 years? Between 5 and 21 years? Between 1 and 25 years?

Solution

To apply the aids for interpreting the value of a standard deviation, we first form the intervals:

$(\bar{x} - s, \bar{x} + s) = (13 - 4, 13 + 4) = (9, 17);$

$(\bar{x} - 2s, \bar{x} + 2s) = (13 - 8, 13 + 8) = (5, 21);$

$(\bar{x} - 3s, \bar{x} + 3s) = (13 - 12, 13 + 12) = (1, 25).$

According to the rule based on Chebyshev's theorem, we may make the following statements:

a. It is possible that none of the measurements will fall within the one standard deviation interval about the mean, (9, 17).

b. At least 3/4 of the measurements fall within (5, 21), the two standard deviation interval about the mean. In terms of the problem, we conclude that at least 3/4 of the homeowners live in their houses between 5 and 21 years.

c. At least 8/9 of the homeowners reside in their homes between 1 and 25 years.

3.17 Suppose that a frequency histogram of the lengths of home residency in a particular region of the country shows the distribution is mound-shaped, with mean 13 years and standard deviation 4 years. What fraction of the lengths of residency would be expected to fall within each of the intervals specified in Example 3.16? Compare your results with those obtained in the previous example.

Solution

We can use the Empirical Rule, which applies to samples with mound-shaped frequency distributions.

a. Approximately 68% of the homeowners reside in their homes between 9 and 17 years; i.e., approximately 68% of the measurements will fall within one standard deviation of the mean.

b. Approximately 95% of the homeowners live in their homes between 5 and 21 years.

c. Essentially all the homeowners in this region live in their homes between 1 and 25 years.

When nothing is known about the shape of the frequency distribution, statement a of Example 3.16 is not very informative. However, if there is evidence that the frequency distribution is mound-shaped, we can make the more meaningful statement that approximately 68% of the measurements will fall within one standard deviation of the mean. Similarly, the rule based on Chebyshev's theorem guarantees only that at least 75% of the measurements will be within two standard deviations of the mean; if the distribution is mound-shaped, we have the stronger conclusion that approximately 95% of the measurements will lie within this interval.

3.18 Recent testing of a popular brand of automobile battery has shown that the distribution of battery lifelengths is approximately mound-shaped, with mean 36 months and standard deviation 6 months. If the batteries are guaranteed to last 2 years, what percentage of all batteries sold will have to be replaced because they fail before expiration of the guarantee period?

Solution

The distribution of battery lifelengths may be visualized as shown at the right.

The distribution is symmetric, with the mean located at the center of the distribution.

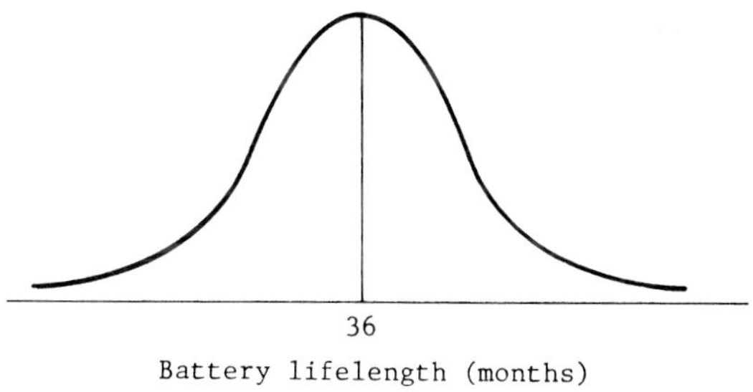

Now, we apply the Empirical Rule to conclude that approximately 95% of the battery lifelengths fall within the interval $(\bar{x} - 2s,\ \bar{x} + 2s) = (36 - 12,\ 36 + 12) = (24,\ 48)$ months:

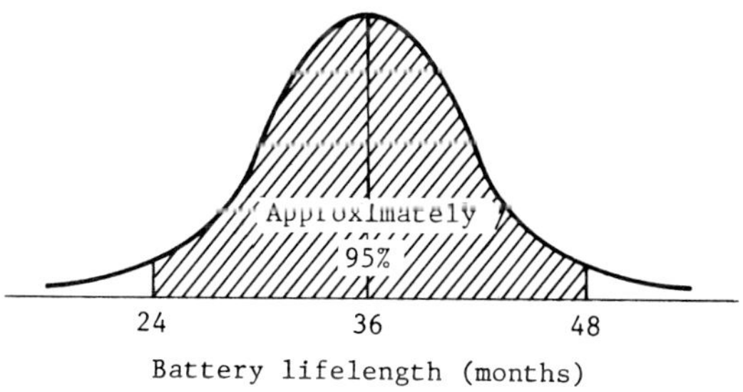

We observe that approximately 5% of the distribution remains to be divided between the two tails. The symmetry of the distribution implies that half of this amount, or approximately 2.5%, will lie below 24 and approximately 2.5% will lie above 48.

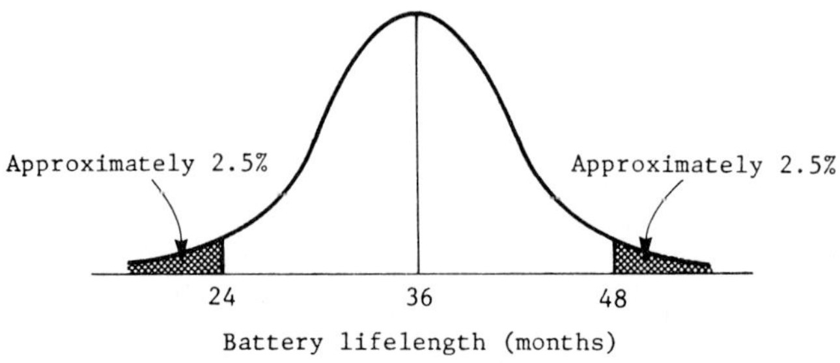

Thus, approximately 2.5% of the batteries sold will fail before 24 months (2 years) and will have to be replaced under the terms of the guarantee. (Note that all measurements of battery lifelength must be made in the same units; thus, the guarantee period was converted from 2 years to 24 months. An equivalent procedure would be to convert all measurements to years: $\bar{x}$ = 3 years, s = .5 year, guarantee period = 2 years.)

Exercises

3.22 First-year sales for textbooks in marketing have had an average volume of 1200 books and a standard deviation of 500 books.

a. What can be said about the fraction of marketing texts that have first-year sales between 700 and 1700 books? Between 200 and 2200 books?

b. Suppose that the distribution of first-year sales for marketing texts is known to be mound-shaped. What percentage of marketing texts would you expect to have first-year sales between 700 and 1700 books? Between 200 and 2200 books?

c. Assume the frequency distribution of first-year sales is mound-shaped. What fraction of marketing texts would you expect to have first-year sales in excess of 2200 books? Less than 700 books?

3.23 A sample of 50 leading economists predicted next year's inflation rate. The average rate predicted was 4.8% and the standard deviation was 1.3%. Assume the distribution of predicted rates was approximately mound-shaped.

a. What fraction of the economists predicted inflation rates of at least 6.1% for next year?

b. What fraction of the economists predicted inflation rates between 3.5% and 7.4%?

3.24 In a test designed to assess small motor coordination, job applicants for some manufacturing positions are timed on their performance of a specific assembly-line task. It is known that the time required to complete the task has an approximately mound-shaped distribution with mean 18 seconds and standard deviation 4 seconds. How long should the test administrator allow for the task if it is desired that approximately 97.5% of the applicants complete the task?

3.25 The chairman of the Greater Miami Chamber of Commerce asked 500 attendees at a political convention to keep records of all expenditures made while in attendance at the three-day convention. A relative frequency histogram of the results showed the distribution of expenditures, which ranged between \$200 and \$750, to be approximately mound-shaped. Use this information to estimate the mean and standard deviation of the distribution of expenditures for this sample.

3.8 CALCULATING A MEAN AND STANDARD DEVIATION FROM GROUPED DATA (Optional)

Example

3.19 The Federal Communications Commission is investigating complaints of irregularities in the broadcasting of commercials by a particular New York radio station. The frequency distribution of the lengths of time for 50 randomly selected commercials broadcast during the station's early morning programming period is given as follows:

LENGTH OF TIME (IN SECONDS)	NUMBER OF RADIO COMMERCIALS
0.5- 6.5	0
6.5 12.5	3
12.5-18.5	18
18.5-24.5	2
24.5-30.5	1
30.5-36.5	10
36.5-42.5	0
42.5-48.5	0
48.5-54.5	2
54.5-60.5	14

Compute the mean and standard deviation of the 50 radio commercial time lengths.

Solution

To simplify the presentation of calculations, we add three columns to the frequency distribution.

CLASS	CLASS MIDPOINT x_i	CLASS FREQUENCY f_i	$x_i f_i$	$x_i^2 f_i$
0.5- 6.5	3.5	0	0.0	0.00
6.5-12.5	9.5	3	28.5	270.75
12.5-18.5	15.5	18	279.0	4324.50
18.5-24.5	21.5	2	43.0	924.50
24.5-30.5	27.5	1	27.5	756.25
30.5-36.5	33.5	10	335.0	11222.50
36.5-42.5	39.5	0	0.0	0.00
42.5-48.5	45.5	0	0.0	0.00
48.5-54.5	51.5	2	103.0	5304.50
54.5-60.5	57.5	14	805.0	46287.50

From the fourth and fifth columns of the table, we obtain

$$\sum_{i=1}^{k} x_i f_i = 0.0 + 28.5 + \cdots + 805.0 = 1621.0$$

and

$$\sum_{i=1}^{k} x_i^2 f_i = 0.00 + 270.75 + \cdots + 46{,}287.50 = 69{,}090.50.$$

Substitution of these values and $n = 50$ into the calculation formulas for grouped data yields:

$$\bar{x} = \frac{\sum_{i=1}^{k} x_i f_i}{n} = \frac{1621.0}{50} = 32.42$$

$$s^2 = \frac{\sum_{i=1}^{k} x_i^2 f_i - \frac{\left(\sum_{i=1}^{k} x_i f_i\right)^2}{n}}{n-1} = \frac{69{,}090.50 - \frac{(1621.0)^2}{50}}{49} = 337.50$$

$$s = \sqrt{337.50} = 18.37$$

The mean and standard deviation of the 50 radio commercial time lengths, based on the grouped data, are 32.42 seconds and 18.37 seconds, respectively.

Exercises

3.26 Refer to Example 2.8. Using the grouped data as shown in the frequency table, calculate the mean and standard deviation of the 50 closing prices.

3.27 Refer to Exercise 3.2. Compute the mean, variance, and standard deviation of the 500 Civil Service examination scores, using the formulas for grouped data. [Hint: It will be necessary to convert relative frequencies to frequencies. Thus, for example, the frequency for the first class (19.5 - 39.5) is $.12 \times 500 = 60$.]

3.9 MEASURES OF RELATIVE STANDING

Examples

3.20 A sample of 200 homes listed for sale in a particular area showed an average selling price of \$67,000 and a standard deviation of \$9000. Suppose your house is selling for \$58,000 and the house you wish to purchase is selling for \$94,000. Compute the z scores for these two prices.

Solution

For this sample of measurements, we have

$$\bar{x} = 67{,}000 \quad \text{and} \quad s = 9000.$$

Thus, for your house,

$$x = 58{,}000 \quad \text{and} \quad z = \frac{x - \bar{x}}{s} = \frac{58{,}000 - 67{,}000}{9000} = -1.$$

The price of your house is one standard deviation *below* the mean selling price for this sample.

For the home you wish to purchase,

$$x = 94{,}000 \quad \text{and} \quad z = \frac{94{,}000 - 67{,}000}{9000} = 3.$$

This home is priced 3 standard deviations *above* the mean selling price for the sample.

3.21 Among all banks in the country, First Security National Exchange Bank (FSNEB) is in the 28th percentile of the distribution of amount of capital used for mortgage loans. Explain how this locates FSNEB in the distribution of capital used for mortgage loans.

Solution

The interpretation is that 28% of all banks use less capital for mortgage loans than does FSNEB, while (100 - 28)% = 72% of all banks use more capital for this purpose.

3.22 In Exercise 3.24, it was stated that the time required to complete a specific assembly-line task has a mound-shaped distribution with mean 18 seconds and standard deviation 4 seconds. Suppose an applicant's z score for the time required was 1.5. How long did he require to complete the assembly-line task?

Solution

Let x denote the time required by the applicant to finish the task. The z score corresponding to this value of x is known to be 1.5. Now, since the mean and standard deviation of the distribution are given, it is required to solve the following equation for x:

$$z = \frac{x - \mu}{\sigma} \quad \text{or} \quad 1.5 = \frac{x - 18}{4}$$

Elementary algebra yields the solution:

$$x = 4(1.5) + 18 = 24$$

Thus, the applicant completed the task in 24 seconds.

3.23 During the past six years, return rates on government-associated investments have followed a mound-shaped distribution with mean 7.8% and standard deviation 1.4%. Suppose a broker is trying to interest you in a government investment for which he predicts a return rate of 13.4%. Why might you be skeptical of his prediction?

Solution

Although the predicted return rate at first looks very attractive, let us consider the relative standing of this prediction in the distribution of return rates on previous investments. The predicted return rate of x = 13.4% has z score:

$$z = \frac{13.4 - 7.8}{1.4} = 4$$

Now, we know that for mound-shaped distributions, essentially *all* the measurements lie within 3 standard deviations of the mean; i.e., almost all measurements have z scores between -3 and 3. A return rate of 13.4% lies 4 standard deviations above the mean and would thus be a very *rare* event. An investor would be advised to carefully scrutinize the subjective statements of the broker.

3.24 Refer to Example 2.7. Find the lower quartile, median, and upper quartile for the twenty-five textbook costs.

Solution

We first rank the twenty-five observations from the smallest to the largest:

127	132	148	152	153
169	169	176	179	180
181	181	195	195	198
203	204	209	209	216
233	248	253	258	277

To find Q_L, calculate $(1/4)(n + 1) = (1/4)(25 + 1) = 6.5$, and round to the integer 7. [Since $(1/4)(n + 1)$ is an integer plus 1/2 in this case, we round upward.] Thus, the lower quartile is the observation with rank 7 in the data set: $Q_L = 169$.

The median is the middle (i.e., the thirteenth) ranked observation: Median = 195.

To find Q_U, calculate $(3/4)(n + 1) = 19.5$. Since this quantity is equal to an integer plus 1/2, we round downward and obtain the upper quartile as the nineteenth ranked observation: $Q_U = 209$.

Exercises

3.28 a. What is the z score corresponding to the 97.5th percentile of a mound-shaped frequency distribution?

b. What is the z score corresponding to the 16th percentile of a mound-shaped frequency distribution?

c. A z score of 0 corresponds to which percentile of a mound-shaped frequency distribution?

3.29 Refer to Example 3.18. Compute the z scores associated with the following battery lifelengths:

a. 28 months
b. 32 months
c. 36 months
d. 45 months
e. 4 years

3.30 Salaries in a certain corporation are known to have a mean of \$18,000 and a standard deviation of \$1600.

a. What is the z score corresponding to a salary of $17,200?

b. Suppose the corporation offers you a starting salary with a z score of -.4. To what starting salary does this z score correspond?

3.31 An oil additive is tested by the Department of Transportation for its effect on gasoline mileage. Test results indicated that the increases in miles per gallon (mpg) obtained with the additive follow an approximately mound-shaped distribution with mean 2.2 mpg and standard deviation .5 mpg. A local service station attendant claims the additive will increase mileage by 4 mpg for most automobiles. Is this a reasonable claim?

3.32 The average loss payment per insurance claim by a sample of 1000 motorcycle owners was $615 and the standard deviation was $85. Would you expect to observe a loss payment as large as $900 in the sample? Assume that the distribution of the amounts of loss payment per claim is approximately mound-shaped.

3.33 Refer to Exercise 2.9. Determine the lower quartile, median, and upper quartile for the data set.

3.34 Refer to the bed size data given in Exercise 2.10. Find the lower quartile, median, and upper quartile for the 54 observations.

3.10 BOX PLOTS: GRAPHICAL DESCRIPTIONS BASED ON QUARTILES (Optional)

Example

3.25 Refer to the textbook cost data for accounting majors, given in Example 2.7. Construct a box plot for the data.

Solution

The first step is to construct a box with Q_L and Q_U located at the lower corners. In Example 3.24, we found Q_L and Q_U to be 169 and 209, respectively. The interquartile range is then

$$IQR = 209 - 169 = 40.$$

The second step is to locate the inner fences, which lie a distance of 1.5(IQR) = 1.5(40) = 60 below Q_L and above Q_U. These values,

$$Q_L - 1.5(IQR) = 169 - 60 = 109 \quad \text{and} \quad Q_U + 1.5(IQR) = 209 + 60 = 269,$$

are located on the box plot.

The third step is to locate the outer fences, which lie a distance of 1.5(IQR) = 60 below the lower inner fence and above the upper inner fence. Thus, the outer fences for this data set are located at 49 and 329, as indicated in the figure.

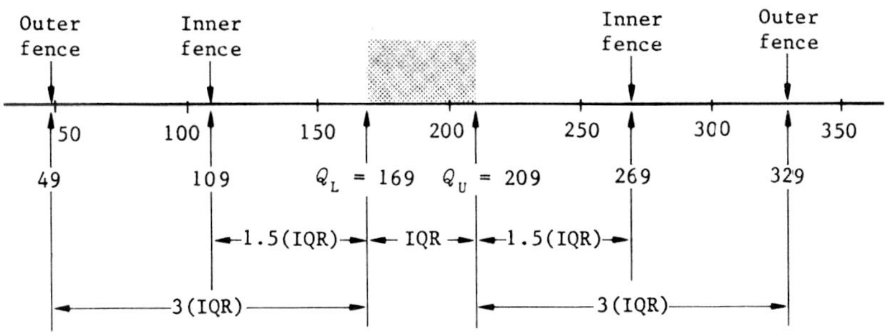

Exercises

3.35 Refer to Exercises 2.9 and 3.33.

a. Compute the interquartile range for the data set.

b. Construct a box plot for the data.

3.36 Refer to Exercises 2.10 and 3.34.

a. Compute the interquartile range for the bed size data.

b. Construct a box plot for the data.

4
PROBABILITY

SUMMARY

This chapter presented the basic concepts and tools of *probability*, which will allow us to make inferences about the population from an observed sample. In addition, the theory of probability will often be used in measuring the reliability of inferences.

The notions of *experiments*, *events*, *event relations*, and *random sampling* were defined. Rules for assigning probabilities to events in the sample space and for computing the probability of an event of interest were presented.

4.1 EVENTS, SAMPLE SPACES, AND PROBABILITY

Examples

4.1 A major department store chain is planning to open a store in a new city. Five cities are being considered: Boston, Atlanta, Dallas, Cleveland, and Los Angeles.

a. List the simple events associated with this experiment.

b. Assign a probability to each simple event, assuming each city has an equal chance of being selected.

c. Compute the probability of each of the following events:

G: {Dallas is chosen}
H: {A "southern" city is chosen}
K: {Los Angeles is not chosen}

Solution

a. Experiment: Choose one city from the five specified.

Simple events:
1. Boston is chosen.
2. Altanta is chosen.
3. Dallas is chosen.
4. Cleveland is chosen.
5. Los Angeles is chosen.

b. Since there are five equally likely simple events, each must be assigned a probability of 1/5; i.e., P(Boston) = P(Atlanta) = P(Dallas) = P(Cleveland) = P(Los Angeles) = 1/5. Note that the two requirements for assigning probabilities to simple events are satisfied: each probability is between 0 and 1, and the probabilities of all the simple events sum to 1.

c. $P(G) = P(\text{Dallas}) = 1/5$

$P(H) = P(\text{Atlanta}) + P(\text{Dallas}) = 1/5 + 1/5 = 2/5$

$P(K) = P(\text{Boston}) + P(\text{Atlanta}) + P(\text{Dallas}) + P(\text{Cleveland})$
$= 1/5 + 1/5 + 1/5 + 1/5 = 4/5$

4.2 The city council of a particular community consists of five elected residents of the community, two of whom are land developers. The city mayor plans to select two members at random from the council to study and make recommendations on land use rezoning requests. The composition of this subcommittee is of particular interest.

a. List the simple events in the sample space for this experiment.

b. Assuming that each pair of city council members has an equal chance of being selected, assign probabilities to each simple event.

c. Compute the probabilities of the following events of interest:

D: {Both land developers are selected}
F: {At least one land developer is selected}
G: {No land developer is selected}

Solution

a. We will label the city council members O_1, O_2, O_3, L_1, and L_2, where the two land developers are represented by L_1 and L_2. To determine the number of simple events, we use the counting rule presented in the text, with $N = 5$ and $n = 2$:

$$\binom{N}{n} = \binom{5}{2} = \frac{5!}{2!3!} = \frac{5 \cdot 4 \cdot 3 \cdot 2 \cdot 1}{2 \cdot 1 \cdot 3 \cdot 2 \cdot 1} = 10$$

Then the ten simple events may be represented as unordered pairs of members:

$$(O_1\ O_2)\quad (O_1\ O_3)\quad (O_1\ L_1)\quad (O_1\ L_2)\quad (O_2\ O_3)$$
$$(O_2\ L_1)\quad (O_2\ L_2)\quad (O_3\ L_1)\quad (O_3\ L_2)\quad (L_1\ L_2)$$

b. The ten simple events are assumed equally likely; thus, each is assigned a probability of 1/10.

c. $P(\text{D}) = P(L_1\ L_2) = 1/10$

$$P(\text{F}) = P(O_1\ L_1) + P(O_1\ L_2) + P(O_2\ L_1) + P(O_2\ L_2) + P(O_3\ L_1) + P(O_3\ L_2) + P(L_1\ L_2) = 7/10$$

$$P(\text{G}) = P(O_1\ O_2) + P(O_1\ O_3) + P(O_2\ O_3) = 3/10$$

4.3 A retail grocer has decided to market organic "health foods" and will purchase a new line of products from each of two suppliers. Unknown to the grocer, the two suppliers are in financial distress. Corporate lawyers have noted that, for firms with similar credit histories, the probability that bankruptcy proceedings will be initiated within one year is .7. We are interested in observing the financial progress of the two firms over the next year. For this experiment, the simple events and their associated probabilities are as follows (B_1: Supplier 1 declares bankruptcy; N_1: Supplier 1 does not declare bankruptcy; and so on):

SIMPLE EVENTS	PROBABILITIES
(B_1, B_2)	.49
(B_1, N_2)	.21
(N_1, B_2)	.21
(N_1, N_2)	.09

Find the probabilities of each of the following events:

D: {Neither supplier declares bankruptcy during the next year}
F: {At least one supplier declares bankruptcy during the next year}

Solution

$$P(\text{D}) = P(N_1, N_2) = .09$$

$$P(\text{F}) = P(B_1, B_2) + P(B_1, N_2) + P(N_1, B_2) = .49 + .21 + .21 = .91$$

Exercises

4.1 Refer to Example 4.1. Suppose the chain will open new stores in two of the candidate cities, and that the selection of the pair of cities will be random.

a. Define the experiment and list the simple events.

b. Compute the probability that neither Boston nor Cleveland is chosen.

4.2 A retailer of stereo equipment has observed that the probability a particular customer will request long-term financing is .8. This afternoon the retailer will make sales to each of three customers, and will note their preferences for financial arrangements. The simple events for this experiment, together with their associated probabilities, are as follows (F_1: Customer 1 requests long-term financing; N_1: Customer 1 does not request long-term financing, and so on):

SIMPLE EVENTS	PROBABILITIES	SIMPLE EVENTS	PROBABILITIES
(F_1, F_2, F_3)	.512	(N_1, F_2, F_3)	.128
(F_1, F_2, N_3)	.128	(N_1, F_2, N_3)	.032
(F_1, N_2, F_3)	.128	(N_1, N_2, F_3)	.032
(F_1, N_2, N_3)	.032	(N_1, N_2, N_3)	.008

Calculate the probabilities of the following events of interest:

A: {At least one customer requests long-term financing}
B: {Exactly one customer requests long-term financing}
C: {No customer requests long-term financing}

4.2 COMPOUND EVENTS

4.3 COMPLEMENTARY EVENTS

Examples

4.4 One hundred students in an introductory statistics course were categorized according to their major and their attitude toward applied statistics; the results are shown in the following table.

MAJOR	ATTITUDE Positive	Negative
Business	46%	12%
Non-Business	17%	25%

Suppose a single student is selected at random from those in the course, and the following events are defined:

A: {Student is a business major}
B. {Student has a negative attitude toward applied statistics}

Describe the characteristics implied by the following compound events:

a. $A \cup B$ b. $A \cap B$ c. A^c d. $A^c \cap B^c$

Solution

a. $A \cup B$: {Student is either a Business major, or has a negative attitude toward applied statistics, or both}

b. $A \cap B$: {Student is a Business major who has a negative attitude toward applied statistics}

c. A^c: {Student is a non-Business major}

d. $A^c \cap B^c$: {Student is a non-Business major who has a positive attitude toward applied statistics}

4.5 Refer to Example 4.4. Calculate the following probabilities by summing the probabilities of the appropriate simple events:

a. $P(A \cup B)$ b. $P(A \cap B)$ c. $P(A^c)$ d. $P(A^c \cap B^c)$ e. $P(A \cup B^c)$

Solution

a. $P(A \cup B) = .46 + .12 + .25 = .83$

b. $P(A \cap B) = .12$

c. $P(A^c) = .17 + .25 = .42$

d. $P(A^c \cap B^c) = .17$

e. $P(A \cup B^c) = .46 + .12 + .17 = .75$

4.6 A listing of 50 houses for sale by a realty firm produced the following breakdown on number of bedrooms and bathrooms:

BATHROOMS	BEDROOMS		
	2	3	4 or More
1	4	7	0
2	5	13	11
3 or More	0	4	6

One of these houses is to be selected at random, and the following events are defined:

A: {House has at least two bathrooms}
B: {House has two or three bedrooms}

Define the following events in terms of the problem and compute their probabilities:

a. A^c b. $A \cup B$ c. $A \cap B^c$

Solution

a. A^c: {House has one bathroom}

$$P(A^c) = \frac{4}{50} + \frac{7}{50} = \frac{11}{50} = .22$$

[Note that the entries within the table are counts and must be converted to probabilities. In this example, there are 11 houses out of 50 that satisfy event A^c; thus, $P(A^c) = 11/50 = .22$.]

b. $A \cup B$: {House has two or three bedrooms *or* at least two bathrooms, or both}

$$P(A \cup B) = \frac{5}{50} + \frac{13}{50} + \frac{11}{50} + \frac{4}{50} + \frac{6}{50} + \frac{4}{50} + \frac{7}{50} = \frac{50}{50} = 1.0$$

[Note that *all* of the houses satisfy either event A or event B or both; thus, $P(A \cup B) = 1.0$.]

c. $A \cap B^c$: {House has 4 or more bedrooms *and* at least two bathrooms}

$$P(A \cap B^c) = \frac{11}{50} + \frac{6}{50} = \frac{17}{50} = .34$$

Exercises

4.3 Assembly line workers in a large factory were rated according to the adequacy of their breakfast and their work efficiency at 10 A.M. Results are shown below.

	EFFICIENCY AT 10 A.M.	
BREAKFAST	Satisfactory	Unsatisfactory
Adequate	28%	23%
Inadequate	20%	29%

One factory worker is selected at random, and the following events are defined:

A: {Worker's efficiency is unsatisfactory}
B: {Worker's breakfast is adequate}

Describe the characteristics implied by the following compound events:

a. $A \cup B$ b. $A \cap B$ c. A^c d. $A \cap B^c$ e. $A^c \cup B$

4.4 Refer to Exercise 4.3. Compute the following probabilities by summing the probabilities of the appropriate simple events:

a. $P(A \cup B)$ b. $P(A \cap B)$ c. $P(A^c)$ d. $P(A \cap B^c)$ e. $P(A^c \cup B)$

4.5 One hundred federal income tax returns from a particular area were classified according to the annual income and age of head of household. The results are shown below.

	INCOME		
AGE	Less than \$20,000	\$20,000-\$40,000	Over \$40,000
Under 25	24	2	4
25-45	14	6	28
Over 45	2	2	18

One of the 100 returns will be randomly selected, and the following events defined:

G: {Head of household is at least 25 years old}
H: {Income is over \$40,000}

Define the following events in terms of the problem and compute their probabilities:

a. $G \cup H$ b. G^c c. $G \cap H$ d. $G \cap H^c$ e. $G^c \cup H^c$

4.4 CONDITIONAL PROBABILITY

Examples

4.7 A local business conducted a survey to determine how their customers first became acquainted with the store. The results are tabulated by sex in the following table.

	SOURCE OF INITIAL INFORMATION	
SEX	Media Advertising (TV, Radio, Newspaper)	Other (Friends, Visit to Store, etc.)
Male	36%	12%
Female	34%	18%

A customer is to be selected randomly from the surveyed group, and the following events are defined:

A: {Customer selected is male}
B: {Customer's first acquaintance with store was through media advertising}

Compute $P(B|A)$ and $P(A|B)$.

Solution

We shall first compute:

$P(A) = .36 + .12 = .48$

$P(B) = .36 + .34 = .70$

$P(A \cap B) = .36$

Then, by the definition of conditional probability,

$$P(B|A) = \frac{P(B \cap A)}{P(A)} = \frac{P(A \cap B)}{P(A)} \quad (\text{since } A \cap B = B \cap A)$$

$$= \frac{.36}{.48} = .75.$$

Thus, given the customer selected is male, the probability his first acquaintance with the store was through media advertising is .75. Similarly,

$$P(A|B) = \frac{P(A \cap B)}{P(B)} = \frac{.36}{.70} \approx .51.$$

4.8 The 500 adult residents of a small town are categorized by sex and employment status, with the following results.

SEX	EMPLOYMENT STATUS: Employed	Unemployed Less than Six Months	Unemployed at Least Six Months
Male	125	75	25
Female	150	50	75

One of the adult residents of this town is selected at random.

a. Given that the person selected is female, what is the probability she is employed?

b. What is the probability that the person selected is male, given that the subject has been unemployed at least six months?

c. Given that the person selected is unemployed, what is the probability the subject is male?

Solution

a. Define the following events of interest:

A: {Adult selected is employed}
B: {Adult selected is female}

Then the required probability is

$$P(A|B) = \frac{P(A \cap B)}{P(B)} = \frac{150/500}{(150 + 50 + 75)/500} = \frac{150}{275} \approx .55.$$

b. Define D: {Subject has been unemployed at least six months}

We desire $P(B^c|D)$, where B is as defined above. Then,

$$P(B^c|D) = \frac{P(B^c \cap D)}{P(D)} = \frac{25/500}{(25 + 75)/500} = \frac{25}{100} = .25.$$

c. $$P(B^c|A^c) = \frac{P(B^c \cap A^c)}{P(A^c)} = \frac{(75 + 25)/500}{(75 + 25 + 50 + 75)/500} = \frac{100}{225} \approx .44$$

Exercises

4.6 Refer to Exercise 4.3. Compute $P(A|B)$ and $P(A^c|B)$.

4.7 Refer to Exercise 4.5.

a. What is the probability that the annual income is \$40,000 or less, given that the head of household is under 25?

b. Given that the head of household is 25 or older, what is the probability that the annual income is at least \$20,000?

4.8 A group of 200 workers on the factory line of a major electronics firm were asked: (1) How do you feel about your job? and (2) How do you feel about your supervisor? Each question had three possible answers: satisfied, dissatisfied, or neutral. The table shows the number of responses in each category:

	JOB		
SUPERVISOR	Satisfied	Dissatisfied	Neutral
Satisfied	60	46	10
Dissatisfied	10	40	18
Neutral	6	5	5

One worker is to be chosen randomly from the surveyed group. Define the following events:

A: {Selected worker is satisfied with the job}
B: {Selected worker is not dissatisfied with the supervisor}

Find $P(A|B)$ and $P(B|A)$.

4.5 PROBABILITIES OF UNIONS AND INTERSECTIONS

Examples

4.9 Suppose events A and B are such that $P(A) = 1/4$, $P(B) = 1/3$, and $P(B|A) = 1/2$.

a. Compute $P(A \cap B)$ and $P(A \cup B)$.

b. Are events A and B independent?

c. Are events A and B mutually exclusive?

Solution

a. We apply the Multiplicative Rule of Probability to obtain

$$P(A \cap B) = P(A)P(B|A) = \frac{1}{4} \cdot \frac{1}{2} = \frac{1}{8}.$$

The Additive Rule of Probability yields

$$P(A \cup B) = P(A) + P(B) - P(A \cap B) = \frac{1}{4} + \frac{1}{3} - \frac{1}{8} = \frac{11}{24}.$$

b. $P(B|A) \neq P(B)\left(\frac{1}{2} \neq \frac{1}{3}\right)$; thus, events A and B are not independent.

c. $P(A \cap B) \neq 0$; thus, events A and B are not mutually exclusive.

4.10 The following experiment is to be performed: A fair six-sided die will be tossed once and we shall observe the number of dots showing face up. Define the following events:

A: {Observe an even number} = {2, 4, 6}
B: {Observe a 1, 2, 3, or 4} = {1, 2, 3, 4}

Are events A and B independent?

Solution

Note that $P(A) = \frac{3}{6} = \frac{1}{2}$, $P(B) = \frac{4}{6} = \frac{2}{3}$, and

$$P(A|B) = \frac{P(A \cap B)}{P(B)} = \frac{P\{2, 4\}}{P(B)} = \frac{1/3}{2/3} = \frac{1}{2}.$$

Since $P(A|B) = P(A)$, events A and B are independent.

4.11 One hundred members of a small suburban country club were surveyed to determine the pattern of use for its recreational facilities, which consist of a golf course and swimming pool. The following results were reported:

92 members regularly use at least one of the facilities,
25 members regularly use the golf course, and
86 members regularly use the swimming pool.

How many members regularly use *both* facilities?

Solution

We shall define the following events of interest:

A: {Member regularly uses golf course}
B: {Member regularly uses swimming pool}

In terms of these events, the following probabilities are known:

$P(A) = .25, \quad P(B) = .86, \quad P(A \cup B) = .92$

To determine $P\{\text{Member regularly uses both facilities}\} = P(A \cap B)$, we shall solve for $P(A \cap B)$ using the Additive Rule of Probability:

$$P(A \cup B) = P(A) + P(B) - P(A \cap B)$$

or $$.92 = .25 + .86 - P(A \cap B)$$

or $$.92 = 1.11 - P(A \cap B)$$

or $$P(A \cap B) = .19.$$

Thus, $P(A \cap B) = .19$ and 19 of the 100 members surveyed regularly use both the golf course and the swimming pool.

4.12 Which of the following statements is/are always true?

Let A and B be any events. Then,

a. $P(A) + P(B) = 1$

b. $P(A) + P(A^c) = 1$

c. $P(A \cup B) = P(A) + P(B)$

d. $P(A \cap B) = P(A) \cdot P(B)$

e. $P(A \cap B) = P(B|A)P(A)$

f. $P(A \cap B) = 0$

g. $P(A|B) = P(B|A)$

Solution

a. False

b. True

c. False (The statement is true only if A and B are mutually exclusive.)

d. False (The statement is true only if A and B are independent.)

e. True

f. False (The statement is true only if A and B are mutually exclusive.)

g. False

4.13 Past records kept on the Dow Jones Index show that on Mondays the index increases 55% of the time. During the remainder of the week, the index increases on 60% of the days when it has increased the previous day, but it increases on only 30% of the days when the previous day's trading has resulted in a decrease of the index. What is the probability that next Tuesday's trading results in an increase in the Dow Jones Index?

Solution

Define the following events:

A: {The Index increases next Monday}
B: {The Index increases next Tuesday}

We wish to find $P(B)$, and are given the following information:

$P(A) = .55, \quad P(B|A) = .6, \quad P(B|A^c) = .3$

Now note that B may be written as the union of two mutually exclusive events, $(A \cap B)$ and $(A^c \cap B)$. (A Venn diagram may be useful to visualize this.) Thus, since the probability of the union of mutually exclusive events is equal to the sum of the probabilities of the respective events, we have:

$$\begin{aligned} P(B) &= P(A \cap B) + P(A^c \cap B) \\ &= P(A)P(B|A) + P(A^c)P(B|A^c) \quad \text{(by the Multiplicative Rule of Probability)} \\ &= (.55)(.6) + (.45)(.3) \quad [\text{Note that } P(A^c) = 1 - P(A) = 1 - .55 = .45.] \\ &= .465 \end{aligned}$$

Thus, the probability is .465 that the Dow Jones Index will increase next Tuesday.

Exercises

4.9 Refer to Exercise 4.3. Use the Additive Rule of Probability to compute $P(A \cup B)$.

4.10 Suppose C and D are events such that $P(C) = 1/2$, $P(D) = 1/4$, and $P(C|D) = 1/3$.

a. Compute $P(C \cap D)$ and $P(C \cup D)$.
b. Are events C and D independent?
c. Are events C and D mutually exclusive?

4.11 In the die toss experiment, define the following events:

A: {Observe a 4}
B: {Observe a 4, 5, or 6}
C: {Observe an odd number}

a. Are events A and C mutually exclusive?
b. Are events A and B independent?
c. Are events B and C independent?

4.12 Suppose A and B are events such that $P(A \cap B) = 0$ and $P(A) = .2$. Are events A and B independent?

4.13 The probability that an automobile salesman sells a new car for the sticker price is .05. If he fails to make a sale at this price, he will reduce the price of the car, and then has a 20% chance of making a sale. Find the probability that the salesman makes a sale to any given customer.

Supplementary Exercises

4.14 Which of the following statements is/are always true?

a. If an experiment consists of 8 simple events, then the probability of each simple event is 1/8.

b. If A and B are independent events with nonzero probabilities, then they cannot be mutually exclusive.

c. If A and B are mutually exclusive events, then A^c and B^c are mutually exclusive.

d. If $P(A \cup B) = 1$ and $P(A \cap B) = 0$, then $B = A^c$.

e. If $P(A) = P(B)$, then $P(A|B) = P(B|A)$.

4.15 An appliance store is going out of business and has ten televisions left: 5 color consoles, 3 portable color sets, and 2 black and white sets. Assume that at each sale, each of the remaining televisions has an equal chance of being selected.

a. Find the probability that the first set sold is a portable color set.

b. Given that the first television sold was a portable color set, find the probability that the second set sold is a portable color set.

c. Find the probability that neither of the first two sets sold is black and white.

d. Find the probability that the first two sets sold are the same model.

4.16 A stockbroker has recommended six stocks to an investor. Unknown to either the stockbroker or investor at the time, two of the stocks will split during the next month. The investor randomly chooses two of the recommended stocks in which to invest his money.

a. List the simple events in this experiment.

b. Assign probabilities to each simple event.

c. Find the probability that at least one of the selected stocks will split during the next month.

4.17 A dairy is planning to introduce two new products to the market: chocolate-flavored buttermilk and bacon-flavored ice-cream. Previous consumer tests have indicated that chocolate-flavored buttermilk will be approved by the public with probability .6 and bacon-flavored ice-cream will be approved with probability .1. (Assume that the success or failure of one product is not affected by the success or failure of the other.) What is the probability that at least one of the new products will be approved by the public?

5
DISCRETE RANDOM VARIABLES

SUMMARY

Numerical measurements of business phenomena are observed values of *random variables*. This chapter presented a general discussion of the characteristics of *discrete* and *continuous* random variables, and identified two discrete variables of particular interest in business experiments: the *binomial* and *Poisson* random variables.

Knowledge of the *probability distribution* of a random variable allows one to calculate the probabilities of specific sample observations. In addition, approximate probability statements about the behavior of a random variable may be based on numerical descriptive measures (mean and standard deviation) of the probability distribution.

5.1 TWO TYPES OF RANDOM VARIABLES

Examples

5.1 Classify the following random variables as discrete or continuous. Specify the possible values the random variables may assume.

a. x = the number of customers who enter a particular bank during the noon hour on a given day.

b. x = the time (in seconds) required for a teller to serve a bank customer.

c. x = the distance (in miles) between a randomly selected home in a community and the nearest pharmacy.

d. x = the number of times a randomly selected head of household goes grocery shopping in a week.

e. x = the number of tosses of a fair coin required to observe at least three heads in succession.

Solution

a. discrete; $x = 0, 1, 2, \ldots$
b. continuous; $0 < x < \infty$
c. continuous; $0 < x < \infty$
d. discrete; $x = 0, 1, 2, \ldots$
e. discrete; $x = 3, 4, 5, 6, \ldots$

5.2 Which of the following describe discrete random variables and which describe continuous random variables?

a. The number of raisins in a 16-ounce package of raisin bran.

b. The number of shares of stock traded on the New York Stock Exchange the day after a presidential State of the Union message.

c. The diameter of a randomly selected ball bearing produced by a machining process.

d. The number of applications for FM radio station licenses received in a week by the Federal Communications Commission.

e. The distance a randomly selected steel-belted radial tire will be driven before it develops a defect.

f. The volume (in cubic feet) of heated space in a randomly selected suburban shopping mall.

Solution

discrete: a, b, d
continuous: c, e, f

Exercises

5.1 Classify each of the following random variables as discrete or continuous. Specify the possible values the random variables may assume.

a. x = the number of small businesses in the metropolitan Atlanta area that will make a profit during the next fiscal year.

b. x = the number of burglary reports received at a local police department during a holiday weekend period.

c. x = the time between emergency shut-downs at a nuclear power plant.

d. x = the total amount of rainfall received during the week of the World Series in the two participating cities.

e. x = the length (in miles) of the daily delivery route of a randomly selected Postal Service employee.

f. x = the number of complaints received by the customer service representatives of a large department store during a given week.

5.2 Give an example of a discrete random variable that may be of interest in each of the following areas:

a. Marketing
b. Management
c. Accounting
d. Finance
e. Economics

5.2 PROBABILITY DISTRIBUTIONS FOR DISCRETE RANDOM VARIABLES

Examples

5.3 Determine whether each of the following represents a valid probability distribution. If not, explain why not.

a.

x	$p(x)$
0	.20
1	.90
2	−.10

b.

x	$p(x)$
−2	.3
−1	.3
1	.3
2	.3

c.

x	$p(x)$
−1	.25
0	.65
1	.10

Solution

a. Not valid; $p(2)$ cannot be negative.

b. Not valid; $\sum_{\text{all } x} p(x)$ must equal 1.

c. Valid.

5.4 It is known that 20% of all light bulbs produced by a certain company have a lifetime of at least 800 hours. You have just purchased two light bulbs manufactured by this company and are interested in the random variable x = the number of the two bulbs that will last at least 800 hours. Construct the probability distribution for x, assuming the two bulbs operate independently.

Solution

It is first required to list the simple events associated with this experiment: (L_1, L_2), (L_1, F_2), (F_1, L_2), and (F_1, F_2), where (L_1, F_2) indicates the first bulb had a lifetime of at least 800 hours and the second bulb failed before 800 hours, and so on.

The random variable x assigns to each simple event the numerical value equal to the number of bulbs that lasted at least 800 hours. (Note that x may assume the values 0, 1, and 2.) Thus, we have:

Simple Event	Value of x Assigned to Simple Event
(L_1, L_2)	2
(L_1, F_2)	1
(F_1, L_2)	1
(F_1, F_2)	0

Now to compute probabilities associated with each value of x, we note that:

$$P(x = 0) = p(0) = P(F_1, F_2) = P(F_1)P(F_2) = (.8)(.8) = .64$$

$$P(x = 1) = p(1) = P(L_1, F_2) + P(F_1, L_2) = P(L_1)P(F_2) + P(F_1)P(L_2)$$
$$= (.2)(.8) + (.8)(.2) = .32$$

$$P(x = 2) = p(2) = P(L_1, L_2) = P(L_1)P(L_2) = (.2)(.2) = .04$$

Finally, the probability distribution for x is written as follows:

x	$p(x)$
0	.64
1	.32
2	.04

5.5 A salesman is paid on a salary-plus-incentive-bonus plan, depending on his sales volume for the month. He has observed that 20% of the months he makes \$2200, 10% of the months he makes \$2500, and the remaining months he makes \$2000. Let x = his income for one randomly chosen month.

a. Construct the probability distribution for the random variable x.

b. What is the probability that the salesman's income for a randomly selected month will be at least \$2200? Less than \$2500?

Solution

a. The random variable x may assume the values 2000, 2200, and 2500, with the following probabilities:

x	$p(x)$
2000	.70
2200	.20
2500	.10

Note that, since $\sum_{\text{all } x} p(x)$ must equal 1, it follows that

$p(2000) = 1 - (.20 + .10) = 1 - .30 = .70.$

b. $P(x \geq 2200) = p(2200) + p(2500) = .20 + .10 = .30$

$P(x < 2500) = p(2000) + p(2200) = .70 + .20 = .90$

Thus, 30% of the months the salesman makes at least $2200 and 90% of the months he makes less than $2500.

Exercises

5.3 The following table gives the probability distribution for a random variable x:

x	$p(x)$
0	.422
1	.422
2	.141
3	?

Compute the value of $p(3)$ for this random variable.

5.4 Insurance experts have determined that the probability of a man under the age of 30 dying within the next year is .001. A 28-year-old man has a $50,000 term life insurance policy. Let x = the amount paid by the insurance company on this policy next year. Find the probability distribution for x, assuming there are no partial payments.

5.5 Past records of a mortgage lending institution indicate that 10% of the people who receive loans default within the first three years after receiving the loan. We shall randomly select the records of two people who received loans in 1989 and record x = the number of people (in our sample of two) who defaulted on their loans within three years. Construct the probability distribution for the random variable x.

5.6 The following is the probability distribution for x - the number of bedrooms in a randomly selected home listed for sale in a particular region of the country:

x	$p(x)$
1	.05
2	.15
3	.30
4	.42
5	.08

Find the probability that a randomly selected home listed for sale will have:

a. At least three bedrooms
b. Fewer than three bedrooms
c. No more than four bedrooms
d. Exactly one bedroom

5.3 EXPECTED VALUES OF DISCRETE RANDOM VARIABLES

Examples

5.6 Refer to the following probability distribution for a random variable x:

x	$p(x)$
-1	.1
0	.1
1	.2
2	.2
5	.4

a. Compute the mean μ and the standard deviation σ for this random variable.

b. Specify the interval $\mu \pm 2\sigma$; what is the probability that x will fall within the interval $\mu \pm 2\sigma$?

Solution

a. $$E(x) = \mu = \sum_{\text{all } x} xp(x) = -1(.1) + 0(.1) + 1(.2) + 2(.2) + 5(.4)$$
$$= -.1 + 0 + .2 + .4 + 2$$
$$= 2.5.$$

Note that $\mu = 2.5$ does not represent a possible value of x. Rather, in many repetitions of the experiment, the *average* value of x that will be observed is 2.5.

Now we shall calculate σ^2, the variance of x:

$$\sigma^2 = E[(x - \mu)^2] = \sum_{\text{all } x} (x - \mu)^2 p(x)$$
$$= (-1 - 2.5)^2(.1) + (0 - 2.5)^2(.1) + (1 - 2.5)^2(.2) + (2 - 2.5)^2(.2) + (5 - 2.5)^2(.4)$$
$$= (-3.5)^2(.1) + (-2.5)^2(.1) + (-1.5)^2(.2) + (-.5)^2(.2) + (2.5)^2(.4)$$
$$= (12.25)(.1) + (6.25)(.1) + (2.25)(.2) + (.25)(.2) + (6.25)(.4)$$

(continued)

$= 1.225 + .625 + .450 + .050 + 2.500$

$= 4.85$

Thus, the standard deviation is $\sigma = \sqrt{4.85} = 2.20$.

b. $\mu \pm 2\sigma = 2.5 \pm 2(2.20) = 2.5 \pm 4.40$, or $(-1.9, 6.9)$.

We observe that the two standard deviation interval about the mean will contain *all* observations on the random variable x, i.e., $P(-1.9 \leqslant x \leqslant 6.9) = 1$.

5.7 A risky investment involves paying \$100 that will return either \$900 (for a net profit of \$800) with probability .2 or \$0 (for a net loss of \$100) with probability .8. What is your expected net profit from this investment?

Solution

Let x = net profit from this investment. We wish to compute $E(x)$ where x has the following probability distribution:

x	$p(x)$
800	.2
-100	.8

(Note that a loss is treated as a negative profit.) Then

$$E(x) = \sum_{\text{all } x} xp(x) = 800(.2) + (-100)(.8) = 160 - 80 = 80.$$

Your expected net profit on an investment of this type is \$80. If you were to make a very large number of such investments, some would result in a net profit of \$800 and others would result in a net loss of \$100. However, in the long run, your *average* net profit per investment would be \$80.

5.8 From past experience, an automobile insurance company knows that a given automobile will suffer a total loss with probability .02, a 50% loss with probability .08, or a 25% loss with probability .15 during a year. What annual premium should the company charge to insure a \$10,000 automobile, if it wishes to "break even" on all policies of this type? (Assume there will be no other partial loss.)

Solution

The company will break even if it charges a premium equal to the *average* payoff on each policy. Thus, we let x = payoff on a policy of this type, and note that x has the following probability distribution:

x	$p(x)$	
10,000	.02	(represents a total loss)
5,000	.08	(represents a 50% loss)
2,500	.15	(represents a 25% loss)
0	.75	

(Note that with probability .75, the automobile will incur no loss, and hence the company will make no payoff on the policy.)

Now,

$$E(x) = 10{,}000(.02) + 5000(.08) + 2500(.15) + 0(.75) = 975.$$

That is, the company will make an *average* payoff of $975 on each policy of this type. In order to break even, a premium of $975 should be assessed.

Exercises

5.7 The probability distribution of x = the number of delivery trucks arriving at the warehouse of a factory during a given hour is as follows:

x	$p(x)$
0	.10
1	.12
2	.31
3	.26
4	.19
5	.02

a. Compute the mean, variance, and standard deviation of the random variable x.

b. What is the probability that a randomly observed value of x will fall within the interval $\mu \pm 2\sigma$?

5.8 A popular automobile advertisement claims that a certain car seats two adults and 2.3 children comfortably, and thus is perfect for the "average" American family. Comment on the statistical sensibility of this advertisement.

5.4 THE BINOMIAL RANDOM VARIABLE

Examples

5.9 For each of the following experiments, decide whether x is a binomial random variable.

a. From past records, it is known that 5% of all electronic calculators manufactured by a certain company will need major repairs within three months. Your company has just purchased 10 calculators from this firm. Let x be the number of these calculators that will require major repairs within three months.

b. Let x be the number of tosses of a fair coin before the first head is observed.

c. Five of the members of a governor's Council on Youth Fitness are female, and five are male. Three of the ten members of this committee will be selected randomly to appear before the state legislature to request funds to support physical education in elementary schools. Let x be the number of females chosen.

d. Past experience indicates that 1% of the tulip bulbs sold by a certain nursery will fail to bloom. A landscaper has just purchased 1500 of these tulip bulbs to beautify a city park. Let x be the number of these bulbs that will fail to bloom.

Solution

a. If we are willing to assume that the 10 calculators were randomly selected from all those produced by the company, and that they operate independently, then x is a binomial random variable with $n = 10$ and $p = .05$, where p = the probability that a randomly selected calculator requires major repairs within three months.

b. The binomial model is not satisfactory since n, the number of identical trials to be performed, cannot be determined in advance.

c. The trials do not satisfy the assumption of independence. To see this, suppose the first member selected is female. Then, the probability that the second member selected is female decreases from 1/2, since only four of the nine remaining members are female. Hence, x is not a binomial random variable.

d. x is a binomial random variable with $n = 1500$ and $p = .01$, where p is the probability that a randomly selected tulip bulb will fail to bloom.

5.10 Most new car dealerships offer a one-year, 12,000 mile warranty on all parts for any new car purchased. Past results have suggested that approximately 20% of all new cars must be serviced while under warranty. Suppose a dealer sells four new cars today, and let x = the number that will require service while under warranty. Tabulate the probability distribution for x.

Solution

We first note that x satisfies the characteristics of a binomial random variable with $n = 4$ and $p = .2$. Then the probability distribution for this random variable is given by

$$p(x) = \binom{n}{x}p^x q^{n-x} = \binom{4}{x}(.2)^x(.8)^{n-x}.$$

Probabilities are then computed as follows:

$$p(0) = \binom{4}{0}(.2)^0(.8)^4 = \frac{4!}{0!4!}(.2)^0(.8)^4 = \frac{4 \cdot 3 \cdot 2 \cdot 1}{1 \cdot 4 \cdot 3 \cdot 2 \cdot 1}(1)(.4096)$$

$$= .4096 \quad [\text{Note that } 0! = 1 \text{ and } (.2)^0 = 1.]$$

$$p(1) = \frac{4!}{1!3!}(.2)^1(.8)^3 = \frac{4 \cdot 3 \cdot 2 \cdot 1}{1 \cdot 3 \cdot 2 \cdot 1}(.2)^1(.8)^3 = 4(.2)(.512) = .4096$$

$$p(2) = \frac{4!}{2!2!}(.2)^2(.8)^2 = 6(.04)(.64) = .1536$$

$$p(3) = \frac{4!}{3!1!}(.2)^3(.8)^1 = 4(.008)(.8) = .0256$$

$$p(4) = \frac{4!}{4!0!}(.2)^4(.8)^0 = 1(.0016)(1) = .0016$$

Thus, the probability distribution of x is:

x	$p(x)$
0	.4096
1	.4096
2	.1536
3	.0256
4	.0016

5.11 Manufactured items that do not pass inspection are often sold as "seconds" or "blemishes" at a reduced price. Quite often, these products may have only a minor defect that does not affect performance. Past testing has shown that 90% of all "seconds" perform as well as "firsts." A random sample of 25 "seconds" from a particular manufacturer is to be selected. We will record x = the number of items in the sample that perform as well as "firsts."

a. Find $P(x \geqslant 20)$.

b. Find $P(18 \leqslant x < 23)$.

c. Compute μ and σ for the random variable x.

d. If this experiment were to be repeated many times, what proportion of the x observations would fall within the interval $\mu \pm 2\sigma$?

Solution

a. We first observe that x is a binomial random variable with $n = 25$ and $p = .9$, where p is the probability that a randomly selected "second" will perform as well as a "first," or, equivalently, the proportion of "seconds" that perform as well as "firsts." We now refer to Table II of Appendix B in the text to find the desired probabilities.

$$P(x \geqslant 20) = 1 - P(x \leqslant 19) = 1 - .033 = .967$$

b. $P(18 \leqslant x < 23) = P(x \leqslant 22) - P(x \leqslant 17) = .463 - .002 = .461$

c. For a binomial random variable x with parameters n and p, $\mu = np$ and $\sigma^2 = npq$. Thus, for our example, $\mu = 25(.9) = 22.5$, $\sigma^2 = 25(.9)(.1) = 2.25$, and $\sigma = \sqrt{2.25} = 1.5$.

d. The two standard deviation interval about the mean is

$$\mu \pm 2\sigma = 22.5 \pm 2(1.5) = 22.5 \pm 3.0, \text{ or } (19.5, 25.5).$$

Now, $P(19.5 \leqslant x \leqslant 25.5) = P(x \geqslant 20)$, since the largest possible value x may assume is 25. From the table of binomial probabilities,

$$P(x \geqslant 20) = 1 - P(x \leqslant 19) = 1 - .033 = .967.$$

Essentially all the observations on this random variable will fall within two standard deviations of the mean.

5.12 Assume x is a binomial random variable with $n = 15$ and $p = .6$. Use the table of binomial probabilities to find:

a. $P(x \leqslant 12)$

b. $P(x < 11)$

c. $P(x > 6)$

d. $P(x \geqslant 5)$

e. $P(4 < x < 12)$

f. $P(4 \leqslant x \leqslant 12)$

g. $P(6 \leqslant x < 12)$

Solution

a. $P(x \leqslant 12) = .973$

b. $P(x < 11) = P(x \leqslant 10) = .783$

c. $P(x > 6) = 1 - P(x \leqslant 6) = 1 - .095 = .905$

d. $P(x \geqslant 5) = 1 - P(x \leqslant 4) = 1 - .009 = .991$

e. $P(4 < x < 12) = P(x \leq 11) - P(x \leq 4) = .909 - .009 = .900$

f. $P(4 \leq x \leq 12) = P(x \leq 12) - P(x \leq 3) = .973 - .002 = .971$

g. $P(6 \leq x < 12) = P(x \leq 11) - P(x \leq 5) = .909 - .034 = .875$

Exercises

5.9 For each of the following experiments, decide whether x is a binomial random variable:

a. A car dealer has 20 used cars, half of which are domestic models and half of which are foreign models. For a weekend special sale, he chooses six of these cars at random and reduces their prices. Let x be the number of domestic models selected for the sale.

b. A local fast-food chain has observed that when they advertise a special in the college newspaper, 60% of their customers order the special. Today they advertised a special in the college paper, and we will observe the orders placed by 30 randomly selected customers. Let x be the number of customers who will order the special.

5.10 A restaurant owner has observed that 30% of the dinner bills are paid with a major credit card. Three bills are randomly chosen during a given evening, and the method of payment will be noted. Let x be the number of these bills that are paid with a major credit card.

a. Tabulate the probability distribution for the random variable x.

b. What is the probability that at least two of the bills will be paid with a major credit card?

5.11 Records kept by a newspaper publisher in a major city indicate that 40% of all subscriptions are for the morning paper. A sample of 15 subscriptions is to be randomly selected from the publisher's records. Let x be the number of these subscriptions that are for the morning paper.

a. Find $P(x < 8)$.

b. Find $P(6 \leq x \leq 11)$.

c. Find $P(x \geq 5)$.

d. Compute the mean and variance of the random variable x.

e. If this experiment were to be repeated many times, what proportion of the x observations would fall within the interval $\mu \pm 2\sigma$?

5.5 THE POISSON RANDOM VARIABLE (Optional)

Examples

5.13 The foreman on the production line of an electronics firm has observed that an average of three defective radios per day pass the production inspection. Let x be the number of defective radios that pass inspection on a given day. Specify the probability distribution of the random variable x.

Solution

The random variable x has the characteristics of a Poisson distribution because it represents the number of events (defective radio passes inspection) occurring over a fixed time period (one day), with a fixed average ($\lambda = 3$). Thus, the probability distribution for x is:

$$p(x) = \frac{\lambda^x e^{-\lambda}}{x!} = \frac{3^x e^{-3}}{x!}, \quad \text{for } x = 0, 1, 2, \ldots .$$

5.14 The number, x, of daily breakdowns of an obsolete university computer has an average of 1.5.

a. What is the probability that there will be no breakdowns on a particular day?

b. What is the probability that there will be at least two breakdowns on a given day?

c. What is the probability that the computer will have no breakdowns for two consecutive days?

d. Specify μ and σ^2 for the random variable x.

Solution

We first note that x possesses the characteristics of a Poisson random variable with $\lambda = 1.5$; thus, the probability distribution is given by:

$$p(x) = \frac{\lambda^x e^{-\lambda}}{x!} = \frac{(1.5)^x e^{-1.5}}{x!}, \quad \text{for } x = 0, 1, 2, \ldots .$$

a. $$P(x = 0) = \frac{(1.5)^0 e^{-1.5}}{0!} = \frac{1 \cdot e^{-1.5}}{1} = .223$$

b. $$\begin{aligned} P(x \geqslant 2) &= P(x = 2) + P(x = 3) + P(x = 4) + \cdots \\ &= 1 - [P(x = 0) + P(x = 1)] \\ &= 1 - \left[\frac{(1.5)^0 e^{-1.5}}{0!} + \frac{(1.5)^1 e^{-1.5}}{1!}\right] \end{aligned}$$

(continued)

$$= 1 - [.223 + (1.5)(.223)]$$

$$= 1 - (.558) = .442$$

c. Define the following events:

A: {No breakdown on Day 1}
B: {No breakdown on Day 2}

Now, if we assume independence of the computer's operation from day to day, we have

$$P(A \cap B) = P(A)P(B) = (.223)(.223) = .050.$$

There is only a 5% chance that the computer will operate for two consecutive days without a breakdown.

d. For a Poisson random variable, $\mu = \lambda$ and $\sigma^2 = \lambda$. In our example, $\mu = \sigma^2 = 1.5$.

Exercises

5.12 An insurance company claims it receives an average of five calls per hour reporting automobile accidents.

a. What is the probability that either four or five accidents are reported during the next hour?

b. What is the probability that at least one accident is reported during the next hour?

5.13 Insurance reports show that the business section in a particular town reports an average of two burglary attempts per month.

a. What is the probability that no burglary attempts are reported during a given month?

b. What is the probability that at least two burglary attempts are reported during each of the next three months?

6
CONTINUOUS RANDOM VARIABLES

SUMMARY

This chapter discussed the methodology used to describe *continuous* random variables, and presented the probability distributions of three such variables with wide applicability in business statistics: the *normal*, *uniform*, and *exponential* distributions. It was also demonstrated that the normal probability distribution provides a good approximation for the binomial distribution when the sample size is sufficiently large.

6.1 CONTINUOUS PROBABILITY DISTRIBUTIONS

6.2 THE UNIFORM DISTRIBUTION

Example

6.1 A machine that is designed to produce bolts with a diameter of .50 inch has been found to produce bolts with diameters that are distributed uniformly between .48 and .52 inch.

a. What fraction of the bolts produced by the machine are at least .49 inch in diameter?

b. Compute the mean and standard deviation of bolt diameters.

c. Find the probability that the diameter of a randomly selected bolt lies within two standard deviations of the mean.

Solution

a. Let x be the diameter of a randomly selected bolt produced by the machine. The probability distribution of x is known to be uniform over the interval $.48 \leqslant x \leqslant .52$; thus, $c = .48$, $d = .52$, and

$$f(x) = \frac{1}{.52 - .48} = \frac{1}{.04} = 25 \qquad (.48 \leqslant x \leqslant .52).$$

This uniform probability function may be visualized as a rectangle with length .04 and height 25:

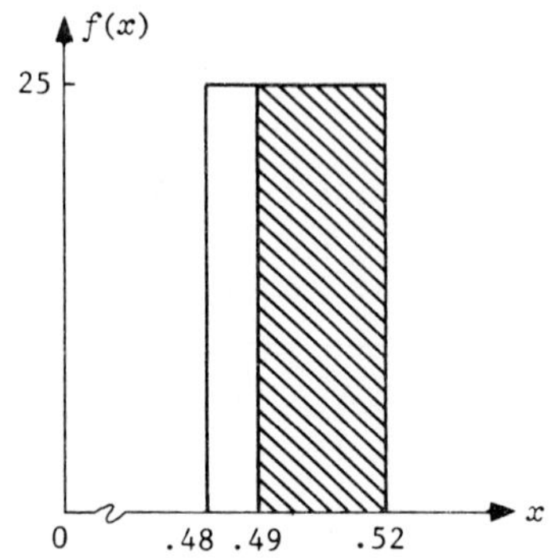

Now, since the area of a rectangle is equal to the base times the height, we have

$$P(x \geqslant .49) = (.52 - .49) \times 25 = .75.$$

Three-fourths of the bolts produced by the machine are at least .49 inch in diameter.

b. For a uniform random variable,

$$\mu = \frac{c + d}{2} \quad \text{and} \quad \sigma = \frac{d - c}{\sqrt{12}}$$

In our example,

$$\mu = \frac{.48 + .52}{2} = .50 \quad \text{and} \quad \sigma = \frac{.52 - .48}{\sqrt{12}} = .012$$

The diameters of bolts produced by this machine have a mean of .50 inch and a standard deviation of .012 inch.

c. The interval $\mu \pm 2\sigma$, or $.50 \pm 2(.012)$, or (.476, .524), covers the entire range of the distribution. Thus, the diameters of *all* bolts produced will lie within two standard deviations of the mean.

Exercises

6.1 A business executive has observed from long experience that his appointments show up any time from 15 minutes early to 30 minutes late. Assume the distribution of appointment arrival times is uniform over the interval between −15 and 30, with 0 representing scheduled appointment time.

a. Find the probability that the executive's next appointment is not late.

b. What fraction of all his appointments arrive within five minutes of the scheduled time?

6.2 Consumer investigations have shown that at auto service centers, jobs for which the customer is given an estimate of one hour of labor will actually require anywhere between 30 and 70 minutes. Assume the distribution of actual labor times is uniform over this interval.

a. If a customer is charged in advance for an estimated labor of one hour, what is the probability that this will represent an excessive charge in terms of the actual labor time required for the job?

b. Compute the mean and standard deviation of the actual labor time required on jobs for which the customer is given an estimate of one hour.

6.3 THE NORMAL DISTRIBUTION

Examples

6.2 Use Table IV in Appendix B of the text to find the following probabilities relating to the standard normal random variable, z.

a. $P(0 \leq z \leq 1.86)$
b. $P(-.52 \leq z \leq 0)$
c. $P(-.30 \leq z \leq 1.76)$
d. $P(z \leq 1.25)$
e. $P(z \geq 2.08)$
f. $P(1.23 \leq z \leq 1.94)$

Solution

It is often helpful to draw a sketch of the normal curve to assist in using Table IV to find the required probabilities.

a. Note that Table IV is designed to provide directly areas (probabilities) of the form $P(0 \leq z \leq z_0)$ for specified values of z_0. Thus, to determine $P(0 \leq z \leq 1.86)$, find the tabled entry at the intersection of the row headed 1.8 and the column headed .06. You will find $P(0 \leq z \leq 1.86) = .4686$.

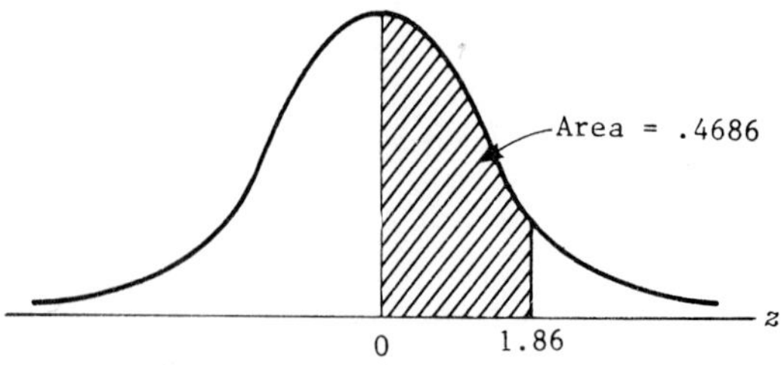

b. Because of the symmetry of the normal distribution, the area between $-.52$ and 0 is equal to the area between 0 and .52.

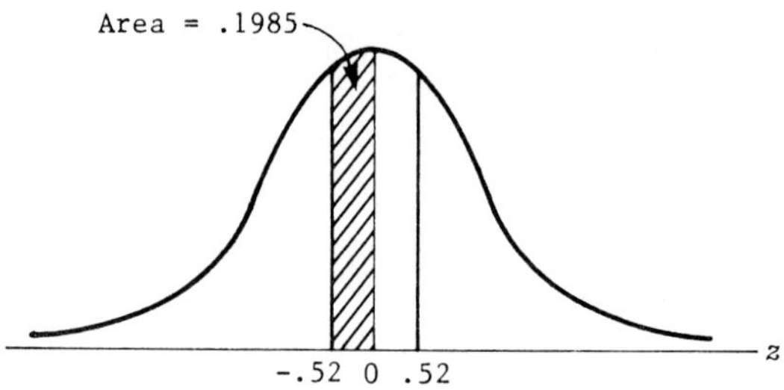

Thus, $P(-.52 \leqslant z \leqslant 0) = P(0 \leqslant z \leqslant .52) = .1985$.

c. $P(-.30 \leqslant z \leqslant 1.76) = P(-.30 \leqslant z \leqslant 0) + P(0 \leqslant z \leqslant 1.76)$

$= .1179 + .4608$

$= .5787$

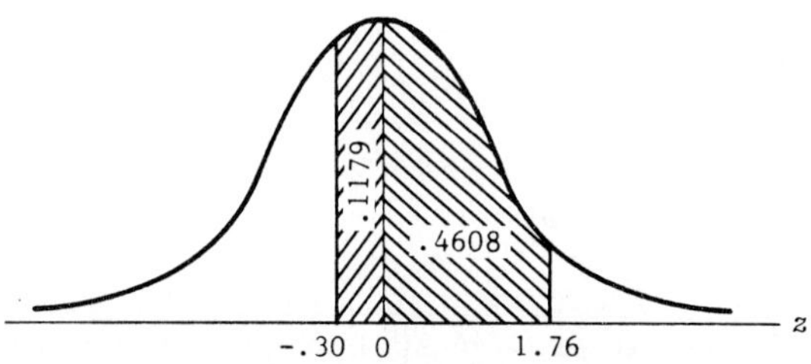

d. Note from Table IV that the area between 0 and 1.25 is .3944. However, to include *all* of the area to the left of 1.25, we write

$$P(z \leqslant 1.25) = P(z \leqslant 0) + P(0 \leqslant z \leqslant 1.25)$$
$$= .5 + .3944 = .8944.$$

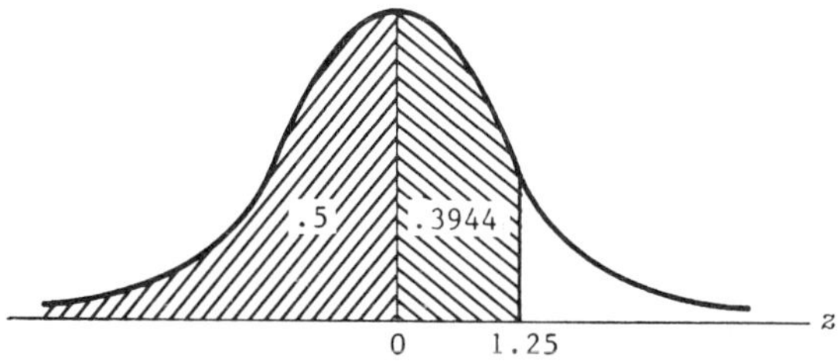

e. To find the required upper-tail area, we note that, since the area between 0 and 2.08 is .4812, the area to the right of 2.08 is .5 - .4812 = .0188. Thus,

$P(z \geqslant 2.08) = .0188.$

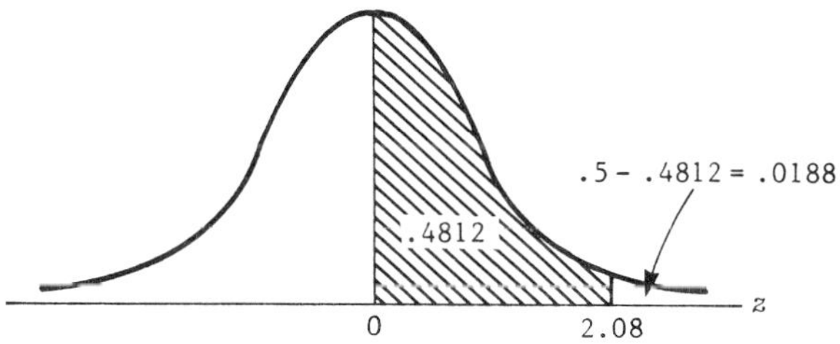

f. To find the area between 1.23 and 1.94, we observe that the area between 0 and 1.94 is $P(0 \leqslant z \leqslant 1.94) = .4738$. However, we want *only* the area between 1.23 and 1.94, so it is required to subtract from .4738 the area between 0 and 1.23, giving

$P(1.23 \leqslant z \leqslant 1.94) = .4738 - .3907 = .0831.$

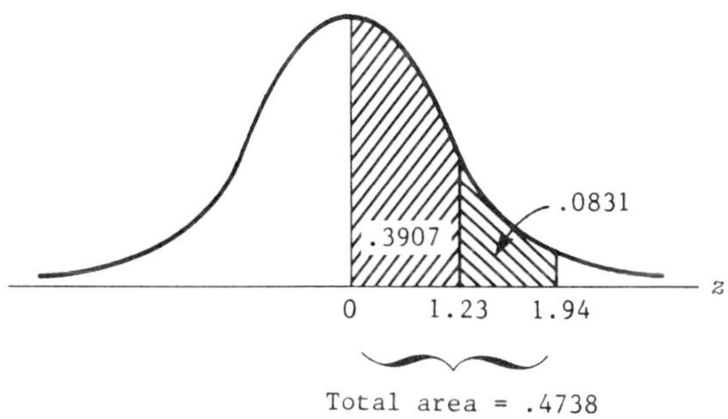

6.3 Find the value of z_0 that makes the following statements true:

a. $P(0 \leqslant z \leqslant z_0) = .3749$

b. $P(-z_0 \leqslant z \leqslant z_0) = .9500$

c. $P(z \geqslant z_0) = .0495$

Solution

a. We know that the area between 0 and z_0 is .3749. Since Table IV is set up to provide areas of this form, it is required to find the entry .3749 in the body of the table. You will find .3749 at the intersection of the 1.1 row and the .05 column; thus,

$$P(0 \leqslant z \leqslant 1.15) = .3749 \quad \text{and} \quad z_0 = 1.15.$$

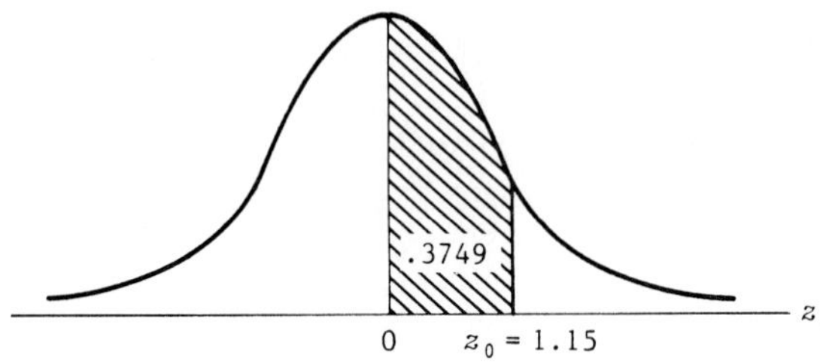

b. We use the symmetry of the normal distribution to conclude that the area within a distance of z_0 on each side of 0 is .9500/2 = .4750.

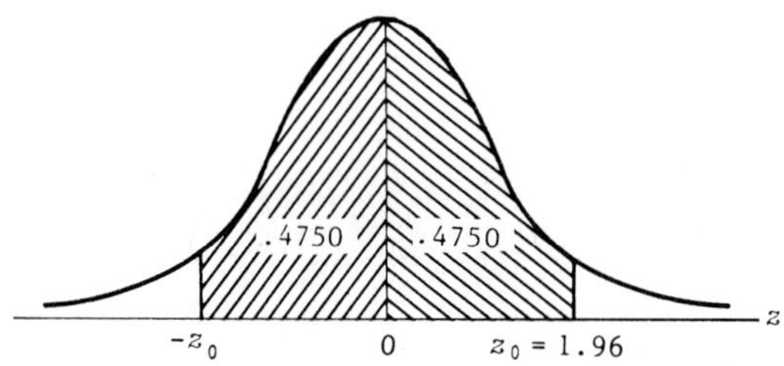

Thus, $P(0 \leqslant z \leqslant z_0) = .4750$ and $z_0 = 1.96$.

c. The first step is to determine on which side of 0 the value z_0 should be. Since $P(z \geqslant 0) = .5$, and we want a smaller probability, z_0 should be to the right of 0. [Note that for $z_0 < 0$, the value of $P(z \geqslant z_0)$ would be greater than .5, which is too large.]

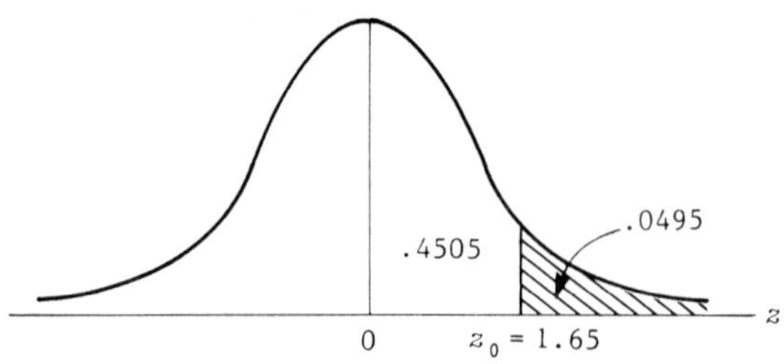

Since the area to the right of z_0 is $P(z \geqslant z_0) = .0495$, this leaves an area of $.5 - .0495 = .4505$ between 0 and z_0. The location of .4505 in the body of Table IV implies $z_0 = 1.65$.

6.4 The assembly time of an item on a production line at a factory is approximately normally distributed with a mean of 90 seconds and a standard deviation of 10 seconds.

a. What is the probability that a randomly selected item takes at least 105 seconds to assemble?

b. What fraction of the items take between 80 and 95 seconds to assemble?

Solution

a. Let x = the assembly time of an item. Since x has an approximately normal distribution, we can transform to the standard normal distribution to compute the required probabilities. The z score corresponding to an assembly time of x = 105 seconds is

$$z = \frac{x - \mu}{\sigma} = \frac{105 - 90}{10} = 1.5.$$

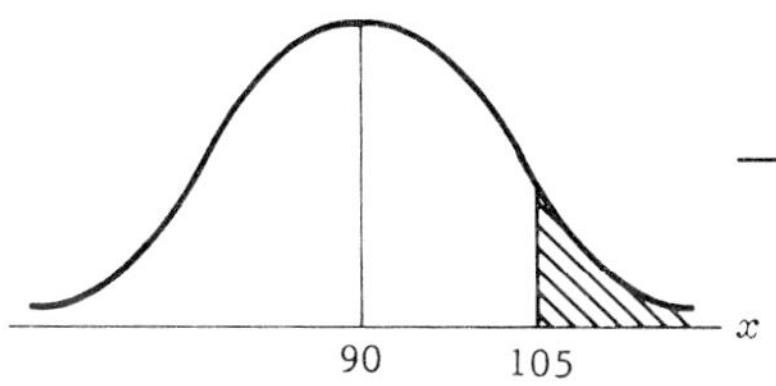

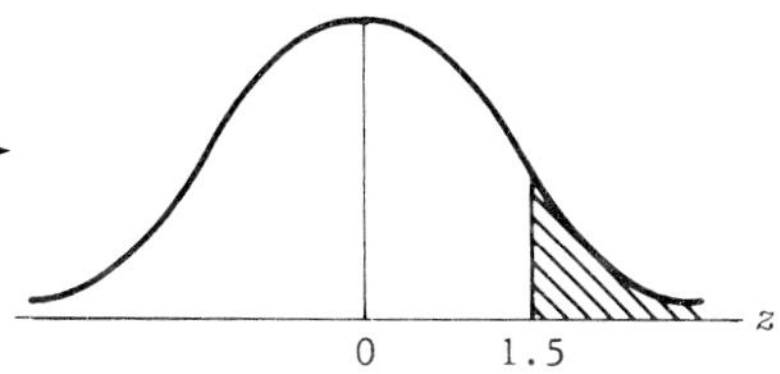

Thus,

$$P(x \geqslant 105) = P(z \geqslant 1.5) = .5 - .4332 = .0668.$$

Almost 7% of all items require at least 105 seconds for assembly.

b. $P(80 < x < 95) = P\left(\frac{80 - 90}{10} < z < \frac{95 - 90}{10}\right)$

$= P(-1.00 < z < .50) = .3413 + .1915 = .5328$

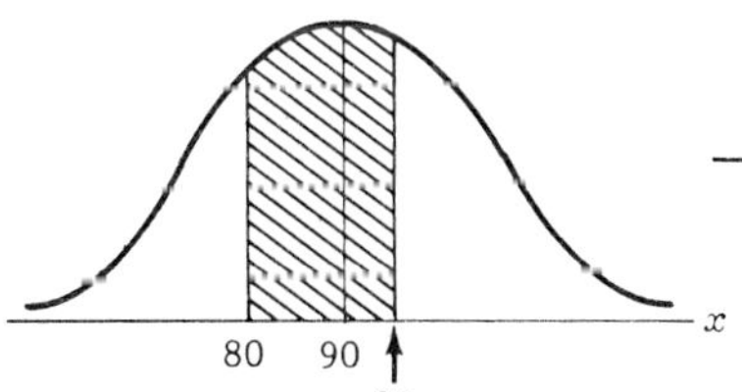

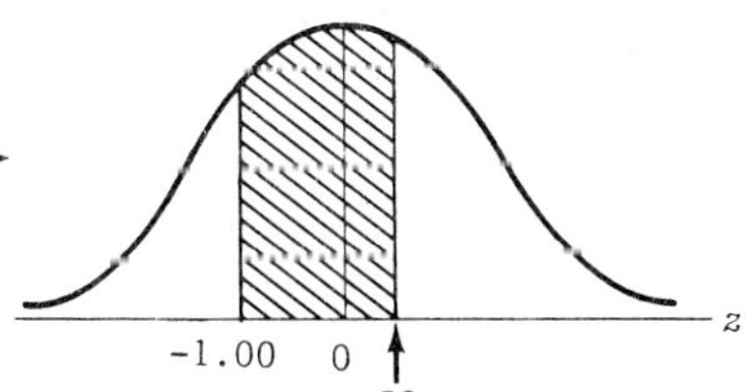

Approximately 54% of all items take between 80 and 95 seconds to assemble.

6.5 The guarantees associated with consumer products must be carefully determined. The manufacturer wants to set the guarantee so that the product looks very attractive, but so that very few items will have to be replaced because of failure before the expiration of the guarantee. Tests on new steel-belted radial tires showed an average tire wear of 40,000 miles and a standard deviation of 3000 miles. If tire wear is assumed to be approximately normally distributed, how much tire wear should be guaranteed if the manufacturer wishes to replace only 1% of the tires sold?

Solution

If we let x = the tire wear for a randomly selected tire and G = the amount of tire wear guaranteed, we can write

$$P(x < G) = .01,$$

since, if the amount of tire wear is less than what the manufacturer guarantees, the tire must be replaced. The next step is to determine how many standard deviations G is from the mean by transforming the normal random variable x to the standard normal random variable z:

$$z = \frac{G - \mu}{\sigma} = \frac{G - 40,000}{3000}$$

Now, since we know the area to the left of z (it is equivalent to the area to the left of G), we can use Table IV to determine the value of z (and hence G).

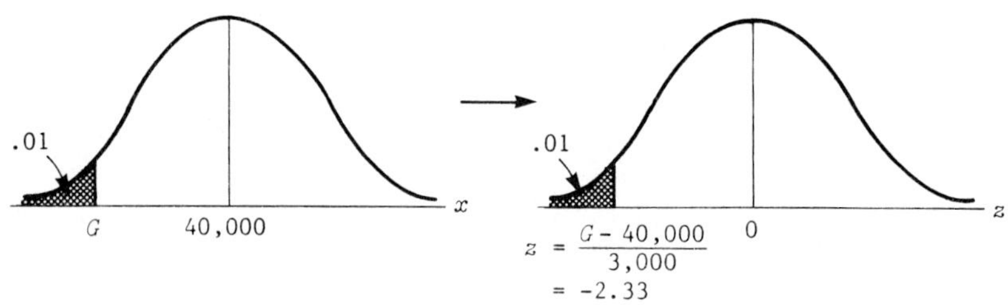

We observe that the area to the left of G (.01) corresponds to the area beneath the z curve to the left of -2.33, since $P(z < -2.33) \approx .01$. Therefore, we can solve the equation

$$\frac{G - 40,000}{3000} = -2.33,$$

which results in

$$G = 40,000 - 2.33(3000) = 33,010.$$

By setting the guarantee at approximately 33,000 miles, the manufacturer will need to replace approximately 1% of all tires sold.

Exercises

6.3 Use Table IV in Appendix B of the text to find the following probabilities:

a. $P(z \geqslant 1.75)$

b. $P(-2.02 \leqslant z \leqslant -1.44)$

c. $P(z \leqslant -1.38)$

d. $P(-1.48 \leqslant z \leqslant 1.03)$

6.4 Find the value of z_0 that makes the following statements true:

a. $P(-z_0 \leqslant z \leqslant z_0) = .9902$

b. $P(z \leqslant z_0) = .0250$

c. $P(z \geqslant z_0) = .7734$

6.5 Teleconferences, electronic mail, and word processors are among the tools that can reduce the length of business meetings. A recent survey indicated that the percent reduction x in time spent by professionals in meetings due to automated office equipment is approximately normally distributed with a mean equal to 15% and a standard deviation equal to 4%.

a. What proportion of all business professionals with access to automated office equipment have reduced their time in meetings by more than 22%?

b. What is the probability that new automated office equipment will reduce a professional's time in meetings by no more than 16%?

6.6 Experience has shown that the advertising revenue of a weekly professional newsletter is normally distributed with a mean of \$7800 per week and a standard deviation of \$620. Find the probability that the advertising revenue in any given week is:

a. Less than \$7000

b. More than \$8000

c. More than \$9000

6.7 A food processor packages instant orange juice in small jars. The weights of the contents of the jars are approximately normally distributed with mean 10.82 ounces and standard deviation .30 ounce.

a. Find the probability that the contents of a randomly selected jar of instant orange juice will be less than 10 ounces.

b. Find the value of c that makes the following statement true:

The contents of 5% of the jars packaged by this food processor weigh less than c ounces.

6.4 THE EXPONENTIAL DISTRIBUTION (Optional)

Example

6.6 An important decision facing bank managers is how many tellers to have available for duty at different times of the day. This decision is based on several factors, one of which is the time required by tellers to service customers. A recent study at a local bank indicated that the service times of the tellers have an exponential distribution with an average service time of four minutes.

a. Find the probability that a customer would require at least six minutes to be served at this bank.

b. What proportion of this bank's customers can be served in less than four minutes?

c. What proportion of the service times fall within two standard deviations of the mean?

<u>Solution</u>

a. If we let x = service time required for a randomly selected customer, then x has an exponential distribution with $\mu = 4$. The probability distribution of x is given by

$$f(x) = \lambda e^{-\lambda x}, \text{ where } \lambda = \frac{1}{\mu} = \frac{1}{4}.$$

We can now write $P(x \geqslant a) = e^{-\lambda a} = e^{-a/4}$. Thus,

$$P(x \geqslant 6) = e^{-6/4} = e^{-1.50} \approx .22.$$

There is an approximate 22% chance that a customer will require at least six minutes to be serviced at this bank.

b. $P(x < 4) = 1 - P(x \geqslant 4) = 1 - e^{-4/4} = 1 - e^{-1.0} \approx 1 - .37 = .63$

Approximately 63% of the bank's customers can be served in less than four minutes.

c. We wish to compute the probability that an x observation falls within the interval $\mu \pm 2\sigma$, or $4 \pm 2(4)$, or $(-4, 12)$. Since x cannot assume negative values, this is equivalent to

$$P(0 < x < 12) = 1 - P(x \geqslant 12) = 1 - e^{-12/4} = 1 - e^{-3.0}$$
$$\approx 1 - .05 = .95.$$

Thus, approximately 95% of the service times will fall within two standard deviations of the mean.

Exercises

6.8 The attendant at a car wash has observed that a car arrives every five minutes, on the average. Assume that the length of time between arrivals has an exponential distribution. A car has just arrived at the car wash.

a. What is the probability that the next car arrives in less than two minutes?

b. What is the probability that the next car arrives in between one and five minutes?

6.9 An advertisement claims that a smoke detector system will last for an average of two years before the batteries have to be replaced. If we assume the lifelength of the system has an exponential distribution, what proportion of all systems sold will last at least two years?

6.5 APPROXIMATING A BINOMIAL DISTRIBUTION WITH A NORMAL DISTRIBUTION

Examples

6.7 From extensive records, a major airline has concluded that 10% of all people with confirmed reservations do not show up for their flight. For a small plane with 96 seats, the airline has decided to book 100 reservations. What is the probability that everyone who shows up with a reservation for the flight gets a seat?

Solution

Let x = the number of people with a reservation who show up for the flight. Then x is a binomial random variable with $n = 100$ and $p = .9$, where p is the probability that a person holding a reservation shows up for the flight. We want to find $P(x \leqslant 96)$, since everyone will get a seat if 96 or fewer people show up for the flight. Binomial tables for $n = 100$ are not available in the text; thus, we will use the normal approximation to the binomial.

The value of $n = 100$ is sufficiently large that x may be well approximated by a normal random variable with

$\mu = np = 100(.9) = 90$ and $\sigma^2 = npq = 100(.9)(.1) = 9$,

and thus, $\sigma = 3$.

(Note that μ and σ^2 are the mean and variance of the original binomial random variable x.)

To apply the continuity correction, we note that it is necessary to include all the area to the left of 96.5 beneath the approximating normal curve in order to include all of the area corresponding to $x = 96$. Thus,

$$P(x \leqslant 96) = P(x \leqslant 96.5) \approx P\left(z \leqslant \frac{96.5 - 90}{3}\right)$$

$$= P(z \leqslant 2.17) = .5 + .4850 = .9850.$$

Therefore, there is a 98.5% chance that all those who show up with reservations for the flight will be accommodated.

6.8 Suppose that x is a binomial random variable for which you wish to find approximate probabilities by using the normal approximation. Indicate the continuity correction that would be appropriate for each of the following situations:

a. $P(x > a)$
b. $P(x < a)$
c. $P(x \geqslant a)$
d. $P(x \leqslant a)$
e. $P(a \leqslant x \leqslant b)$
f. $P(a < x < b)$

Solution

It may be useful to sketch the binomial histograms and the approximating normal curves in order to visualize each situation.

a. $P(x > a) = P(x > a + \frac{1}{2})$

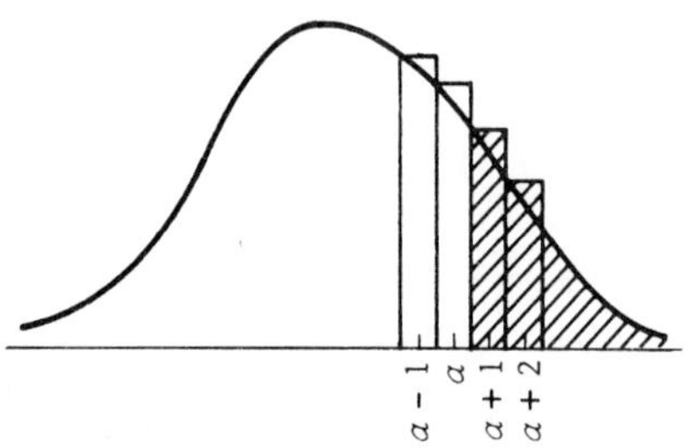

b. $P(x < a) = P(x < a - \frac{1}{2})$

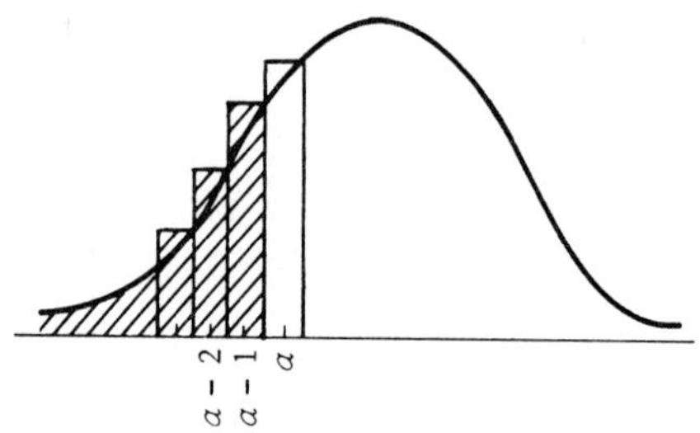

c. $P(x \geqslant a) = P(x \geqslant a - \frac{1}{2})$

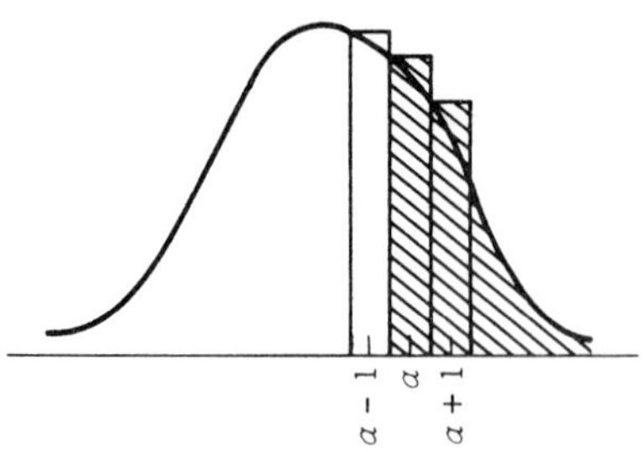

d. $P(x \leqslant a) = P(x \leqslant a + \frac{1}{2})$

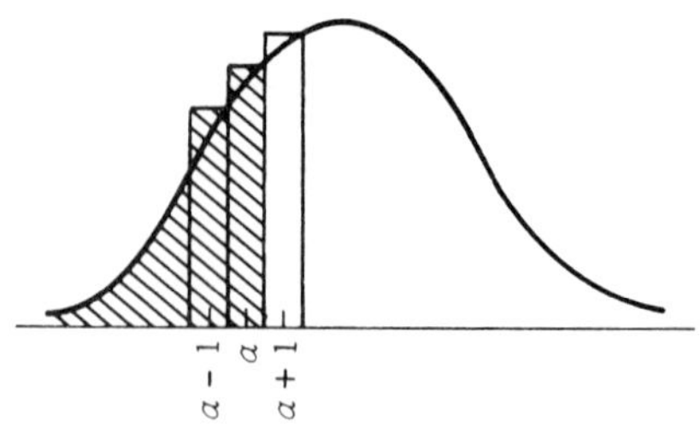

e. $P(a \leqslant x \leqslant b)$
$= P(a - \frac{1}{2} \leqslant x \leqslant b + \frac{1}{2})$

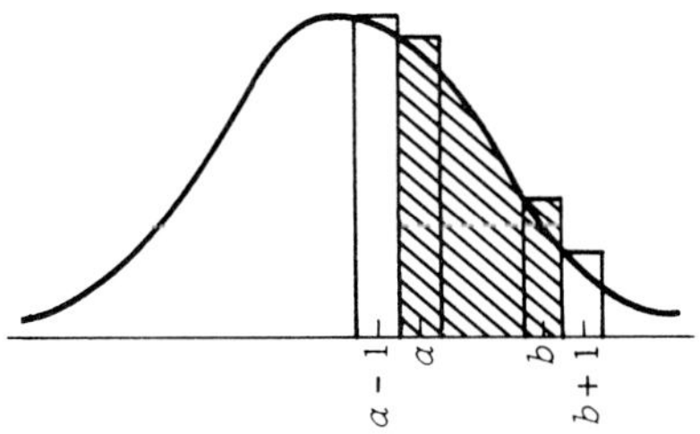

f. $P(a < x < b)$
$= P(a + \frac{1}{2} < x < b - \frac{1}{2})$

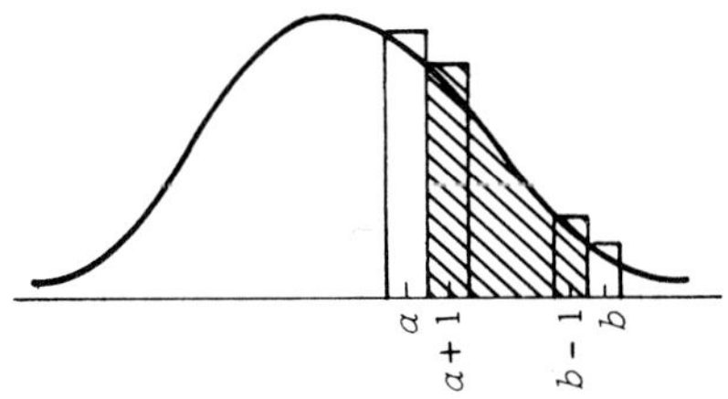

Exercises

6.10 A television dealer has observed that 75% of all televisions he sells are portable. Find the approximate probability that, of the next 50 sold, at least 35 will be portable.

6.11 A major weekly business magazine claims that it has subscriptions from 40% of all major companies across the country. In a sample of 150 companies, what is the approximate probability that at least 50 subscribe to the magazine, if the claim is valid?

7
SAMPLING DISTRIBUTIONS

SUMMARY

The objective of most statistical investigations is to make an inference about the population *parameter*, θ. To do this, we use sample data to compute a sample *statistic* which contains information about θ. The *sampling distribution* of a statistic characterizes the distribution of values of the statistic over a very large number of samples.

Unbiasedness and *minimum variance* are desirable properties of the probability distribution of a sample statistic. In terms of these criteria, the sample mean provides the "best" estimator when the parameter of interest is the population mean, μ. Further, the *Central Limit Theorem* guarantees that the sampling distribution for the sample mean will be approximately normal, regardless of the distribution of the sampled population, when the sample size is sufficiently large.

For all the statistics used in this text, the variance of the sampling distribution of the statistic is inversely related to the sample size.

7.1 INTRODUCTION TO SAMPLING DISTRIBUTIONS

7.2 PROPERTIES OF SAMPLING DISTRIBUTIONS: UNBIASEDNESS AND MINIMUM VARIANCE

Example

7.1 Consider the random variable x, whose probability distribution is as follows:

x	$p(x)$
1	.2
2	.2
3	.2
4	.2
5	.2

Construct the sampling distribution (or probability distribution) of $\bar{x}$, the mean of a random sample of $n = 3$ observations selected without replacement from this population.

Solution

We first note the form of the probability distribution for the random variable x:

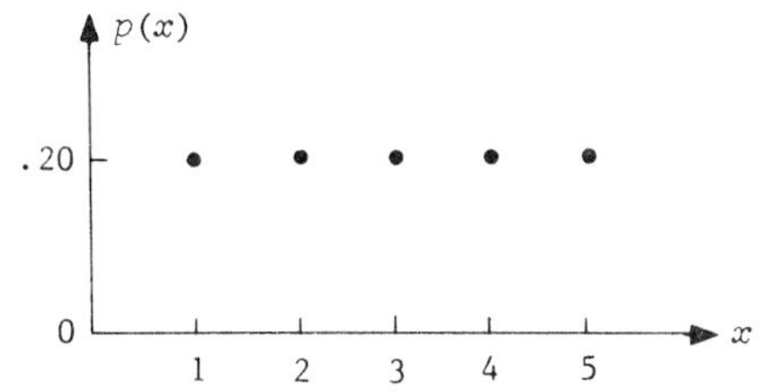

In addition, you should verify that $\mu = E(x) = 3.00$.

A random sample of size $n = 3$ is to be selected without replacement from this population. The 10 possible samples and their associated values of $\bar{x}$ are as follows:

POSSIBLE SAMPLE	VALUE OF $\bar{x}$
1, 2, 3	2.00
1, 2, 4	2.33
1, 2, 5	2.67
1, 3, 4	2.67
1, 3, 5	3.00
1, 4, 5	3.33
2, 3, 4	3.00
2, 3, 5	3.33
2, 4, 5	3.67
3, 4, 5	4.00

Since the selection is made at random, each possible sample is equally likely and has probability .1.

To construct the probability distribution of $\bar{x}$, we observe that:

$P(\bar{x} = 2.00) = P(\text{sample } 1, 2, 3) = .1;$

$P(\bar{x} = 2.33) = P(\text{sample } 1, 2, 4) = .1;$

$P(\bar{x} = 2.67) = P(\text{sample } 1, 2, 5) + P(\text{sample } 1, 3, 4) = .1 + .1 = .2;$

etc.

Thus, the probability distribution of $\bar{x}$ for this particular situation is given by:

$\bar{x}$	$p(\bar{x})$
2.00	.1
2.33	.1
2.67	.2
3.00	.2
3.33	.2
3.67	.1
4.00	.1

The mean of the probability distribution of $\bar{x}$ is equal to

$$\mu_{\bar{x}} = E(\bar{x}) = 2.00(.1) + 2.33(.1) + 2.67(.2) + 3.00(.2) + 3.33(.2) + 3.67(.1) + 4.00(.1)$$
$$= 3.00.$$

We have demonstrated that the mean of the sampling distribution of $\bar{x}$ is equal to the mean of the sampled population; i.e., $E(\bar{x}) = \mu$, and thus the sample mean $\bar{x}$ is an unbiased estimator of the population mean μ.

It should also be noted that the values of $\bar{x}$ cluster more closely about their mean than do the values of x; for example,

$P(2.5 \leqslant x \leqslant 3.5) = .2,$

whereas

$P(2.5 \leqslant \bar{x} \leqslant 3.5) = .6.$

In other words, the variation of the $\bar{x}$ values is less than the variation of the x values. It can be shown that, among all possible unbiased estimators of a population mean, $\bar{x}$ is the unbiased estimator with minimum variance.

Exercises

7.1 Refer to Example 7.1.

a. Construct the sampling distribution of m, the median of a random sample of size $n = 3$ selected without replacement from the population in Example 7.1.

b. Show that $E(m) = \mu$ (i.e., m is an unbiased estimator of μ) *in this particular situation.*

c. Use the probability distribution for $\bar{x}$ shown in Example 7.1 to compute $\sigma^2_{\bar{x}}$. Use the probability distribution for m found in part a of this exercise to compute σ^2_m. Show that $\sigma^2_{\bar{x}} < \sigma^2_m$; i.e., for these two unbiased estimators of the population mean, $\bar{x}$ has a smaller variance than m.

7.2 Consider the random variable x, whose probability distribution is as follows:

x	$p(x)$
1	.2
3	.2
4	.2
5	.2
10	.2

a. Construct the sampling distribution of m, the median of a random sample of size $n = 3$ selected without replacement from this population.

b. Verify that $E(m) \neq \mu$, and thus the sample median is *not*, in general, an unbiased estimator of the population mean.

7.3 THE SAMPLING DISTRIBUTION OF THE SAMPLE MEAN

7.4 THE RELATIONSHIP BETWEEN SAMPLE SIZE AND A SAMPLING DISTRIBUTION

Examples

7.2 Due to the problems with foam during the filling process, beer bottles are not always filled to capacity. A certain brewery advertises that their bottles contain, on the average, 12 ounces of beer. A random sample of 100 bottles off their production line yielded a sample mean fill of 11.9 ounces, and a standard deviation of .4 ounce. Compute the probability of observing a sample mean fill of 11.9 ounces or less, assuming the brewery's claim is valid.

Solution

Let x be the amount of fill (in ounces) of a randomly selected beer bottle from this brewery. Then x has a probability distribution (the exact form of which is unspecified) with mean $\mu = 12$, according to the brewery's claim.

We wish to compute $P(\bar{x} \leqslant 11.9)$, where $\bar{x}$ is the mean of a random sample of $n = 100$ observations from the distribution of x. The Central Limit Theorem assures us that $\bar{x}$ has an approximately normal distribution, with

$$\text{mean } \mu_{\bar{x}} = \mu = 12$$

and

$$\text{standard deviation } \sigma_{\bar{x}} = \frac{\sigma}{\sqrt{n}} \approx \frac{s}{\sqrt{n}} = \frac{.4}{\sqrt{100}} = .04.$$

(Note that the value of σ, the standard deviation of the sampled population, is unknown; hence, we estimate it using the value of s, the sample standard deviation.)

Now we apply a result from Chapter 6 to conclude that

$$z = \frac{\bar{x} - \mu_{\bar{x}}}{\sigma_{\bar{x}}}$$

is a standard normal random variable. Thus,

$$P(\bar{x} \leqslant 11.9) = P\left(z \leqslant \frac{11.9 - 12}{.04}\right) = P(z \leqslant -2.5) = .0062.$$

The probability of observing a sample mean fill of 11.9 ounces or less is only .0062, if the brewery's claim that $\mu = 12$ is true. We have strong evidence that the brewery's claim is untrue, because the observed sample result is very unlikely if the claim is true.

7.3 A study of the residential housing in a particular state showed that the average appraised value of a house in the state is \$85,000 and the standard deviation is \$8000. A random sample of 40 homes is to be selected from the state.

a. Describe the sampling distribution of the sample mean appraised value of the 40 homes.

b. Compute $P(\bar{x} > \$86{,}000)$.

c. Compute $P(\$82{,}000 \leqslant \bar{x} \leqslant \$86{,}000)$.

Solution

a. Let x be the appraised value of a randomly selected home from this state. Then the probability distribution of x (although the exact form is unknown) has mean $\mu = 85{,}000$ and standard deviation $\sigma = 8000$. Now, by an application of the Central Limit Theorem, the sampling distribution of $\bar{x}$, the mean of a random sample of size $n = 40$, is approximately normal with

$$\text{mean } \mu_{\bar{x}} = \mu = 85{,}000$$

and

$$\text{standard deviation } \sigma_{\bar{x}} = \frac{\sigma}{\sqrt{n}} = \frac{8000}{\sqrt{40}} = 1264.9.$$

b. $P(\bar{x} > 86{,}000) = P\left(z > \dfrac{86{,}000 - 85{,}000}{1264.9}\right) = P(z > .79) = .2148$

c. $P(82{,}000 \leqslant \bar{x} \leqslant 86{,}000) = P\left(\dfrac{82{,}000 - 85{,}000}{1264.9} \leqslant z \leqslant \dfrac{86{,}000 - 85{,}000}{1264.9}\right)$

$= P(-2.37 \leqslant z \leqslant .79) = .7763$

7.4 Refer to Example 7.3. Suppose it is desired to reduce the standard deviation of the sampling distribution of $\bar{x}$ by 1/3, to

$$\sigma_{\bar{x}} = \frac{1264.9}{3} = 421.63.$$

What size sample must be selected to accomplish this?

Solution

Since we desire $\sigma_{\bar{x}} = 421.63$, it is necessary to solve the following equation for n:

$$\sigma_{\bar{x}} = \frac{\sigma}{\sqrt{n}} = \frac{8000}{\sqrt{n}} = 421.63$$

or

$$n = \left(\frac{8000}{421.63}\right)^2 = 360.$$

Note that, in order to reduce $\sigma_{\bar{x}}$ to 1/3 of its original value, it is necessary to include nine times as many observations in the sample. In general, to reduce the standard deviation of the sampling distribution of $\bar{x}$ to $1/K$ times its original value, nK^2 observations must be included in the sample.

Exercises

7.3 Suppose we select a random sample of 40 recently issued building permits for improvements to existing residential structures, and record the value x of each permit. Prior experience has shown that, in a particular county, the relative frequency distribution of the values of such building permits has a mean of μ = \$8000 and a standard deviation of σ = \$1500.

a. Describe the sampling distribution of $\bar{x}$, the mean value of a sample of 40 building permits.

b. What is the probability that the mean value of permits in the sample will be less than \$7500?

c. What is the probability that the mean value of permits in the sample will be between \$7500 and \$8500?

7.4 A grocery store advertises that its ground beef contains no more than 30% fat. A random sample of 64 one-pound packages of ground beef was cooked and then weighed electronically to determine fat content. The weights of the cooked beef had an average of $\bar{x}$ = .68 pound and a standard deviation of s = .075 pound. (Note that, if the store's advertisement is accurate, then the population mean cooked weight, μ, of all such one-pound packages sold at the store would be at least .70 pound.) Compute the probability of observing a sample mean cooked weight of .68 pound or less for these 64 packages, assuming μ does in fact equal .70 pound.

7.5 For families living in a particular housing district, the average annual income is \$31,000 and the standard deviation is \$15,000.

a. Describe the sampling distribution of $\bar{x}$, the sample mean annual income of n = 25 families selected at random from the housing district.

b. Suppose it is desired to reduce the standard deviation of the sampling distribution in part **a** by one-half. What size sample must be selected to accomplish this?

c. Compute $P(\$26{,}000 \leq \bar{x} \leq \$34{,}900)$ for each of the sampling distributions in parts **a** and **b**.

8
INFERENCES BASED ON A SINGLE SAMPLE: ESTIMATION

SUMMARY

This chapter presented the inference-making technique of *estimation* based on a single sample selected from a population; measures of the uncertainty of the inference, based on the sampling distribution of the sample statistic, were discussed.

An interval estimate, called a *confidence interval*, is used to estimate a population parameter with a prespecified probability of coverage, called the *confidence coefficient*.

When using the sample mean $\bar{x}$ to make inferences about the population mean μ, the standard normal z statistic is employed when the sample size is sufficiently large ($n > 30$). For small samples drawn from a normal population with an unknown value of σ, the t statistic is used in making the inference. The z statistic is also used to form confidence intervals for a binomial proportion p, based on a sample fraction of successes, $\hat{p}$.

The sample size required for estimating a population parameter can be determined by specifying the desired confidence level and the bound on the error of estimation.

8.1 LARGE-SAMPLE ESTIMATION OF A POPULATION MEAN

Examples

8.1 For each of the following confidence coefficients, determine the value of $z_{\alpha/2}$ which would be used in constructing a $100(1 - \alpha)\%$ confidence interval for μ:

a. .80 b. .85 c. .95

Solution

a. For a confidence coefficient of .80, we have

$$1 - \alpha = .80,$$

or $\alpha = .20,$

or $\alpha/2 = .10.$

Thus, we desire the value of $z_{\alpha/2} = z_{.10}$ that locates an area of .10 in the upper tail of the distribution of z (see figure):

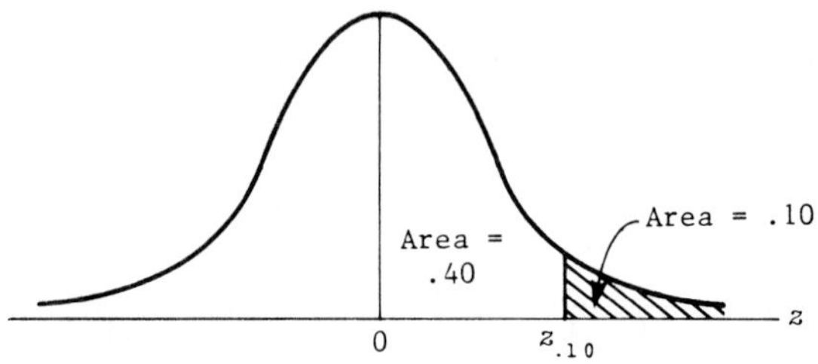

Now recall that the table in the text gives areas beneath the standard normal curve between 0 and the specified z value. From the figure, it can be seen that the area between 0 and $z_{.10}$ is .50 - .10 - .40; thus, it is necessary to locate the area .4000 in the body of the table to determine the corresponding value of $z_{.10}$. The tabled entry .3997 is the value closest to the desired area of .4000, and its corresponding z value is $z_{.10} = 1.28$. Hence, the value of $z_{\alpha/2}$ used in the construction of an 80% confidence interval for μ is $z_{.10} = 1.28$.

b. For a confidence coefficient of .85,

$$1 - \alpha = .85,$$

or $\alpha = .15,$

or $\alpha/2 = .075$

The required value of z is the one that locates an upper tail area of .075 beneath the z distribution:

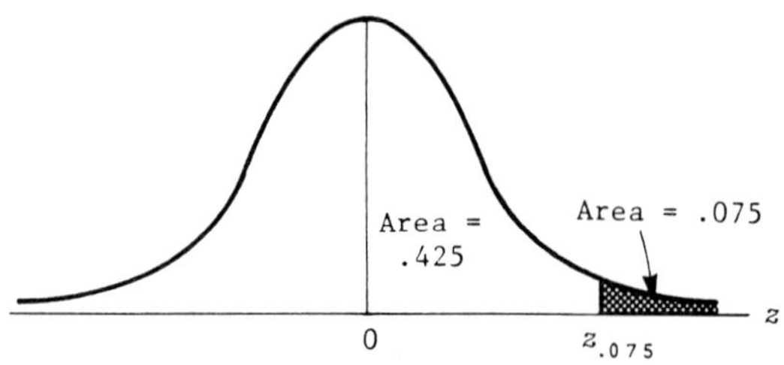

The area between 0 and the desired value of $z_{.075}$ is $.5 - .075 = .425$. The closest entry in the body of the table is .4251, and it corresponds to a z value of 1.44. In the construction of an 85% confidence interval for μ, the appropriate z value is $z_{.075} = 1.44$.

c. For a confidence coefficient of .95,

$$1 - \alpha = .95,$$

or $\alpha = .05,$

or $\alpha/2 = .025.$

The area between 0 and $z_{\alpha/2} = z_{.025}$ is equal to $.5 - .025 = .475$:

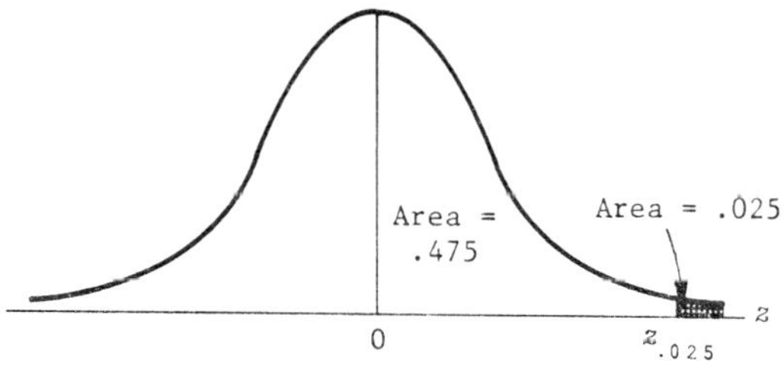

From the table of areas beneath the standard normal distribution, it is seen that the desired z value is $z_{.025} = 1.96$.

8.2 Automotive corporations are now required by federal regulations to reveal estimates of gasoline mileage for each new car model marketed. Recent testing of 36 automobiles of a new model yielded $\bar{x} = 28.6$ miles per gallon (mpg) and $s = 2.4$ mpg.

a. Construct a 95% confidence interval for μ, the true (but unknown) mean number of miles per gallon of gasoline that will be obtained by all new cars of this model.

b. Interpret the confidence interval obtained in part a.

Solution

a. The general form of a large-sample 95% confidence interval for a population mean μ is

$$\bar{x} \pm z_{.025}\sigma_{\bar{x}} \quad \text{or} \quad \bar{x} \pm 1.96(\sigma/\sqrt{n}).$$

In our example, we have

$$\bar{x} = 28.6, \; s = 2.4, \; n = 36.$$

Since the value of σ (the population standard deviation of the number of miles per gallon for all new cars of this model) is unknown, we will estimate it with the sample standard deviation, s. Then the 95% confidence interval is given by

$$28.6 \pm 1.96(\sigma/\sqrt{36}) \approx 28.6 \pm 1.96(2.4/6) = 28.6 \pm .78,$$

or (27.82, 29.38).

b. If we were to select repeated random samples of 36 new automobiles of this particular model, compute $\bar{x}$ for each sample, and construct a 95% confidence interval each time, then approximately 95% of the intervals so constructed would contain the true value of the population mean μ. We are thus 95% confident that the interval (27.82, 29.38) contains μ, although we do not know whether this *particular* interval is one of the 95% which contain μ, or one of the remaining 5% which fail to contain μ.

Exercises

8.1 For each of the following confidence coefficients, specify the value of $z_{\alpha/2}$ that would be used in the construction of a large-sample $100(1-\alpha)\%$ confidence interval for a population mean μ.

a. .90 b. .98 c. .99

8.2 An examination of the yearly premiums for a random sample of 80 automobile insurance policies from a major company showed an average of \$329 and a standard deviation of \$49.

a. Give a precise definition of what the population parameter μ represents in terms of this problem.

b. Construct a 99% confidence interval for μ.

c. Interpret the interval constructed in part b.

8.3 A publisher was interested in estimating the mean retail cost of its best-selling hardbound novel. A random sample of 50 retail outlets gave the following results on retail cost: $\bar{x} = \$19.80$; $s = \$2.40$. Estimate the mean retail cost of the publisher's best-selling hardbound novel. Use a 95% confidence interval.

8.2 DETERMINING THE SAMPLE SIZE NECESSARY TO ESTIMATE A POPULATION MEAN

Example

8.3 Each year, when automotive makers introduce the new models, the Environmental Protection Agency (EPA) calculates an estimate of the average gasoline mileage rating for each new model. For a particular new model, the EPA intends to provide an estimate of the average mileage rating that is accurate to within .5 mile per gallon (mpg) with 95% confidence. How many cars should be tested by EPA in order to achieve the desired accuracy? Assume that the standard deviation of mpg ratings for this model was $\sigma = 2.5$ mpg last year.

Solution

The EPA desires to estimate μ, the true mean gasoline mileage rating for this model, correct to within $B = .5$ mpg with 95% confidence. The required sample size is

$$n = \frac{(z_{\alpha/2})^2\sigma^2}{B^2},$$

where $z_{\alpha/2} = z_{.025} = 1.96$, $\sigma = 2.5$, and $B = .5$. The solution is then computed as follows:

$$n = \frac{(1.96)^2(2.5)^2}{(.5)^2} = 96.04.$$

Thus, the EPA must test at least 97 automobiles to estimate μ with the desired accuracy.

Exercise

8.4 The credit manager of a large department store wishes to estimate μ, the mean amount of purchases charged to a credit account during a one-month period. How many charge accounts should be sampled in order to be 90% confident that the estimate obtained will be within \$2.50 of the true value of μ? (Previous records indicate that the standard deviation of the amount of monthly purchases charged to a credit account is \$15.50.)

8.3 SMALL-SAMPLE ESTIMATION OF A POPULATION MEAN

Examples

8.4 Use the table of critical values of the t distribution to find the particular values of t_0 that make the following statements true:

a. $P(t > t_0) = .05$ when $df = 12$.

b. $P(t < t_0) = .025$ when $df = 20$.

c. $P(t > t_0 \text{ or } t < -t_0) = .01$ when $df = 8$.

Solution

a. We first note that the table of critical values of the t distribution in the text gives values t_α such that $P(t > t_\alpha) = \alpha$. Now, at the intersection of the column labeled $t_{.05}$ and the row corresponding to 12 degrees of freedom, we find the entry 1.782; thus,

$P(t > 1.782) = .05$ when $df = 12$

(see figure), i.e., $t_0 = 1.782$.

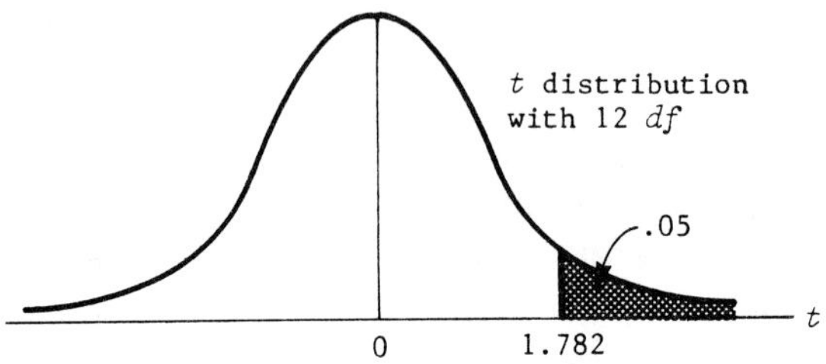

b. From the table, we observe that $P(t > 2.086) = .025$ when $df = 20$ (see figure below).

We use the symmetry of the t distribution to conclude that

$P(t < -2.086) = .025$ when $df = 20$,

i.e., $t_0 = -2.086$.

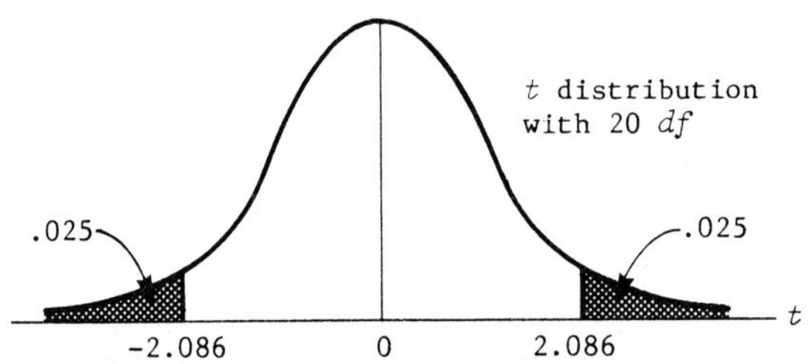

c. We wish to locate the critical values t_0 and $-t_0$ such that the total area in the two tails of the t distribution with 8 degrees of freedom is .01 (see figure below).

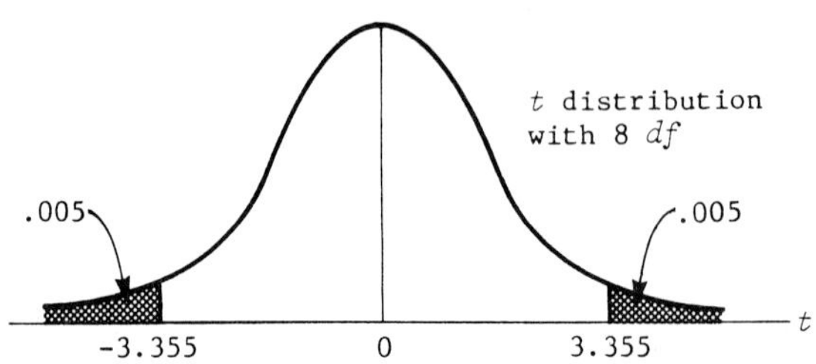

Because of the symmetry of the t distribution, an area of .01/2 = .005 in each tail is required. Thus, we determine the value of t_0 by locating the entry at the intersection of the column labeled $t_{.005}$ and the row corresponding to df = 8: t_0 = 3.355. Thus,

$P(t > 3.355 \text{ or } t < -3.355) = .01$ when df = 8.

8.5 With inflation and rising operational costs, medical bills have risen rapidly over the past 10 years. A newspaper study recently reported that the nationwide average cost of a hospital room in a semi-private ward is \$250 per day. To test this claim, an insurance company conducted its own survey in California, the only state in which it is licensed to sell hospitalization policies. The daily cost of a semi-private room was recorded for a random sample of 20 major hospitals, and the following statistics were computed: $\bar{x}$ = \$236; s = \$23. Construct a 98% confidence interval for the true mean cost of a hospital room in a semi-private ward.

Solution

The general form of a small-sample confidence interval for μ is

$\bar{x} \pm t_{\alpha/2}(s/\sqrt{n})$

where t is based on $n - 1$ degrees of freedom. In our example, $\bar{x}$ = 236, s = 23, n = 20, and $t_{\alpha/2} = t_{.01}$ = 2.539, based on 19 df. Thus, the required confidence interval is

$236 \pm 2.539(23/\sqrt{20})$,
or $236 \pm 2.539(5.14)$,
or 236 ± 13.05,
or (222.95, 249.05).

The insurance company can be 98% confident that the true mean cost of a hospital room in a semi-private ward is between \$222.95 and \$249.05.

8.6 A trans-oceanic airline conducted a study to determine whether the mean weight of baggage checked by a passenger on its Miami to London flight differs significantly from 45 pounds. A random sample of 25 passengers was selected, and the weight of each passenger's checked baggage was recorded. The following results were obtained: $\bar{x}$ = 43.5 pounds; s = 6 pounds. Construct a 95% confidence interval for the true mean weight of checked baggage of passengers on the Miami to London flight.

Solution

The general form of a small-sample confidence interval for μ is

$\bar{x} \pm t_{\alpha/2}(s/\sqrt{n})$,

where t is based on $n - 1$ degrees of freedom. In our example, $\bar{x} = 43.5$, $s = 6$, $n = 25$, and $t_{\alpha/2} = t_{.025} = 2.064$, based on 24 df. Thus, the required confidence interval is

$$43.5 \pm 2.064(6/\sqrt{25}),$$

or $43.5 \pm 2.064(1.2)$,

or 43.5 ± 2.48,

or $(41.02, 45.98)$.

The airline can be 95% confident that the true mean weight of checked baggage of passengers going from Miami to London is between 41.02 and 45.98 pounds.

Note that this confidence interval procedure requires the assumption that the relative frequency distribution of baggage weights for passengers on the Miami to London flight is approximately normal.

Exercises

8.5 Determine the values of t_0 that make the following statements true:

a. $P(t < t_0) = .01$ when $df = 18$.

b. $P(t > t_0) = .05$ when $df = 7$.

c. $P(t < -t_0 \text{ or } t > t_0) = .10$ when $df = 22$.

8.6 The off-campus housing office at a major university has published an apartment-finder's guide which states that the average cost of a two-bedroom, unfurnished apartment located within three miles of the campus is \$400 per month. However, for a random sample of 16 apartment complexes contacted by a prospective renter, the mean and standard deviation of the monthly rental rates for such apartments were found to be \$420 and \$28, respectively.

a. Construct a 99% confidence interval for the mean cost of a two-bedroom, unfurnished apartment within three miles of the campus.

b. State any assumptions required for the validity of the test procedure used in part **a**.

8.7 A random sample of 22 new homes built last year in a particular state was selected, and the number of square feet of heated floor space was recorded for each. The sample mean and standard deviation were computed as follows: $\bar{x} = 1712$; $s = 250$.

a. Construct a 95% confidence interval for the mean square footage of new homes being built in this state.

b. State any assumptions required for the validity of the procedures used in part **a**.

8.4 LARGE-SAMPLE ESTIMATION OF A BINOMIAL PROBABILITY

Examples

8.8 Each year, the Internal Revenue Service (IRS) conducts a study of the accuracy of tax returns for the purpose of possible simplification (or other revision) of forms for subsequent tax years. In this year's study, a random sample of 500 tax returns showed that 90 contained at least one error. Construct a 99% confidence interval for p, the proportion of all tax returns that contain at least one error.

Solution

The general form of a large-sample confidence interval for p is

$$\hat{p} \pm z_{\alpha/2}\sqrt{pq/n} \approx \hat{p} \pm z_{\alpha/2}\sqrt{\hat{p}\hat{q}/n},$$

where $\hat{p}$ is the proportion of successes in the sample, and $\hat{q} = 1 - \hat{p}$.

In this example, we are interested in p = the true proportion of all tax returns submitted this year that contain at least one error. The best estimate of the binomial parameter p is

$$\hat{p} = \frac{\text{Number of returns in sample that contain at least one error}}{\text{Number of returns in sample}}$$

$$= \frac{90}{500} = .18.$$

Now, we substitute the values

$$\hat{p} = .18,\ z_{\alpha/2} = z_{.005} = 2.58,\ \hat{q} = 1 - \hat{p} = .82,\ n = 500$$

into the general formula to obtain the desired confidence interval:

$$.18 \pm 2.58\sqrt{(.18)(.82)/500} = .18 \pm 2.58(.017)$$

$$= .18 \pm .044 \quad \text{or} \quad (.136, .224).$$

The IRS can be 99% confident that the proportion of this year's tax returns that contain at least one error lies within the interval (.136, .224).

8.9 In previous years, a mail-order company observed that 10% of its customers placed an additional order within six months of their original order. However, the records for a random sample of 1000 recent customers indicate that only 80 customers placed an additional order within six months of their original order. Construct a 95% confidence interval for p, the proportion of customers who place an additional order within six months.

Solution

The general form of a large-sample confidence interval for p is

$$\hat{p} \pm z_{\alpha/2}\sqrt{pq/n} \approx \hat{p} \pm z_{\alpha/2}\sqrt{\hat{p}\hat{q}/n},$$

where $\hat{p}$ is the proportion of successes in the sample, and $\hat{q} = 1 - \hat{p}$.

We are interested in p = the true proportion of customers who place an additional order within six months. The best estimate of p is

$$\hat{p} = \frac{80}{1000} = .08.$$

Now we substitute the values

$$\hat{p} = .08,\ \hat{q} = 1 - \hat{p} = .92,\ z_{\alpha/2} = z_{.025} = 1.96,\ n = 1{,}000$$

into the general formula to obtain the desired confidence interval:

$$\begin{aligned} .08 \pm 1.96\sqrt{(.08)(.92)/1{,}000} &= .08 \pm 1.96(.009) \\ &= .08 \pm .018 \text{ or } (.062,\ .098) \end{aligned}$$

The retail chain can be 95% confident that the true proportion of customers who place additional orders within six months is between .062 and .098.

Exercises

8.8 A local dairy is considering the possibility of ceasing home deliveries in an effort to minimize cost increases for its products. In a survey of 100 randomly selected customers who currently receive home delivery, 64 customers indicated that they were in favor of this economy measure. Construct a 99% confidence interval for the proportion of all home delivery customers who favor the proposed measure.

8.9 Refer to Exercise 8.8. The dairy will cease home deliveries if the results of the survey indicate (at $\alpha = .01$) that at least 60% of all home delivery customers favor the proposal. What decision should the dairy make?

8.8 DETERMINING THE SAMPLE SIZE NECESSARY TO ESTIMATE A BINOMIAL PROBABILITY

Examples

8.10 Before a company commits funds for advertising during a television show, they need an accurate estimate of p, the proportion of area viewers who watch the particular show. How many area viewers should be sampled in order to produce an estimate of p that is correct within .02 with 90% confidence?

Solution

The required sample size is

$$n = \frac{(z_{\alpha/2})^2 pq}{B^2},$$

where $z_{\alpha/2} = z_{.05} = 1.645$ and $B = .02$. Since we have no prior knowledge about the value of p, we will substitute $p = q = .5$ into the sample size formula. (This is a conservative procedure which will yield a value for n that is at least as large as required.)

Substitution yields:

$$n = \frac{(1.645)^2(.5)(.5)}{(.02)^2} = 1691.3.$$

The company must sample 1692 viewers in order to estimate p with the desired accuracy.

8.11 A national retail chain wishes to estimate p, the proportion of charge customers who are more than one month behind in their payments. If they want to be 95% confident that their estimate is within .01 of the true value of p, how many accounts should be sampled? (Past evidence indicates that the proportion of delinquent accounts is approximately .15.)

Solution

The required sample size is

$$n = \frac{(z_{\alpha/2})^2 pq}{B^2},$$

where $z_{\alpha/2} = z_{.025} = 1.96$, $B = .01$, and we use our prior estimate of $p = .15$ ($q = .85$) in the computation. Thus,

$$n = \frac{(1.96)^2(.15)(.85)}{(.01)^2} = 4898.04.$$

The retail chain must sample the accounts of 4899 charge customers in order to be 95% confident that their estimate is within .01 of the true value of p.

Exercise

8.10 A manufacturer of desk calculators believes that the proportion of calculators that require service within one month of sale is no more than .04. The firm's quality control engineer wishes to estimate p, the actual proportion of all calculators sold by the firm that require service within one month of sale, accurate to within .005 with 90% confidence. The sale/repair records for how many calculators should be sampled in order to obtain the desired accuracy?

9
INFERENCES BASED ON A SINGLE SAMPLE: TESTS OF HYPOTHESES

SUMMARY

This chapter presented the inference-making technique of hypothesis testing based on a single sample selected from the population; measures of the uncertainty of the inference, based on the sampling distribution of the sample statistic, were discussed.

Two methods for reporting the results of a hypothesis test were presented. In the first method, the experimenter fixes the probability α of falsely rejecting the *null hypothesis* in favor of the *research (alternative) hypothesis*. The second method reports the *observed significance level*, or *p-value*, which is the extent to which the test statistic disagrees with the null hypothesis, and leaves to the reader the decision whether to reject the null hypothesis.

When using the sample mean $\bar{x}$ to perform a test of hypothesis about the population mean μ, the standard normal z statistic is employed when the sample size is sufficiently large ($n > 30$). For small samples drawn from a normal population with an unknown σ, the t statistic is used to perform the hypothesis test. The z statistic is also used to perform a test of hypothesis for a binomial proportion p, based on the sample fraction of successes, $\hat{p}$.

9.1 THE ELEMENTS OF A TEST OF HYPOTHESIS

9.2 LARGE-SAMPLE TEST OF A HYPOTHESIS ABOUT A POPULATION MEAN

Examples

9.1 A college recruiter claimed that the average monthly starting salary for 1989 college graduates with business degrees would be \$2300. The monthly starting salaries for a sample of 75 companies selected randomly from the placement files were recorded, with the following results: $\bar{x} = \$2281$; $s = \$91$. Is this evidence that the average starting salary is less than \$2300 per month? Use a significance level of $\alpha = .05$.

Solution

The elements of this large-sample test of an hypothesis are as follows:

The null hypothesis is

$H_0: \mu = 2300$,

where μ is the true (but unknown) mean monthly starting salary (in dollars) for all 1989 college graduates with degrees in business.

The alternative (or research) hypothesis that we wish to establish is

$H_a: \mu < 2300$,

i.e., the average starting salary is less than \$2300 per month.

The rejection region consists of all values of z such that

$z < -z_\alpha$,

or $z < -z_{.05}$,

or $z < -1.645$.

Thus, we will reject H_0 if the computed value of the test statistic z is less than -1.645.

The test statistic is

$$z = \frac{\bar{x} - \mu_0}{\sigma_{\bar{x}}} = \frac{\bar{x} - \mu_0}{\sigma/\sqrt{n}},$$

where μ_0 is the value assigned to μ in the null hypothesis, and the value of σ will be estimated by s. Thus,

$$z = \frac{2281 - 2300}{91/\sqrt{75}} = -1.81.$$

Since this value of the test statistic falls within the rejection region, we reject H_0. There is sufficient evidence to conclude that the mean starting salary is less than \$2300 per month. We recognize the possibility of having made a Type I error; if the null hypothesis is in fact true, the probability that we have incorrectly rejected H_0 is $\alpha = .05$.

9.2 A local pizza parlor advertises that their average time for delivery of a pizza is within 30 minutes of receipt of the order. The delivery times for a random sample of 64 orders were recorded, with the following results: $\bar{x}$ = 34 minutes; s = 21 minutes. Is there sufficient evidence to conclude that the actual mean delivery time is larger than what is claimed by the pizza parlor? Use a significance level of $\alpha = .01$.

Solution

The hypothesis test is composed of the following elements:

H_0: $\mu = 30$
H_a: $\mu > 30$

where μ is the true mean delivery time (in minutes) for all orders placed at the pizza parlor. Note that we are interested in establishing the alternative hypothesis that the true mean delivery time exceeds the value advertised by the pizza parlor.

The rejection region consists of all values of z such that

$$z > z_\alpha,$$

or $z > z_{.01}$,

or $z > 2.33$.

The null hypothesis H_0 will be rejected if the computed value of the test statistic z exceeds 2.33.

The test statistic is

$$z = \frac{\bar{x} - \mu_0}{\sigma_{\bar{x}}} = \frac{\bar{x} - \mu_0}{\sigma/\sqrt{n}} = \frac{34 - 30}{21/\sqrt{64}} = 1.52.$$

This value of the test statistic does not fall within the rejection region; thus, there is insufficient evidence to conclude that the true mean delivery time is significantly greater than the 30 minutes claimed by the pizza parlor.

9.3 A machine is designed to fill cereal boxes with a net weight of 16 ounces. It is important that the machine operate accurately: if it fills too much, the company wastes excess cereal; if it underfills the boxes, the company risks a penalty from the Food and Drug Administration. The company has instituted a new quality control program to monitor the amount of fill of its cereal boxes. Every four hours, a random sample of 100 boxes is selected from the production line, and the amounts of fill are noted. If there is evidence (at $\alpha = .05$) that the mean amount of fill differs from 16 ounces, then the filling machine is reset.

Suppose one such inspection yielded the following results: $\bar{x}$ = 15.98 ounces; s = .21 ounce. Should the machine be reset?

Solution

We wish to perform a test of the hypothesis

H_0: $\mu = 16$

against

H_a: $\mu \neq 16$

where μ is the true mean amount of fill (in ounces) of the cereal boxes. We perform a two-tailed test to be able to detect the possibility that the machine either underfills (i.e., $\mu < 16$) or overfills (i.e., $\mu > 16$) the cereal boxes.

The rejection region consists of the following sets of z values:

$$z < -z_{\alpha/2} \quad \text{or} \quad z > z_{\alpha/2},$$

$$\text{i.e.,} \quad z < -z_{.025} \quad \text{or} \quad z > z_{.025},$$

$$\text{i.e.,} \quad z < -1.96 \quad \text{or} \quad z > 1.96.$$

The test statistic is

$$z = \frac{\bar{x} - \mu_0}{\sigma/\sqrt{n}} \approx \frac{\bar{x} - \mu_0}{s/\sqrt{n}} = \frac{15.98 - 16}{.21/\sqrt{100}} = -.95.$$

Since the value of the test statistic does not fall within the rejection region, we do not reject H_0. There is insufficient evidence to conclude that the mean amount of fill differs significantly from 16 ounces; there is no need to reset the machine based on this inspection.

Exercises

9.1 A random sample of 49 plastic bags with an advertised breaking strength of 10 pounds were tested, yielding an average breaking strength of 9.7 pounds and a standard deviation of .7 pound. Does this experiment provide sufficient evidence (at $\alpha = .01$) to conclude that the true mean breaking strength of all such plastic bags is less than the manufacturer's claim of 10 pounds?

9.2 A manufacturing process was designed to make pistons with a mean diameter of 11.5 centimeters. In the most recent quality control test of the process, a random sample of 81 pistons was selected from the production line, and their diameters were measured, with the following results: $\bar{x} = 11.54$ centimeters; $s = .25$ centimeter. Do the test results suggest (at $\alpha = .05$) that the mean diameter of the pistons being produced differs from 11.5 centimeters?

9.3 OBSERVED SIGNIFICANCE LEVELS: p-VALUES

Examples

9.4 For the given hypotheses and computed value of the test statistic, determine the observed significance level of the large-sample test.

a. H_0: $\mu = 50$, H_a: $\mu > 50$; $z = 1.79$

b. H_0: $\mu = 75$; H_a: $\mu < 75$; $z = -2.04$

c. H_0: $\mu = 4.8$, H_a: $\mu \neq 4.8$; $z = 1.32$

Solution

a. Since the test is upper-tailed (H_a: $\mu > 50$), values of the test statistic even more contradictory to H_0 than the computed value would be values larger than 1.79. Thus, the observed significance level (p-value) for this test is

$$p = P(z \geqslant 1.79) = .5 - .4633 = .0367.$$

b. The test is lower-tailed (H_a: $\mu < 75$); values of the test statistic that are contradictory to H_0 are those in the lower tail of the distribution. The observed significance level for this test is

$$p = P(z \leqslant -2.04) = .5 - .4793 = .0207.$$

c. For this two-tailed test (H_a: $\mu \neq 4.8$), values of the test statistic at least as contradictory to the null hypothesis as the computed value are those less than -1.32 *or* greater than 1.32. Thus,

$$p = P(z \leqslant -1.32 \text{ or } z \geqslant 1.32) = 2P(z \geqslant 1.32) = 2(.0934) = .1868.$$

9.5 Refer to Example 9.1. Compute the observed significance level for the test and interpret its value.

Solution

Example 9.1 presented a test of the hypothesis

$$H_0: \mu = 2300$$

against the alternative hypothesis

$$H_a: \mu < 2300.$$

The computed value of the test statistic was $z = -1.81$. For this lower-tailed test, the observed significance level is

$$p = P(z \leqslant -1.81) = .5 - .4649 = .0351.$$

This p-value implies that we would reject the null hypothesis for any value of α greater than .0351. In Example 9.1, we preselected the significance level $\alpha = .05$, and thus rejected the null hypothesis. However, at a preselected significance level of $\alpha = .01$, the null hypothesis would not be rejected, based on this sample.

9.6 Refer to Example 9.3. Compute the observed significance level for the test and interpret its value.

Solution

In Example 9.3, we conducted a two-tailed test of the hypothesis

H_0: $\mu = 16$

against the alternative hypothesis

H_a: $\mu \neq 16$.

The value of the test statistic computed from the observed sample was $z = -.95$. Values of the test statistic that would be even more contradictory to H_0 than the computed value are those less than $-.95$ *or* greater than .95. Thus, the observed significance level for this test is

$$p = P(z < -.95 \text{ or } z > .95) = 2P(z \geqslant .95) = 2(.1711) = .3422.$$

This large p-value does not cast doubt on the null hypothesis; we would be able to reject H_0 only for the preselected values of α greater than .3422.

Exercises

9.3 Refer to Exercise 9.1. Compute the observed significance level for the test of hypothesis and interpret its value.

9.4 Refer to Exercise 9.2. Report the p-value for the test and give an interpretation.

9.4 SMALL-SAMPLE TEST OF HYPOTHESIS ABOUT A POPULATION MEAN

Examples

9.7 Refer to Example 8.5. Can we conclude (at the $\alpha = .05$ level) that the average cost of a semi-private room in California hospitals is less than the nationwide average?

Solution

It is desired to make an inference about the value of μ, the true mean cost of a semi-private room in all California hospitals. In particular, we wish to test

H_0: $\mu = 250$ (i.e., the average cost in California equals the nationwide average)

against

H_a: $\mu < 250$ (i.e., the average cost in California is less than the nationwide average).

Since the sample size is $n = 20$, we cannot use the large-sample z statistic; thus, we must make the assumption that the distribution of semi-private room costs in California hospitals is approximately normal. The test will then be based on a t distribution with $n - 1 = 19$ degrees of freedom. The rejection region consists of all values of t such that

$t < -t_{\alpha}$,

or $t < -t_{.05}$,

or $t < -1.729$,

where t is based on 19 df.

The test statistic is

$$t = \frac{\bar{x} - \mu_0}{s/\sqrt{n}} = \frac{236 - 250}{23/\sqrt{20}} = -2.72.$$

This value of the test statistic falls within the rejection region. We thus reject H_0 and conclude that the average daily cost of a semi-private room in California hospitals is significantly less than the nationwide average of $250.

9.8 A trans-oceanic airline conducted a study to determine whether the mean weight of baggage checked by a passenger on its Miami to London flight differs significantly from 45 pounds. A random sample of 25 passengers was selected, and the weight of each passenger's checked baggage was recorded. The following results were obtained: $\bar{x} =$ 43.5 pounds; $s = 6$ pounds. If the airline is willing to risk a Type I error with probability $\alpha = .05$, what should they conclude from this study?

Solution

The airline wishes to perform a test of

$H_0: \mu = 45$

against

$H_a: \mu \neq 45$

where μ is the true mean weight of checked baggage of all passengers on the Miami to London flight.

The test will be based on a t statistic, since $n < 30$, and the large-sample z statistic is inappropriate. We must make the assumption that the baggage weights on Miami to London flights have an approximate normal distribution. Then, for $\alpha = .05$, the rejection region consists of the following sets of t values:

$$t < -t_{\alpha/2} \quad \text{or} \quad t > t_{\alpha/2},$$

$$\text{i.e.,} \quad t < -t_{.025} \quad \text{or} \quad t > t_{.025},$$

$$\text{i.e.,} \quad t < -2.064 \quad \text{or} \quad t > 2.064,$$

where t is based on $n - 1 = 24$ degrees of freedom.

The value of the test statistic is

$$t = \frac{\bar{x} - \mu_0}{s/\sqrt{n}} = \frac{43.5 - 45}{6/\sqrt{25}} = -1.25.$$

The computed value of the test statistic does not fall within the rejection region. There is insufficient evidence to conclude that the mean weight of checked baggage of passengers going from Miami to London is significantly different from 45 pounds.

Exercises

9.5 Refer to Exercise 8.6. Is there sufficient evidence (at $\alpha = .05$) to conclude that the true mean monthly rental rate for two-bedroom, unfurnished apartments in the area exceeds \$400? State any assumptions required for the validity of this hypothesis test.

9.6 A random sample of 22 new homes built last year in a particular state was selected, and the number of square feet of heated floor space was recorded for each. The sample mean and standard deviation were computed as follows: $\bar{x} = 1712$; $s = 250$.

a. The average number of square feet of heated floor space for new homes being built nationwide is 1800. Is there evidence that the new homes in this state have a mean square footage that differs significantly from the nationwide average? Use $\alpha = .05$.

b. State any assumptions required for the validity of the procedure used in part a.

9.5 LARGE-SAMPLE TEST OF HYPOTHESIS ABOUT A BINOMIAL PROBABILITY

Examples

9.9 Refer to Example 8.9. Is there evidence (at $\alpha = .05$) that the proportion of customers who place additional orders has decreased from previous years?

Solution

The mail-order company is interested in a test of the hypothesis

H_0: $p = .10$ (i.e., the proportion has not changed)

against

H_a: $p < .10$ (i.e., the proportion has decreased),

where p is the proportion of recent customers who place an additional order within six months of the original order.

The test will be based on a z statistic, since the sample size $n = 1000$ is large enough so that the sampling distribution of $\hat{p}$ is approximately normal. For $\alpha = .05$, the rejection region consists of z values such that

$z < -z_{\alpha}$,

or $z < -z_{.05}$,

or $z < -1.645$.

The test statistic is

$$z = \frac{\hat{p} - p_0}{\sqrt{pq/n}} \approx \frac{\hat{p} - p_0}{\sqrt{p_0 q_0/n}}.$$

In our example,

$$\hat{p} = \frac{80}{1000} = .08,\ \hat{q} = 1 - \hat{p} = .92,\ n = 1000,\ p_0 = .10.$$

Thus,

$$z \approx \frac{.08 - .10}{\sqrt{(.10)(.90)/1000}} = -2.11.$$

Since the computed value of z falls within the rejection region, we reject H_0 and conclude that the proportion of recent customers who place additional orders within six months of the original order is significantly less than .10.

Exercises

9.7 A local dairy is considering the possibility of ceasing home deliveries in an effort to minimize cost increases for its products. In a survey of 100 randomly selected customers who currently receive home delivery, 64 customers indicated that they were in favor of this economy measure. The dairy will cease home deliveries if the results of the survey indicate (at $\alpha = .01$) that at least 60% of all home delivery customers favor the proposal. What decision should the dairy make?

9.8 Refer to Example 8.8. A study of last year's returns showed that 10% of all returns contained at least one error. Is there sample evidence (at $\alpha = .01$) that the proportion of this year's returns with at least one error has increased?

9.6 CALCULATING TYPE II ERROR PROBABILITIES: MORE ABOUT β (Optional)

Example

9.10 A manufacturing process is tested to determine whether a new machine produces nails with a mean length of 1.2 inches. The test set-up is as follows:

H_0: $\mu = 1.2$
H_a: $\mu \neq 1.2$ (i.e., $\mu < 1.2$ or $\mu > 1.2$)

Test statistic: $z = \dfrac{\bar{x} - 1.2}{\sigma_{\bar{x}}}$

Rejection region: For $\alpha = .05$, $z < -1.96$ or $z > 1.96$.
For $\alpha = .01$, $z < -2.575$ or $z > 2.575$.

Note that two rejection regions have been specified corresponding to values of $\alpha = .05$ and $\alpha = .01$, respectively. Assume that $n = 100$ and $s = .5$.

a. Suppose that the nails have a mean length of 1.1 inches, i.e., $\mu = 1.1$. Calculate the values of β corresponding to the two rejection regions. Discuss the relationship between the values of α and β.

b. Calculate the power of the test for each of the rejection regions when $\mu = 1.1$.

Solution

a. We first consider the rejection region corresponding to $\alpha = .05$. The first step is to calculate the border values of $\bar{x}$ corresponding to the two-tailed rejection region, $z < -1.96$ or $z > 1.96$:

$$\bar{x}_{0,L} = \mu_0 - 1.96\sigma_{\bar{x}} \approx \mu_0 - 1.96s/\sqrt{n} = 1.2 - 1.96(.5/10) = 1.102$$
$$\bar{x}_{0,U} = \mu_0 + 1.96\sigma_{\bar{x}} \approx \mu_0 + 1.96s/\sqrt{n} = 1.2 + 1.96(.5/10) = 1.298$$

These border values are shown in the accompanying figure, part **a**. Next, we convert these values to z values in the alternative distribution with $\mu_a = 1.1$.

$$z_L = \frac{\bar{x}_{0,L} - \mu_a}{\sigma_{\bar{x}}} \approx \frac{1.102 - 1.1}{.05} = .04$$

$$z_U = \frac{\bar{x}_{0,U} - \mu_a}{\sigma_{\bar{x}}} \approx \frac{1.298 - 1.1}{.05} = 3.96$$

These z values are shown in the figure, part **b**, and you can see that the acceptance (or nonrejection) region is the area between them. Using Table IV of the Appendix, we find that the area between $z = 0$ and $z = .04$ is .0160, and the area between $z = 0$ and $z = 3.96$ is (approximately) .5 (since $z = 3.96$ is off the scale of Table IV). Then the area between $z = .04$ and $z = 3.96$ is, approximately,

$$\beta = .5 - .0160 = .484.$$

Thus, the test with $\alpha = .05$ will lead to a Type II error about 48% of the time when the nail mean length is .1 inch less than the expected mean length.

For the rejection region corresponding to $\alpha = .01$, $z < -2.575$ or $z > 2.575$, we find:

$$\bar{x}_{0,L} = 1.2 - 2.575(.5/10) = 1.0712$$
$$\bar{x}_{0,U} = 1.2 + 2.575(.5/10) = 1.3288$$

These border values of the rejection region are shown in the figure, part **c**.

Converting these to z values in the alternative distribution with $\mu_a = 1.1$, we find $z_L = .58$ and $z_U = 4.58$. The area between these values is, approximately,

$$\beta = .2190 + .5 = .719.$$

Thus, the chance that the test procedure with $\alpha = .01$ will lead to an incorrect acceptance of H_0 is about 72%.

Note that the value of β increases from .4840 to .7190 when we decrease the value of α from .05 to .01. This is a general property of the relationship between α and β; as α is decreased (increased), β is increased (decreased).

b. The power is defined to be the probability of (correctly) rejecting the null hypothesis when the alternative is true. When μ = 1.1 and α = .05, we find

Power = 1 - β = 1 - .4840 = .5160.

When μ = 1.1 and α = .01, we find

Power = 1 - β = 1 - .7190 = .2810.

The powers are shown in the figure, parts **b** and **c**, respectively. You can see that the power of the test is decreased as the level of α is decreased. This means that as the probability of incorrectly rejecting the null hypothesis is decreased, the probability of correctly accepting the null hypothesis for a given alternative is also decreased. Thus, the value of α must be selected carefully, with the realization that a test is made less powerful to detect departures from the null hypothesis when the value of α is decreased.

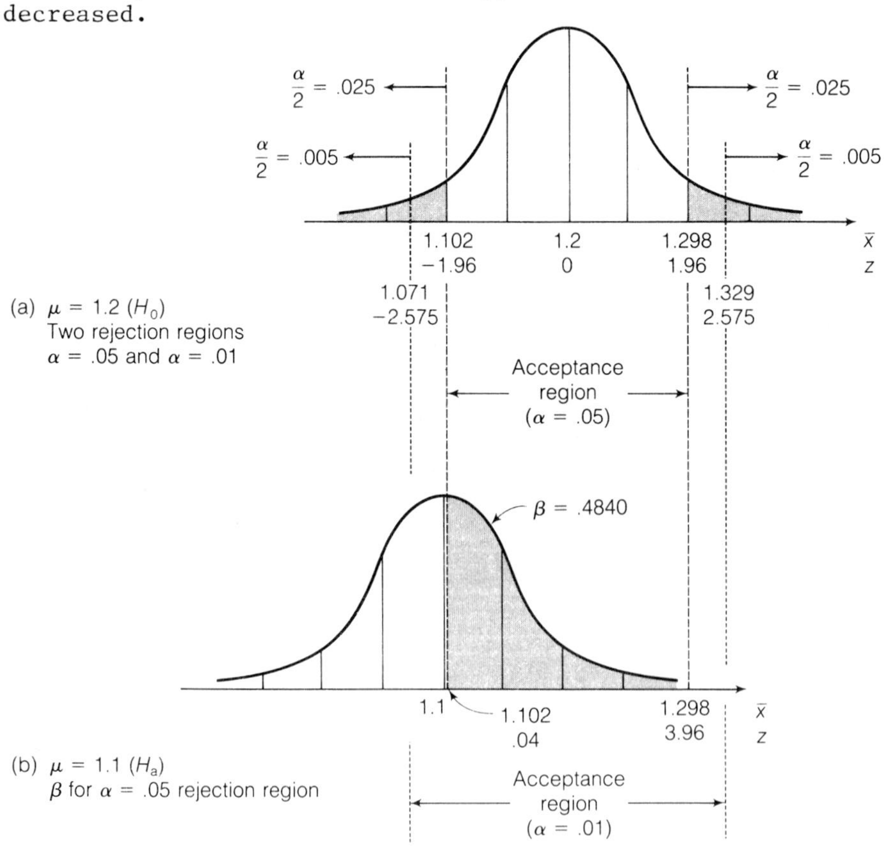

(a) $\mu = 1.2$ (H_0)
Two rejection regions
$\alpha = .05$ and $\alpha = .01$

(b) $\mu = 1.1$ (H_a)
β for $\alpha = .05$ rejection region

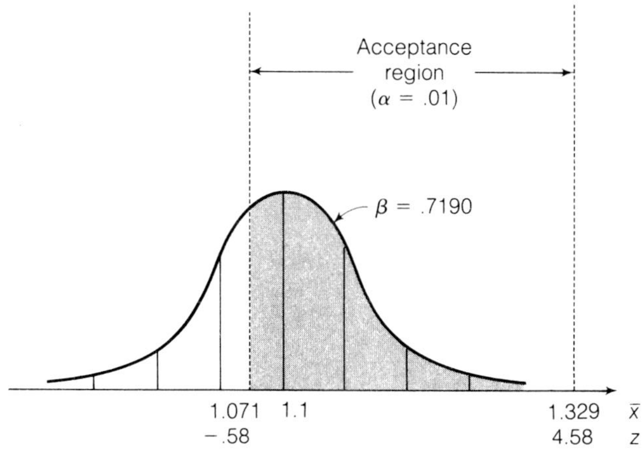

(c) $\mu = 1.1$ (H_a)
β for $\alpha = .01$ rejection region

Exercise

9.9 Refer to Example 8.7. Suppose the nails have a mean length of 1.35 inches. Calculate β for each of the rejection regions used in the example.

10
INFERENCES BASED ON TWO SAMPLES: ESTIMATION AND TESTS OF HYPOTHESES

SUMMARY

This chapter presented techniques for making inferences about the difference between population parameters, based on the information contained in two samples.

Large-sample inferences about the difference $(\mu_1 - \mu_2)$ between population means, or the difference $(p_1 - p_2)$ between binomial proportions, require minimal assumptions about the sampled populations and use a *two-sample z statistic*. Small-sample inferences about $(\mu_1 - \mu_2)$ may be based on an independent samples design (which requires the assumptions of normality and equal population variances) and a *two-sample t statistic*. Alternatively, it is often advantageous to employ a *paired difference design* (to eliminate the effect of variability due to the dimension(s) on which the observations are paired) and a single-sample t statistic to analyze the differences. An *F test* may be used to compare two population variances, σ_1^2 and σ_2^2.

The chapter demonstrated the calculation of the sample size required to estimate $(\mu_1 - \mu_2)$ or $(p_1 - p_2)$ with a specified degree of accuracy.

10.1 LARGE-SAMPLE INFERENCES ABOUT THE DIFFERENCE BETWEEN TWO POPULATION MEANS: INDEPENDENT SAMPLING

Examples

10.1 A major electrical corporation has recently developed a new 100 watt lightbulb which, it claims, has a longer mean lifelength than the leading competitor's 100 watt bulb. To test this claim, a consumer agency conducted a test with independent random samples of 100 of the new bulbs and 150 bulbs manufactured by the leading competitor. The lifelength for each of the bulbs was recorded, with the following results:

	NEW BULB	LEADING COMPETITOR'S BULB
$\bar{x}$	2197 hours	2134 hours
s	123 hours	99 hours
n	100	150

Is this sufficient evidence (at $\alpha = .05$) to support the claim that the new lightbulb lasts longer, on the average, than the leading competitor's bulb?

Solution

The elements of the relevant hypothesis test are as follows:

H_0: $\mu_1 - \mu_2 = 0$ (i.e., $\mu_1 = \mu_2$)
H_a: $\mu_1 - \mu_2 > 0$ (i.e., $\mu_1 > \mu_2$)

where μ_1 and μ_2 are the true average lifelengths of the new bulb and the leading competitor's bulb, respectively.

The sample sizes $n_1 = 100$ and $n_2 = 150$ are sufficient to permit use of a large-sample procedure based on a z statistic. Thus, for a significance level of $\alpha = .05$, we will reject H_0 if

$z > z_\alpha$,

or $z > z_{.05}$,

or $z > 1.645$.

The test statistic is

$$z = \frac{(\bar{x}_1 - \bar{x}_2) - 0}{\sqrt{\frac{\sigma_1^2}{n_1} + \frac{\sigma_2^2}{n_2}}} \approx \frac{(\bar{x}_1 - \bar{x}_2) - 0}{\sqrt{\frac{s_1^2}{n_1} + \frac{s_2^2}{n_2}}}$$

(The sample sizes are sufficient so that σ_1^2 and σ_2^2 may be well approximated by s_1^2 and s_2^2.) For our example, the computed value of z is:

$$z = \frac{2197 - 2134}{\sqrt{\frac{(123)^2}{100} + \frac{(99)^2}{150}}} = 4.28.$$

The value of the test statistic falls within the rejection region. We thus reject H_0 and conclude that the average lifelength of the new bulb is significantly greater than that of the leading competitor's bulb.

10.2 Independent random samples of records of new car sales for which a trade-in was accepted were obtained from the local General Motors dealership and from the Ford dealership across the street. The following data were tabulated on the mileage of the trade-in car:

	GENERAL MOTORS	FORD
$\bar{x}$	67,250	58,989
s	22,010	12,308
n	59	45

Construct a 90% confidence interval for the difference between the mean mileages on trade-in cars accepted by the General Motors and Ford dealerships.

Solution

The sample sizes are sufficient to employ the large-sample confidence interval for $(\mu_1 - \mu_2)$, where μ_1 and μ_2 denote the mean mileages on trade-in cars accepted by the General Motors and Ford dealerships, respectively. The confidence interval is given by:

$$(\bar{x}_1 - \bar{x}_2) \pm z_{\alpha/2}\sqrt{\frac{\sigma_1^2}{n_1} + \frac{\sigma_2^2}{n_2}} \approx (\bar{x}_1 - \bar{x}_2) \pm z_{\alpha/2}\sqrt{\frac{s_1^2}{n_1} + \frac{s_2^2}{n_2}}$$

$$= (67{,}250 - 58{,}989) \pm 1.645\sqrt{\frac{(22{,}010)^2}{59} + \frac{(12{,}308)^2}{45}}$$

$$= 8261 \pm 5597 \quad \text{or} \quad (2664,\ 13{,}858).$$

We can be 90% confident that the mean mileage on trade-ins accepted by the General Motors dealership is between 2664 and 13,858 miles higher than the mean mileage on trade-ins accepted by the Ford dealership.

10.3 Under what conditions will the sampling distribution of $(\bar{x}_1 - \bar{x}_2)$ be approximately normal?

Solution

The Central Limit Theorem guarantees that the sampling distribution of $(\bar{x}_1 - \bar{x}_2)$ will be approximately normal for sufficiently large values of n_1 and n_2, say, $n_1 \geqslant 30$ and $n_2 \geqslant 30$.

Further, it can be shown that the mean and variance of the sampling distribution of $(\bar{x}_1 - \bar{x}_2)$ are, respectively,

$$\mu_{(\bar{x}_1 - \bar{x}_2)} = E(\bar{x}_1 - \bar{x}_2) = \mu_1 - \mu_2 \quad \text{and} \quad \sigma^2_{(\bar{x}_1 - \bar{x}_2)} = \frac{\sigma_1^2}{n_1} + \frac{\sigma_2^2}{n_2},$$

assuming the two samples are randomly selected in an independent manner from the two populations.

Exercises

10.1 A study was conducted to investigage the difference in the fees charged by land surveyors in two neighboring states. Independent random samples of the fees assessed to survey residential properties in the two states were obtained; the results are presented in the table.

LAND SURVEYOR FEES	
State A	State B
$n_1 = 50$	$n_2 = 50$
$\bar{x}_1 = \$85$	$\bar{x}_2 = \$92$
$s_1 = \$4$	$s_2 = \$10$

Is there sufficient evidence (at $\alpha = .05$) to conclude that the mean fees assessed to survey residential properties in the two states are significantly different?

10.2 Refer to Exercise 10.1. Construct a 95% confidence interval for the difference between the mean fees assessed to survey residential properties in the two states. Interpret the confidence interval.

10.2 SMALL-SAMPLE INFERENCES ABOUT THE DIFFERENCE BETWEEN TWO POPULATION MEANS: INDEPENDENT SAMPLING

Examples

10.4 A company with a conventional sales training program experimented with a new program to see if it would improve sales. Out of 10 new salesmen, 6 were trained under the conventional program and 4 received the new program. The sales commission for each salesman was then recorded for the month following completion of the program. The following descriptive statistics were computed from the data:

	CONVENTIONAL	NEW
$\bar{x}$	\$1482	\$1680
s	\$112	\$146

Is there evidence (at $\alpha = .05$) that the new program may be more effective than the conventional training program?

Solution

Since the sample sizes are small, the test must be based on a two-sample t statistic, and the following assumptions are required:

1) The populations of sales commissions during the month following completion of the training program must be approximately normally distributed, for both the conventional and new program.

2) The variances of the two populations must be equal.

3) The two samples are randomly selected in an independent manner from the two populations. (In our example, it is reasonable to assume that the first-month sales commissions for the 10 salesmen represent independent random samples from the populations of the first-month sales commissions that would conceivably be generated by all potential trainees under both programs.)

The company is then interested in a test of

$H_0\colon \mu_1 - \mu_2 = 0 \quad (\text{i.e., } \mu_1 = \mu_2)$

against

$H_a\colon \mu_1 - \mu_2 < 0 \quad (\text{i.e., } \mu_1 < \mu_2)$

where μ_1 and μ_2 are the mean sales commissions for the month following completion of the training program, for all salesmen in the conventional and new training programs, respectively. Note that the alternative hypothesis of interest ($H_0\colon \mu_1 - \mu_2 < 0$) states that the mean first-month sales commission for those trained with the conventional program is lower than that for salesmen trained with the new program.

At $\alpha = .05$, we will reject H_0 if $t < -t_{.05}$, where t has $n_1 + n_2 - 2 = 6 + 4 - 2 = 8$ degrees of freedom. From the table of critical values for the t distribution, we see that for $df = 8$, $t_{.05} = 1.860$. The rejection region thus consists of all values of t such that $t < -1.860$. It is now required to compute s_p^2, the pooled estimate of the common population variance. We obtain:

$$s_p^2 = \frac{(n_1 - 1)s_1^2 + (n_2 - 1)s_2^2}{n_1 + n_2 - 2} = \frac{(6 - 1)(112)^2 + (4 - 1)(146)^2}{6 + 4 - 2}$$

$$= \frac{5(12{,}544) + 3(21{,}316)}{8} = 15{,}833.5$$

Then the value of the test statistic is

$$t = \frac{(\bar{x}_1 - \bar{x}_2) - 0}{\sqrt{s^2\left(\frac{1}{n_1} + \frac{1}{n_2}\right)}} = \frac{1482 - 1680}{\sqrt{15833.5\left(\frac{1}{6} + \frac{1}{4}\right)}} = \frac{-198}{81.22} = -2.44.$$

Since the computed value of the test statistic falls within the rejection region, we reject H_0 and conclude that the mean first-month sales commission is significantly higher for those salesmen trained under the new program, i.e., the new training program appears to be more effective than the conventional program.

10.5 Independent random samples of two well-advertised brands of house paint produced the following results on coverage (in square feet of surface) per gallon:

	PAINT A	PAINT B
$\bar{x}$	615	570
s	42	31
n	10	10

Estimate the difference in mean coverage for the two paints with a 90% confidence interval.

Solution

The following assumptions must be made in order to employ the small-sample confidence interval procedure:

1) The populations of coverage per gallon values must be normally distributed for both Paint A and Paint B.

2) The population variances must be equal for the two populations.

3) The samples must be obtained randomly and in an independent manner from the two populations.

Let us define μ_1 and μ_2 to be the mean coverage (in square feet of surface) per gallon for Paint A and Paint B, respectively. We wish to obtain a 90% confidence interval for $\mu_1 - \mu_2$, the difference in mean coverage for the two paints.

The pooled estimate of the common population variance is

$$s_p^2 = \frac{(n_1 - 1)s_1^2 + (n_2 - 1)s_2^2}{n_1 + n_2 - 2} = \frac{9(42)^2 + 9(31)^2}{18} = 1362.5.$$

Now, the 90% confidence interval is based on the critical value of $t_{\alpha/2} = t_{.05} = 1.734$, where t has $n_1 + n_2 - 2 = 18$ degrees of freedom. The desired confidence interval is:

$$(\bar{x}_1 - \bar{x}_2) \pm t_{.05}\sqrt{s_p\left(\frac{1}{n_1} + \frac{1}{n_2}\right)} = (615 - 570) \pm 1.734\sqrt{(1362.5)\left(\frac{1}{10} + \frac{1}{10}\right)}$$

$$= 45 \pm 28.6 \quad \text{or} \quad (16.4,\ 73.6).$$

We can be 90% confident that the mean coverage obtained per gallon of Paint A exceeds the mean coverage per gallon of Paint B by between 16.4 and 73.6 square feet.

Exercises

10.3 Automotive researchers have recently been interested in comparing the amount of air pollution for rotary engine and piston engine cars. A test designed to measure the amount of pollution (in milligrams per cubic yard of exhaust) produced the following results:

	ROTARY ENGINE	PISTON ENGINE
$\bar{x}$	70.8	79.0
s	29.0	23.0
n	8	4

a. Test the hypothesis (at $\alpha = .01$) that the mean pollution emitted by rotary engine cars is significantly lower than the mean pollution emitted by piston engine cars.

b. What assumptions are required for the validity of the procedure used in part **a**?

10.4 Refer to Exercise 10.3. Construct a 95% confidence interval for the difference in the mean amounts of pollution emitted by rotary engine and piston engine cars. Interpret the confidence interval.

10.3 COMPARING TWO POPULATION VARIANCES: INDEPENDENT RANDOM SAMPLES

Examples

10.6 Obtain the critical values of the F distribution for the following situations:

a. $F_{.01}$, numerator $df = 8$, denominator $df = 6$

b. $F_{.01}$, numerator $df = 5$, denominator $df = 120$

c. $F_{.05}$, numerator $df = 12$, denominator $df = 24$

Solution

a. In the table of percentage points of the F distribution for $\alpha = .01$, we locate the entry at the intersection of the column for 8 numerator degrees of freedom and the row for 6 denominator degrees of freedom: $F_{.01} = 8.10$. Thus, for an F distribution with 8 numerator and 6 denominator degrees of freedom, $P(F > 8.10) = .01$.

b. In the table of percentage points of the F distribution for $\alpha = .01$, we locate the entry at the intersection of the column for 5 numerator degrees of freedom and the row for 120 denominator degrees of freedom: $F_{.01} = 3.17$.

c. In the table of percentage points of the F distribution for $\alpha = .05$, we find $F_{.05} = 2.18$, where F has 12 numerator and 24 denominator degrees of freedom.

10.7 Two major executives have turned in last month's receipts for business expenses. The following summarizes the information regarding expenses for "business lunches" by the two executives:

	EXECUTIVE A	EXECUTIVE B
$\bar{x}$	\$18.42	\$20.75
s	\$5.40	\$3.70
n	13	10

To perform the t test (Section 10.2) for the difference between mean expenditures for business lunches by the two executives, we must make the assumption of equal population variances. Is such an assumption reasonable, based on these results? Use a significance level of $\alpha = .10$.

Solution

We wish to test the hypothesis

$$H_0\text{: } \sigma_1^2/\sigma_2^2 = 1 \quad (\text{i.e., } \sigma_1^2 = \sigma_2^2)$$

against

$$H_a\text{: } \sigma_1^2/\sigma_2^2 \neq 1 \quad (\text{i.e., } \sigma_1^2 \neq \sigma_2^2)$$

where σ_1^2 and σ_2^2 are the population variances of the expenses for business lunches by Executive A and Executive B, respectively.

The test requires the following assumptions.

1) The populations of business lunch expenses are normally distributed for each executive.

2) The samples are obtained randomly and independently from the two populations.

The rejection region consists of values of the F statistic for which

$$F > F_{\alpha/2} \quad \text{or} \quad F > F_{.05},$$

where F has $n_1 - 1 = 12$ numerator degrees of freedom and $n_2 - 1 = 9$ denominator degrees of freedom. From the table of percentage points for $\alpha = .05$, we obtain the critical value $F_{.05} = 3.07$. We will thus reject H_0 if $F > 3.07$.

The value of the test statistic is

$$F = \frac{\text{Larger sample variance}}{\text{Smaller sample variance}} = \frac{(5.40)^2}{(3.70)^2} = 2.13.$$

The computed value of the test statistic does not lie within the rejection region. There is insufficient evidence to conclude that the population variances are significantly different at $\alpha = .10$.

Exercises

10.5 Obtain the critical values of the F distribution in each of the following situations.

a. $F_{.01}$, numerator df = 3, denominator df = 20

b. $F_{.05}$, numerator df = 30, denominator df = 60

c. $F_{.05}$, numerator df = 24, denominator df = 9

10.6 Refer to Exercise 10.3. One of the assumptions required for the hypothesis test is that the population variances of pollution amounts emitted by rotary engines and piston engines are equal. Do the data provide sufficient evidence (at $\alpha = .02$) to refute the assumption of equal population variances?

10.4 INFERENCES ABOUT THE DIFFERENCE BETWEEN TWO POPULATION MEANS: PAIRED DIFFERENCE EXPERIMENTS

Examples

10.8 The federal government has been funding researchers to investigate and develop alternative sources of fuel. A new product, methanol, is currently being tested in California. It costs much less than regular gasoline and, if judged successful, will require fewer natural oil resources than gasoline does. A test was run on five cars of different sizes to compare the mileage per gallon obtained using methanol with the mileage per gallon obtained with a standard brand of gasoline. The following results were obtained:

	MILEAGE PER GALLON		
CAR	Methanol	Regular Gasoline	Difference d_i
1	14.0	12.3	1.7
2	20.0	17.8	2.2
3	21.4	20.9	0.5
4	27.1	25.7	1.4
5	35.6	33.0	2.6

Can we conclude (at $\alpha = .01$) that the mean mileage per gallon of methanol is significantly greater than the mean mileage per gallon of regular gasoline?

Solution

Based on this paired difference experiment, we wish to test the hypothesis

$H_0: \mu_D - 0 \quad (\text{i.e., } \mu_1 - \mu_2 = 0)$

against

$H: \mu_D > 0 \quad (\text{i.e., } \mu_1 - \mu_2 > 0)$

where μ_1 and μ_2 are the population mean mileage per gallon ratings obtained by cars using methanol and regular gasoline, respectively, and $\mu_D = \mu_1 - \mu_2$.

The assumptions required are:

1) The population of differences in mileage per gallon ratings is normally distributed.

2) The sample differences are randomly selected from the population of differences.

At $\alpha = .01$, we will reject H_0 for all values of t such that $t > t_{.01} = 3.747$, where t has $n_D - 1 = 4$ degrees of freedom.

It is necessary to compute $\bar{x}_D$ and s_D from the sample differences:

$$\bar{x}_D = \frac{1.7 + 2.2 + 0.5 + 1.4 + 2.6}{5} = 1.68,$$

and

$$s_D = \sqrt{\frac{\Sigma d_i^2 - \frac{(\Sigma d_i)^2}{n_D}}{n_D - 1}} = \sqrt{\frac{(1.7)^2 + (2.2)^2 + (0.5)^2 + (1.4)^2 + (2.6)^2 - \frac{(8.4)^2}{5}}{4}}$$

$$= \sqrt{\frac{16.7 - 14.112}{4}} = \sqrt{0.647} - .8044.$$

Then the test statistic is

$$t = \frac{\bar{x}_D - 0}{s_D/\sqrt{n_D}} = \frac{1.68}{.8044/\sqrt{5}} = 4.67.$$

Since the value of the test statistic is within the rejection region, we reject H_0 and conclude that the mean mileage per gallon rating for cars using methanol is significantly greater (at $\alpha = .01$) than the mean mileage rating for cars using regular gasoline.

10.9 To compare sales for two local fast-food chains, a marketing researcher recorded the number of hamburgers sold during the noon hour for each day during a randomly selected week. The following results were obtained:

	CHAIN		
DAY	A	B	DIFFERENCE
Monday	137	97	40
Tuesday	98	63	35
Wednesday	69	59	10
Thursday	72	48	24
Friday	83	62	21
Saturday	142	101	41
Sunday	126	105	21
			$\bar{x}_D = 27.43$
			$s_D = 11.53$

Construct a 95% confidence interval for $\mu_1 - \mu_2$, where μ_1 and μ_2 are the mean noon-hour sales (number of hamburgers) for fast-food chains A and B, respectively.

Solution

The confidence interval procedure for the paired difference experiment requires the following assumptions:

1) The population of differences in noon-hour sales is normally distributed.

2) The sample differences are randomly selected from the population of differences.

The general form of a 95% confidence interval for $\mu_1 - \mu_2$ is

$\bar{x}_D \pm t_{.025}(s_D/\sqrt{n_D})$,

where t is based on $n_D - 1 = 6$ degrees of freedom. For this example, we have

$27.43 \pm 2.447(11.53/\sqrt{7}) = 27.43 \pm 10.66$ or $(16.77, 38.09)$.

The marketing researcher can be 95% confident that the mean number of hamburgers sold during the noon hour in the Chain A store is between 16.77 and 38.09 higher than the mean noon-hour sales in the Chain B store.

Exercises

10.7 A local health spa advertises that its clients lose an average of 10 pounds during their four-week weight reduction program. An investigation by the Better Business Bureau produced the following data on four people enrolled in the program:

INDIVIDUAL	WEIGHT BEFORE PROGRAM	WEIGHT AFTER PROGRAM
1	203	195
2	144	132
3	157	155
4	128	120

a. Is there evidence (at $\alpha = .01$) to refute the claim of the health spa? (Hint: Perform a test of the hypothesis $H_0: \mu_D = 10$ against $H_a: \mu_D < 10$.)

b. What assumptions are required for the validity of the procedure used in part **a**?

10.8 Due to many complaints about the high cost of textbooks at the campus bookstore, a student opened an off-campus bookstore. He claims that the average price of textbooks at his store is less than the average price charged at the campus bookstore. A comparison of prices for 10 high-volume textbooks revealed the information presented in the following table.

TEXTBOOK	PRICE Campus Bookstore	Off-Campus Bookstore
1	$27.95	$25.95
2	23.00	22.00
3	20.50	21.00
4	26.00	24.95
5	31.00	29.95
6	23.00	22.50
7	28.50	27.00
8	19.95	18.50
9	22.95	20.75
10	27.00	25.50

a. Construct a 95% confidence interval for the mean difference in textbook prices charged by the two bookstores.

b. State the assumptions upon which the confidence interval procedure in part **a** is based.

10.9 A company pays its salesmen on a commission basis and trains them to sell the product either on a door-to-door basis or by telephone contact. They wish to perform an experiment to compare the effectiveness of these two techniques; the following designs have been proposed:

Design A: Select ten salesmen, five of whom will be randomly assigned to sell door-to-door for one week and the remaining five will sell by telephone contact for one week. Compare the mean sales for the two methods.

Design B: Select five salesmen, and randomly assign the method of sale for the first week; the other method will be used the following week. Compare the results for the two methods.

a. Identify the two types of designs and state the assumptions required for making inferences from each.

b. Which design do you think is preferable in this situation? Why?

10.5 INFERENCES ABOUT THE DIFFERENCE BETWEEN POPULATION PROPORTIONS: INDEPENDENT BINOMIAL EXPERIMENTS

Examples

10.10 For several years there has been an advertising war between two of the largest firms that market insect-killing sprays. A consumer agency recently set up a test to determine if one spray was more effective than the other. Two large containers, each with 1500 insects, were sprayed according to the manufacturer's instruction, one with Spray A and one with Spray B. After 10 minutes, the numbers of live insects were recorded for each container. There were 87 survivors in the container of Spray A and 112 survivors in the container of Spray B. Is there evidence (at $\alpha = .01$) of a difference in the effectiveness of the two sprays?

Solution

One measure of the effectiveness of a spray is the proportion of insects killed by the spray. Therefore, we are interested in a test of

$$H_0: p_1 - p_2 = 0 \quad (\text{i.e., } p_1 = p_2)$$

against

$$H_a: p_1 - p_2 \neq 0 \quad (\text{i.e., } p_1 \neq p_2)$$

where p_1 and p_2 are the proportions of insects killed by Spray A and Spray B, respectively.

The sample sizes are sufficiently large that we can employ a z statistic. For $\alpha = .01$, we will reject H_0 if

$$z < -z_{.005} \quad \text{or} \quad z > z_{.005},$$

i.e., if $z < -2.58$ or $z > 2.58$.

The following quantities are required for computation of the test statistic:

$$\hat{p} = \frac{\text{Number of insects killed in Spray A container}}{\text{Number of insects in Spray A container}}$$

$$= \frac{1500 - 87}{1500} = \frac{1413}{1500} = .9420$$

$$\hat{p} = \frac{\text{Number of insects killed in Spray B container}}{\text{Number of insects in Spray B container}}$$

$$= \frac{1500 - 112}{1500} = \frac{1388}{1500} = .9253$$

$$\hat{p} = \frac{\text{Total number of insects killed}}{\text{Total number of insects in both containers}}$$

$$= \frac{1413 + 1388}{1500 + 1500} = \frac{2801}{3000} = .9337$$

$$\hat{q}_1 = 1 - \hat{p}_1 = 1 - .9420 = .0580$$
$$\hat{q}_2 = 1 - \hat{p}_2 = 1 - .9253 = .0747$$
$$\hat{q} = 1 - \hat{p} = 1 - .9337 = .0663$$

Thus,

$$z = \frac{(\hat{p}_1 - \hat{p}_2) - 0}{\sqrt{\hat{p}\hat{q}\left(\frac{1}{n_1} + \frac{1}{n_2}\right)}} = \frac{(.9420 - .9253) - 0}{\sqrt{(.9337)(.0663)\left(\frac{1}{1500} + \frac{1}{1500}\right)}} = 1.84$$

This value of the test statistic does not lie within the rejection region. There is insufficient evidence (at $\alpha = .01$) to conclude that there is a difference in the effectiveness of the two sprays.

10.11 A life insurance salesman wishes to compute the proportion of contacts to married and single individuals that result in sales. An examination of his records for the past three months revealed that he had sold policies to 24 out of 52 married people contacted, and to 19 out of 60 single people contacted. Construct a 95% confidence interval for the difference in the proportions of married and single individuals who purchase policies.

Solution

Let p_1 and p_2 be the proportions of married people and single people, respectively, who purchase policies from the salesman. A 95% confidence interval for $p_1 - p_2$ is given by

$$(\hat{p}_1 - \hat{p}_2) \pm z_{.025}\sqrt{\frac{\hat{p}_1\hat{q}_1}{n_1} + \frac{\hat{p}_2\hat{q}_2}{n_2}}$$

where

$$\hat{p}_1 = \frac{24}{52} = .46,\ \hat{p}_2 = \frac{19}{60} = .32,$$

$$\hat{q}_1 = 1 - .46 = .54,\ \hat{q}_2 = 1 - .32 = .68,$$

$$n_1 = 52,\ n_2 = 60,$$

and

$$z_{.025} = 1.96.$$

Substitution of these values yields:

$$(.46 - .32) \pm 1.96\sqrt{\frac{(.46)(.54)}{52} + \frac{(.32)(.68)}{60}}$$

$$= .14 \pm .18 \quad \text{or} \quad (-.04, .32).$$

We estimate that p_2, the proportion of single people who purchase policies, could be larger than p_1, the proportion of married people who purchase policies, by as much as .04, or p_2 could be less than p_1 by as much as .32.

Exercises

10.10 A survey was taken to compare the opinions of Republicans and Democrats on cutting the defense budget. The results are summarized below.

	REPUBLICANS	DEMOCRATS
Number of people surveyed	400	500
Number of people who favor cutting the defense budget	120	180

Is there sufficient evidence (at $\alpha = .01$) to conclude that the proportion of Democrats who favor cutting the defense budget is significantly higher than the proportion of Republicans in favor of this measure?

10.11 Refer to Exercise 10.10. Construct a 95% confidence interval for the difference in the proportions of Republicans and Democrats in favor of cutting the defense budget.

10.6 DETERMINING THE SAMPLE SIZE

Examples

10.12 A study is being designed to compare the scores on the Graduate Management Aptitude Test (GMAT) for Business and non-Business majors. Past testing has shown that the standard deviation of scores for all people taking the test is approximately 80 points. How many students should be sampled in order to estimate the difference in mean GMAT scores between Business and non-Business majors, if we want to be 95% confident that the estimate is within 10 points of the true mean difference?

Solution

It is required to solve the equation

$$z_{\alpha/2}\sqrt{\frac{\sigma_1^2}{n_1} + \frac{\sigma_2^2}{n_2}} = B$$

where $z_{\alpha/2} = z_{.025} = 1.96$ and $B = 10$.

We will assume that $\sigma_1^2 = \sigma_2^2 = 80^2$, where σ_1^2 and σ_2^2 are the population variances of scores for Business and non-Business majors, respectively. If the two sample sizes are to be equal $(n_1 = n_2 = n)$, then

$$1.96\sqrt{\frac{80^2}{n} + \frac{80^2}{n}} = 10.$$

We now solve for n:

$$1.96\sqrt{\frac{2(80)^2}{n}} = 10, \quad \text{or } n = 491.7.$$

Thus, we should randomly sample 492 Business and 492 non-Business majors in order to be 95% confident that the estimated difference in mean GMAT scores is correct to within 10 points.

10.13 A tobacco company wishes to estimate the difference in the proportions of men and women who smoke cigarettes. How many men and women must be included in their samples if the company wishes to be 90% confident that the estimated difference is within .02 of the true difference in proportions? Past studies indicate that the fraction of smokers among both sexes is approximately .25.

Solution

We wish to estimate $(p_1 - p_2)$, where p_1 and p_2 are the proportions of men and women, respectively, who smoke cigarettes. For the desired confidence, $z_{\alpha/2} = z_{.05} = 1.645$. Then, with $p_1 = p_2 = .25$ and equal sample sizes $n_1 = n_2 = n$, the required sample sizes are found by solving the following equation for n:

$$z_{\alpha/2}\sqrt{\frac{p_1 q_1}{n_1} + \frac{p_2 q_2}{n_2}} = B$$

$$1.645\sqrt{\frac{(.25)(.75)}{n} + \frac{(.25)(.75)}{n}} = .02$$

$$1.645\sqrt{\frac{2(.25)(.75)}{n}} = .02, \quad \text{or } n = 2536.9.$$

The tobacco company should sample at least 2537 men and 2537 women in order to estimate $p_1 - p_2$ with the specified level of reliability.

Exercises

10.12 A television station wishes to estimate the difference in the proportions of viewers who watch their 6 P.M. and 11 P.M. newscasts. How many 6 P.M. and 11 P.M. viewers should be sampled in order to be 95% confident that the estimated difference is within .07 of the true difference in proportions? Past surveys indicate that approximately 60% of 6 P.M. viewers and 80% of 11 P.M. viewers watch the station's newscasts.

10.13 A state welfare agency is interested in estimating the difference in mean weekly food costs between families with one child and families with no children. How many one-child and no-child families should be sampled in order to be 90% confident that the estimated difference is within $2.00 of the true difference in mean costs? Previous studies have shown that the standard deviation of weekly food costs is approximately $7.50 for no-child and one-child families.

11
SIMPLE LINEAR REGRESSION

SUMMARY

This chapter presented the five steps required in a *regression analysis*, a procedure for fitting a prediction equation to a set of data and making inferences from the results. We restricted attention to the particular case where a dependent variable y is related to a single independent variable x. The five steps are summarized below:

1. *A probabilistic model* is hypothesized. Straight-line models are of the form $y = \beta_0 + \beta_1 x + \varepsilon$.

2. The unknown parameters in the *deterministic component*, $\beta_0 + \beta_1 x$, are estimated using *the method of least squares*. The sum of squared errors for the resulting least squares model is smaller than that for any other straight-line model.

3. The probability distribution of ε, the *random error component*, is specified.

4. Inferences about the slope β_1, and the calculation of the coefficient of correlation r and the coefficient of determination r^2 are performed to assess the utility of the model.

5. If judged to be satisfactory, the model may be used to estimate $E(y)$, the mean y value for a given x value, or to predict an individual y value for a specific value of x.

11.1 PROBABILISTIC MODELS

11.2 FITTING THE MODEL: THE METHOD OF LEAST SQUARES

Examples

11.1 a. Plot the graph of the (deterministic) straight line $y = 1 + .5x$.

b. Give the slope and y-intercept of the line defined in part **a**.

Solution

a.

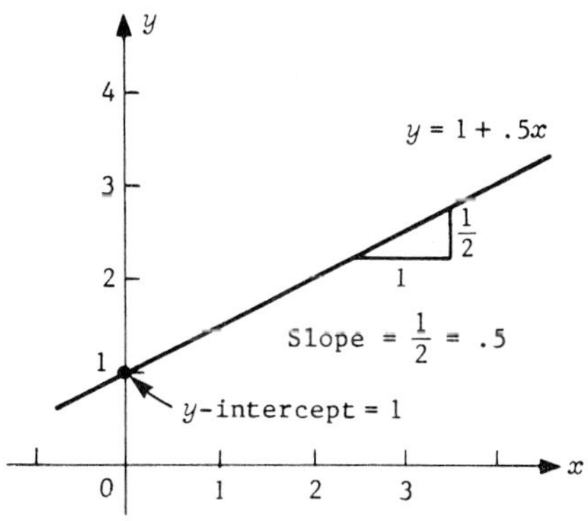

b. For a straight line of the form $y = \beta_0 + \beta_1 x$, the y-intercept is β_0 and the slope is β_1. In our example,

y-intercept = 1 and slope = .5.

Note from the figure that the y-intercept (1) is the point at which the line crosses the y-axis. Also, the slope (.5) is the amount of increase in y for a unit increase in x.

11.2 A real estate broker has been collecting data on home sales so that he can investigate the relationship between the dependent variable,

y = value of the purchased home,

and the independent variable,

x = annual family income of buyer.

Data from six recent sales are shown in the following table.

ANNUAL FAMILY INCOME, x (Thousands of Dollars)	VALUE OF HOME, y (Thousands of Dollars)
15.2	33.8
17.4	48.9
22.0	49.5
24.6	61.0
29.8	63.8
38.0	92.5

a. Plot a scattergram of the data.

b. Use the method of least squares to fit a straight line to the $n = 6$ data points. Graph the least squares line on a scattergram.

Solution

a.

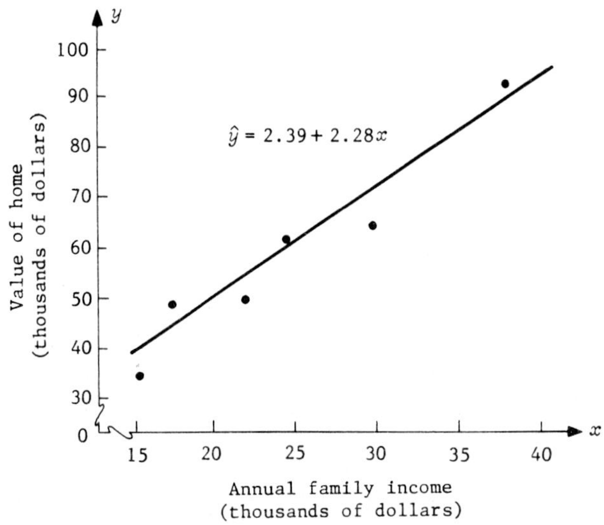

Note that the scattergram suggests a general tendency for y to increase as x increases.

b. We will set up a table to assist in performing the required calculations:

x_i	y_i	x_i^2	$x_i y_i$
15.2	33.8	231.04	513.76
17.4	48.9	302.76	850.86
22.0	49.5	484.00	1089.00
24.6	61.0	605.16	1500.60
29.8	63.8	888.04	1901.24
38.0	92.5	1444.00	3515.00
$\Sigma x_i = 147.0$	$\Sigma y_i = 349.5$	$\Sigma x_i^2 = 3955.00$	$\Sigma x_i y_i = 9370.46$

We now calculate:

$$SS_{xy} = \Sigma x_i y_i - \frac{(\Sigma x_i)(\Sigma y_i)}{n} = 9370.46 - \frac{(147.0)(349.5)}{6}$$

$$= 9370.46 - 8562.75 = 807.71$$

$$SS_{xx} = \Sigma x_i^2 - \frac{(\Sigma x_i)^2}{n} = 3955.00 - \frac{(147.0)^2}{6}$$

$$= 3955.00 - 3601.50 = 353.50$$

$$\bar{y} = \frac{\Sigma y_i}{n} = \frac{349.5}{6} = 58.25$$

$$\bar{x} = \frac{\Sigma x_i}{n} = \frac{147.0}{6} = 24.50$$

Now, the slope of the least squares line is

$$\hat{\beta}_1 = \frac{SS_{xy}}{SS_{xx}} = \frac{807.71}{353.50} = 2.28$$

and the y-intercept is

$$\hat{\beta}_0 = \bar{y} - \hat{\beta}_1\bar{x} = 58.25 - 2.28(24.50) = 2.39.$$

Thus, the least squares line is

$$\hat{y} = \hat{\beta}_0 + \hat{\beta}_1 x = 2.39 + 2.28x.$$

This line in graphed on the scattergram in part **a**.

11.3 Refer to Example 11.2. Compute SSE, the sum of squared errors for the least squares model.

Solution

The following table presents the calculations required for SSE:

x	y	$\hat{y} = 2.39 + 2.28x$	$(y - \hat{y})$	$(y - \hat{y})^2$
15.2	33.8	37.046	-3.246	10.5365
17.4	48.9	42.062	6.838	46.7582
22.0	49.5	52.550	-3.050	9.3025
24.6	61.0	58.478	2.522	6.3605
29.8	63.8	70.334	-6.534	42.6932
38.0	92.5	89.030	3.470	12.0409
				SSE = 127.6918

This value of SSE = 127.6918 is smaller than the SSE for any other straight-line model that could be fit to the data.

11.4 Refer to Example 11.2. According to your least squares line, approximately how much would a buyer whose annual family income is \$27,000 be expected to spend on a home?

Solution

The least squares prediction equation obtained in Example 11.2 is

$\hat{y} = 2.39 + 2.28x.$

For a family whose annual income is \$27,000 (i.e., $x = 27$), the predicted home value (in thousands of dollars) is

$\hat{y} = 2.39 + 2.28(27) = 63.95.$

We would expect the family to buy a home worth approximately \$63,950. (A measure of the reliability of our prediction will be developed in a subsequent section.)

Exercises

11.1 a. Plot the graph of the straight line

$y = 1.5 - 2x.$

b. Give the slope and y-intercept of the line defined in part a. Interpret these values.

11.2 A study was conducted to investigate the relationship between a student's score on the Graduate Management Aptitude Test (GMAT) and his or her grade point average (GPA). It is hoped that a useful equation will be developed for predicting a student's GMAT score from his or her GPA. Records for ten students yielded the following data:

GMAT SCORE, y	GPA, x
710	3.8
690	3.6
650	3.7
630	3.4
490	2.7
680	3.1
500	3.0
550	2.9
660	3.5
430	2.4

a. Plot a scattergram of the data.

b. Use the method of least squares to fit a straight line to the data points. Graph the least squares line on the scattergram.

c. Compute the value of SSE for the least squares model.

d. According to your least squares prediction equation, approximately what GMAT score would you expect for a student whose GPA is 3.3?

11.3 MODEL ASSUMPTIONS

11.4 AN ESTIMATOR OF σ^2

Examples

11.5 Refer to Example 11.3. Calculate s^2, the estimator of σ^2, the variance of the random error component ε of the probabilistic model $y = \beta_0 + \beta_1 x + \varepsilon$.

Solution

In the real estate example, we previously calculated SSE = 127.6918 for the least squares line $\hat{y} = 2.39 + 2.28x$. Since there were $n = 6$ data points, there are $(n - 2) = 4$ degrees of freedom available for estimating σ^2. Thus,

$$s^2 = \frac{\text{SSE}}{n - 2} = \frac{127.6918}{4} = 31.92$$

is our estimate of the variance of ε. The estimated standard deviation of ε, $s = \sqrt{s^2}$, will later be used to evaluate the error of prediction when using the least squares line to predict a value of y for a specified value of x.

(Note that in the calculation of SSE, it may often be easier to use the computational formula

$$\text{SSE} = \text{SS}_{yy} - \hat{\beta}_1 \text{SS}_{xy},$$

because the quantities $\hat{\beta}_1$ and SS_{xy} were computed during the fitting of the least squares line.)

11.6 A major appliance store has obtained the following data on daily high temperature and number of air-conditioning units sold for eight randomly selected business days during the summer:

DAILY HIGH TEMPERATURE x, °F	NUMBER OF UNITS SOLD y
83	4
88	5
73	1
76	0
92	5
79	3
81	2
77	2

a. Fit a least squares line to the data.

b. Plot the data and graph the least squares line.

c. Compute SSE.

d. Calculate s^2.

Solution

a. The following table shows the required calculations:

x_i	y_i	x_i^2	$x_i y_i$
83	4	6889	332
88	5	7744	440
73	1	5329	73
76	0	5776	0
92	5	8464	460
79	3	6241	237
81	2	6561	162
77	2	5929	154
$\Sigma x_i = 649$	$\Sigma y_i = 22$	$\Sigma x_i^2 = 52933$	$\Sigma x_i y_i = 1858$

Thus,

$$SS_{xy} = \Sigma x_i y_i - \frac{(\Sigma x_i)(\Sigma y_i)}{n} = 1858 - \frac{(649)(22)}{8} = 73.25,$$

$$SS_{xx} = \Sigma x_i^2 - \frac{(\Sigma x_i)^2}{n} = 52933 - \frac{(649)^2}{8} = 282.875,$$

$$\bar{y} = \frac{\Sigma y_i}{n} = \frac{22}{8} = 2.75,$$

$$\bar{x} = \frac{\Sigma x_i}{n} = \frac{649}{8} = 81.125.$$

The slope of the least squares line is

$$\hat{\beta}_1 = \frac{SS_{xy}}{SS_{xx}} = \frac{73.25}{282.875} = .258948$$

and the y-intercept is

$$\hat{\beta}_0 = \bar{y} - \hat{\beta}_1\bar{x} = 2.75 - .258948(81.125) = -18.257157.$$

Thus, the least squares line is

$$\hat{y} = \hat{\beta}_0 + \hat{\beta}_1 x \quad \text{or} \quad \hat{y} = -18.26 + .26x.$$

b. A graph of the data points and the least squares line follows:

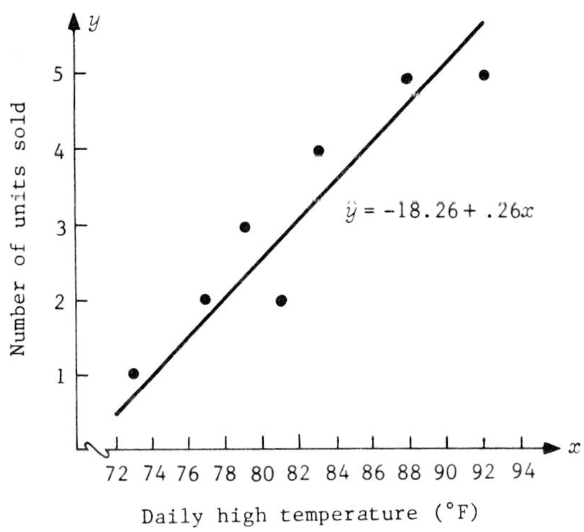

c. We will use the computational formula for SSE:

$$SSE = SS_{yy} - \hat{\beta}_1 SS_{xy},$$

where

$$SS_{yy} = \Sigma y_i^2 - \frac{(\Sigma y_i)^2}{n}$$

$$= (4^2 + 5^2 + 1^2 + 0^2 + 5^2 + 3^2 + 2^2 + 2^2) - \frac{(22)^2}{8}$$

$$= 84 - 60.5 = 23.5.$$

Hence, $SSE = 23.5 - (.258948)(73.25) = 4.532059.$

(Note that we have retained six significant digits in the value for $\hat{\beta}_1$ to avoid substantial rounding errors in the calculation of SSE.)

d. Our estimate of the variance of the random error component ε is:

$$s^2 = \frac{\text{SSE}}{n - 2} = \frac{4.532059}{8 - 2} = .755343.$$

Exercises

11.3 Refer to Exercise 11.2. Obtain an estimate of σ^2, the variance of the random error component in the model.

11.4 Refer to Exercise 11.2. Recompute SSE using the computational formula:

$$\text{SSE} = \text{SS}_{yy} - \hat{\beta}_1 \text{SS}_{xy}.$$

11.5 ASSESSING THE USEFULNESS OF THE MODEL: MAKING INFERENCES ABOUT THE SLOPE β_1

Examples

11.7 Refer to Examples 11.2-11.5.

a. State the assumptions about ε in the model

$$y = \beta_0 + \beta_1 x + \varepsilon,$$

where y = home value at time of purchase and x = annual family income.

b. Test the null hypothesis that x contributes no information (at $\alpha = .05$) for the prediction of y against the alternative that home value y tends to increase as the annual family income x increases.

Solution

a. In order to make inferences about the usefulness of the model, the following four assumptions are made about the probability distribution of ε:

1) The probability distribution of ε is normal.

2) The expected value or mean of the probability distribution is zero.

3) The variance of the probability distribution is equal to a constant σ^2 for all values of x.

4) The errors associated with different observations of y are independent.

b. The hypothesis test has the following elements:

H_0: $\beta_1 = 0$
H_a: $\beta_1 > 0$

where β_1 is the true slope of the straight line relating y and x. At $\alpha = .05$, we will reject H_0 if $t > t_{.05} = 2.132$, where t is based on $n - 2 = 6 - 2 = 4$ df.

The value of the test statistic is:

$$t = \frac{\hat{\beta}_1 - 0}{s_{\hat{\beta}_1}} = \frac{\hat{\beta}_1 - 0}{s/\sqrt{SS_{xx}}}$$

We have previously obtained $\hat{\beta}_1 = 2.28$, $s = \sqrt{s^2} = \sqrt{31.92} \approx 5.65$, and $SS_{xx} = 353.50$. Substitution yields

$$t = \frac{2.28 - 0}{5.65/\sqrt{353.50}} = 7.59.$$

The calculated t value falls within the rejection region; we thus reject H_0 and conclude that β_1 is significantly greater than zero. The sample evidence suggests that y tends to increase as x increases, and that x contributes useful information for the prediction of y.

11.8 Refer to Example 11.7. Construct a 90% confidence interval for β_1.

Solution

The general form for a 90% confidence interval for β_1 is

$$\hat{\beta}_1 \pm t_{.05}\, s_{\hat{\beta}_1},$$

where $t_{.05} = 2.132$ is based on $n - 2 = 4$ df and

$$s_{\hat{\beta}_1} = s/\sqrt{SS_{xx}} \approx 5.65/\sqrt{353.50} = .301.$$

The required confidence interval is

$$2.28 \pm 2.132(.301) = 2.28 \pm .642 \quad \text{or} \quad (1.638, 2.922).$$

We are 90% confident that the slope parameter β_1 is contained in this interval. That is, we estimate (with 90% confidence) that the mean increase in the value of a home at the time of purchase for each unit ($1000) increase in annual family income is between $1638 and $2922.

11.9 For five popular American-made cars, the following information on engine size and mileage ratings was recorded:

ENGINE SIZE, x (Cubic Inches)	MILEAGE RATING, y (Miles per Gallon of Gasoline)
144	28
232	21
306	23
388	17
414	15

For these data, $SS_{xx} = 49684.8$, $SS_{yy} = 104.8$, $SS_{xy} = -2119.2$, $\Sigma x_i = 1484$, and $\Sigma y_i = 104$.

Test the null hypothesis that x contributes no information for the prediction of y against the alternative hypothesis that these variables are linearly related with a slope significantly different from zero. Use a significance level of $\alpha = .01$.

Solution

The hypothesized probabilistic model is

$$y = \beta_0 + \beta_1 x + \varepsilon,$$

where y = mileage rating, x = engine size, and the errors ε are assumed to be independent and normally distributed with mean 0 and constant variance σ^2.

The least squares line is given by

$$\hat{y} = \hat{\beta}_0 + \hat{\beta}_1 x,$$

where

$$\hat{\beta}_1 = \frac{SS_{xy}}{SS_{xx}} = \frac{-2119.2}{49684.8} = -.043$$

and

$$\hat{\beta}_0 = \bar{y} - \hat{\beta}_1\bar{x} = \frac{104}{5} - (-.043)\left(\frac{1484}{5}\right) = 20.80 + 12.76 = 33.56.$$

The hypotheses of interest are:

H_0: $\beta_1 = 0$
H_a: $\beta_1 \neq 0$

At $\alpha = .01$, we will reject H_0 if $t < -t_{.005}$ or $t > t_{.005}$, i.e., if $t < -5.841$ or $t > 5.841$, where t is based on $n - 2 = 5 - 2 = 3$ df.

The form of the test statistic is

$$t = \frac{\hat{\beta}_1 - 0}{s_{\hat{\beta}_1}} = \frac{\hat{\beta}_1}{s/\sqrt{SS_{xx}}}$$

where

$$s = \sqrt{\frac{SSE}{n - 2}} = \sqrt{\frac{SS_{yy} - \hat{\beta}_1 SS_{xy}}{n - 2}} = \sqrt{\frac{104.8 - (-.043)(-2119.2)}{3}}$$

$$= \sqrt{4.5581} = 2.13.$$

The computed value of t is then

$$t = \frac{-.043}{2.13/\sqrt{49684.8}} = -4.50.$$

At $\alpha = .01$, there is insufficient evidence to conclude that the value of β_1 differs significantly from zero.

11.10 Refer to Example 11.9. Construct a 99% confidence interval for β_1.

Solution

The general form of a 99% confidence interval for β_1 is

$$\hat{\beta}_1 \pm t_{.005}\, s_{\hat{\beta}_1},$$

where $t_{.005} = 5.841$ is based on $n - 2 = 3$ df, and

$$s_{\hat{\beta}_1} = s/\sqrt{SS_{xx}} = 2.13/\sqrt{49684.8} = .00956.$$

Now, the desired confidence interval is:

$$-.043 \pm 5.841(.00956) = -.043 \pm .0558 \quad \text{or} \quad (-.0988, .0128).$$

Note that the interval contains the value zero, which reflects a lack of sufficient evidence that x contributes information for the prediction of y. This is consistent with the result of the previous example, in which we failed to reject H_0: $\beta_1 = 0$.

Exercises

11.5 Refer to Exercises 11.2 11.3. Test the null hypothesis that x contributes no information for the prediction of y against the alternative hypothesis that these variables are linearly related with positive slope, i.e., that GMAT scores tend to increase as GPA increases. Use $\alpha = .025$.

11.6 Refer to Exercises 11.2-11.3. Construct a 95% confidence interval for β_1, the mean increase in GMAT score for a unit increase in GPA.

11.7 Advertising constitutes a large portion of many companies' budgets. To determine if there is a linear relationship between the amount of money spent on advertising and the amount of sales, ten drug and cosmetic companies were surveyed, with the following results:

COMPANY	ADVERTISING EXPENDITURE, x (Millions of Dollars)	SALES, y (Millions of Dollars)
1	115.0	955.0
2	72.0	870.5
3	62.0	182.6
4	44.5	880.2
5	30.0	438.6
6	27.5	128.8
7	20.3	68.4
8	16.8	769.4
9	48.0	231.8
10	83.9	490.6

For these data,

SS = 8887.04, $\bar{x}$ = 52.00,

SS = 1,061,998.689, $\bar{y}$ = 501.59,

SS_{xy} = 45,466.48.

Do the data provide sufficient evidence to indicate that advertising expenditures contribute information for predicting sales? Use $\alpha = .05$.

11.6 CORRELATION: ANOTHER MEASURE OF THE USEFULNESS OF THE MODEL

11.7 THE COEFFICIENT OF DETERMINATION

Examples

11.11 Refer to Examples 11.2-11.5.

a. Compute the coefficient of correlation, r, for the real estate data. Interpret its value.

b. Compute the coefficient of determination, r^2, for the sample data. Interpret its value.

Solution

a. The coefficient of correlation, r, is computed as follows:

$$r = \frac{SS_{xy}}{\sqrt{SS_{xx} SS_{yy}}},$$

where we previously obtained the values $SS_{xy} = 807.71$ and $SS_{xx} = 353.50$. Now,

$$SS_{yy} = \Sigma y_i^2 - \frac{(\Sigma y_i)^2}{n}$$

$$= (33.8^2 + 48.9^2 + 49.5^2 + 61^2 + 63.8^2 + 92.5^2) - \frac{(349.5)^2}{6}$$

$$= 22331.59 - 20358.375 = 1973.215.$$

Thus,

$$r = \frac{807.71}{\sqrt{(353.50)(1973.215)}} = .967.$$

The large, positive value of r implies a strong linear relationship between y and x, in which y tends to increase as x increases.

b. The coefficient of determination is

$$r^2 = (.967)^2 = .935.$$

Note that this value may also be obtained as follows:

$$r^2 = \frac{SS_{yy} - SSE}{SS_{yy}} = \frac{1973.215 - 127.692}{1973.215} = .935.$$

This represents the proportion of the sum of squares of the deviations of the sample y values about their mean that may be attributed to a linear relation between y and x. In other words, there is a 93.5% reduction in the sum of squared prediction errors when the least squares line $\hat{y} = \hat{\beta}_0 + \hat{\beta}_1 x$, instead of $\bar{y}$, is used to predict y.

11.12 A radio station has experimented with contests that give away money and prizes in an attempt to increase the size of its listening audience, as measured by a listener rating service. Results from the last two weeks are shown in the following table.

VALUE OF PRIZES, x (Hundreds of Dollars)	LISTENER RATING, y
0	11.1
3	11.5
7	14.0
0	12.0
1	9.0
6	11.0
20	23.0
10	22.4
5	19.3
10	18.6
12	18.5
20	21.3
0	17.8
12	15.7

For these data, the following values have been computed:

$SS_{xx} = 605.428$, $\bar{x} = 7.57$,

$SS_{yy} = 283.437$, $\bar{y} = 16.09$,

$SS_{xy} = 305.314$.

a. Obtain the least squares prediction equation.

b. Compute the value of r, the coefficient of correlation.

c. Do the data provide sufficient evidence to indicate a nonzero population correlation between x and y? Use $\alpha = .05$.

Solution

a. The slope of the least squares line is

$$\hat{\beta}_1 = \frac{SS_{xy}}{SS_{xx}} = \frac{305.314}{605.428} = .50$$

and the y-intercept is

$$\hat{\beta}_0 = \bar{y} - \hat{\beta}_1\bar{x} = 16.09 - .50(7.57) = 12.31.$$

Thus, the least squares prediction equation is $\hat{y} = 12.31 + .50x$.

b. $$r = \frac{SS_{xy}}{\sqrt{SS_{xx}\,SS_{yy}}} = \frac{305.314}{\sqrt{(605.428)(283.437)}} = .74$$

c. The test of

H_0: population coefficient of correlation $\rho = 0$

against

H_a: $\rho \neq 0$

is equivalent to the test of

H_0: $\beta_1 = 0$

against

H_a: $\beta_1 \neq 0$.

At $\alpha = .05$, the null hypothesis will be rejected if

$$t < -t_{.025} \quad \text{or} \quad t > t_{.025},$$

i.e., $t < -2.179$ or $t > 2.179$,

where the distribution of t has $n - 2 = 12$ degrees of freedom.

It is necessary to compute the value of s:

$$s = \sqrt{\frac{\text{SSE}}{n-2}} = \sqrt{\frac{\text{SS}_{yy} - \hat{\beta}_1 \text{SS}_{xy}}{n-2}} = \sqrt{\frac{283.437 - .50(305.314)}{12}}$$

$$= \sqrt{10.8983} = 3.30$$

The test statistic is:

$$t = \frac{\hat{\beta}_1 - 0}{s_{\hat{\beta}_1}} = \frac{\hat{\beta}_1}{s/\sqrt{\text{SS}_{xx}}} = \frac{.50}{3.30/\sqrt{605.428}} = 3.73$$

Since the value of t falls within the rejection region, we reject H_0 and conclude that x does contribute information for the prediction of y. In other words, there is sufficient evidence in the sample to conclude that the population coefficient of correlation between x and y is significantly nonzero.

Exercises

11.8 Refer to Exercises 11.2-11.3.

a. Compute the coefficient of correlation, r, between GMAT score and GPA for this sample. Interpret its value.

b. Compute the coefficient of determination, r^2, for the data. Interpret its value.

11.9 Refer to Exercise 11.8. Do the data provide sufficient evidence to conclude that the population coefficient of correlation between x and y is significantly greater than zero? Use $\alpha = .01$.

11.10 Refer to Exercise 11.7. Determine the coefficient of determination and explain its significance in terms of the problem.

11.8 USING THE MODEL FOR ESTIMATION AND PREDICTION

Examples

11.13 For the real estate data of Example 11.2, find a 95% confidence interval for the mean value of a home purchase when the annual family income is $27,500.

Solution

For an annual family income of $27,500, $x_p = 27.5$, and a 95% confidence interval for the mean value of y is

$$y \pm t_{.025}\, s\sqrt{\frac{1}{n} + \frac{(x_p - \bar{x})^2}{SS_{xx}}}$$

where $t_{.025} = 2.776$ is based on $n - 2 = 4$ degrees of freedom.

Recall that $s = 5.65$, $\bar{x} = 24.50$, $n = 6$, and $SS_{xx} = 353.50$ for the real estate data. Now, the estimated value of y when $x_p = 27.5$ is

$\hat{y} = \hat{\beta}_0 + \hat{\beta}_1(27.5) = 2.39 + 2.28(27.5) = 65.09$.

Substitution into the general formula for the confidence interval yields:

$$65.09 \pm 2.776(5.65)\sqrt{\frac{1}{6} + \frac{(27.5 - 24.5)^2}{353.50}} = 65.09 \pm 6.87$$

or (58.22, 71.96).

We estimate, with 95% confidence, that the interval from $58,220 to $71,960 encloses the mean value of a home purchase when the annual family income is $27,500.

11.14 Predict the value of a home purchase by a particular family with an annual income of $23,000. Use a 95% prediction interval.

Solution

To predict the value of a home to be purchased by a particualr family for whom $x_p = 23$, we calculate the 95% prediction interval as

$$\hat{y} \pm t_{.025}\, s\sqrt{1 + \frac{1}{n} + \frac{(x_p - \bar{x})^2}{SS_{xx}}},$$

where $t_{.025} = 2.776$ (4 df), $s = 5.65$, $n = 6$, $\bar{x} = 24.50$, $SS_{xx} = 353.50$, and

$$\hat{y} = \hat{\beta}_0 + \hat{\beta}_1(23) = 2.39 + 2.28(23) = 54.83.$$

Thus, the desired prediction interval is

$$54.83 \pm 2.776(5.65)\sqrt{1 + \frac{1}{6} + \frac{(23 - 24.5)^2}{353.50}} = 54.83 \pm 16.99$$

or (37.84, 71.82).

We predict, with 95% confidence, that the value of the home purchased by this family will fall in the interval from \$37,840 to \$71,820.

11.15 Refer to Example 11.12. Predict the listener rating for tomorrow if the value of prizes to be given away is \$1500. Use a 90% prediction interval.

Solution

To predict the listener rating for a particular day on which $x_p = 15$, we compute the 90% prediction interval as

$$\hat{y} \pm t_{.05}\, s\sqrt{1 + \frac{1}{n} + \frac{(x_p - \bar{x})^2}{SS_{xx}}},$$

where $t_{.05} = 1.782$ (12 df), $s = 3.30$, $n = 14$, $\bar{x} = 7.57$, $SS_{xx} = 605.428$, and

$$\hat{y} = \hat{\beta}_0 + \hat{\beta}_1(15) = 12.31 + .50(15) = 19.81.$$

Thus, the prediction interval is

$$19.81 \pm 1.782(3.30)\sqrt{1 + \frac{1}{14} + \frac{(15 - 7.57)^2}{605.428}} = 19.81 \pm 6.34$$

or (13.47, 26.15).

We predict that tomorrow's listener rating will fall in the interval from 13.47 to 26.15.

Exercises

11.11 Refer to Exercise 11.2. Construct a 90% confidence interval for the mean GMAT score when the GPA is 3.6.

11.12 Predict the GMAT score for a student whose GPA is 3.6. Use a 90% prediction interval.

11.13 Compare the lengths of the intervals obtained in Exercises 11.11 and 11.12.

11.9 SIMPLE LINEAR REGRESSION: AN EXAMPLE

Example

11.16 The financial director of a private college was interested in the relationship between the amount of money donated to the school per year by an alumnus (y) and the number of years the alumnus has been out of school (x). A random sample of 15 alumni donors yielded the following information:

x	4	8	30	24	18	10	21	7	15	28	2	17	12	21	14
y (\$)	25	20	50	150	100	10	75	30	25	60	10	25	30	50	10

a. Develop a simple linear model for the relationship between y and x.

b. Use the data in the table to obtain the least squares prediction equation.

c. Do the data provide sufficient evidence to indicate that the number of years since graduation contributes information about the amount of money donated? Use a significance level of $\alpha = .05$.

d. Calculate and interpret the value of r^2 for these data.

e. If an alumnus has been out of school for 20 years, form a 90% prediction interval for the amount of money he will donate to the college per year.

f. Find a 90% confidence interval for the mean amount contributed per year by an alumnus who has been out of school for 20 years.

Solution

a. We hypothesize the following straight-line probabilistic model:

$$y = \beta_0 + \beta_1 x + \varepsilon,$$

where y = dollar amount contributed per year by an alumnus and x = number of years the alumnus has been out of school.

b. We perform the following preliminary calculations:

$$SS_{xx} = 995.6, \qquad \bar{x} = 15.4,$$
$$SS_{yy} = 21{,}173.333, \quad \bar{y} = 44.667,$$
$$SS_{xy} = 2777.$$

Now, the least squares line has slope

$$\hat{\beta}_1 = \frac{SS_{xy}}{SS_{xx}} = \frac{2777}{995.6} = 2.789$$

and y-intercept

$$\hat{\beta}_0 = \bar{y} - \hat{\beta}_1\bar{x} = 44.667 - 2.789(15.4) = 1.716.$$

Thus, the least squares prediction equation is

$$\hat{y} = 1.716 + 2.789x.$$

c. It is necessary to perform a test of the null hypothesis

$$H_0\text{: } \beta_1 = 0$$

against the alternative hypothesis

$$H_a\text{: } \beta_1 \neq 0.$$

At the significance level $\alpha = .05$, we will reject H_0 if

$$t < -t_{.025} \quad \text{or} \quad t > t_{.025},$$
i.e., $$t < -2.160 \quad \text{or} \quad t > 2.160,$$

where t has $n - 2 = 13$ df.

The test statistic is

$$t = \frac{\hat{\beta}_1 - 0}{s_{\hat{\beta}_1}} = \frac{\hat{\beta}_1}{s/\sqrt{SS_{xx}}},$$

where

$$s = \sqrt{\frac{SSE}{n-2}} = \sqrt{\frac{SS_{yy} - \hat{\beta}_1 SS_{xy}}{n-2}} = \sqrt{\frac{21173.333 - 2.789(2777)}{13}}$$
$$= \sqrt{1032.945} = 32.139.$$

Thus,

$$t = \frac{2.789}{32.139/\sqrt{995.6}} = 2.74.$$

The computed value of the test statistic lies within the rejection region. We thus conclude that the number of years since graduation contributes information for the prediction of the amount of money donated.

(Note that this test procedure requires the assumptions that ε is normally distributed with mean 0, constant variance σ^2, and that the errors are independent.)

d. The coefficient of determination is

$$r^2 = \frac{SS_{yy} - SSE}{SS_{yy}},$$

where

$$SSE = SS_{yy} - \hat{\beta}_1 SS_{xy} = 21{,}173.333 - 2.789(2777) = 13{,}428.28.$$

Then,

$$r^2 = \frac{21{,}173.333 - 13{,}428.28}{21{,}173.333} = .366.$$

There is a 36.6% reduction in the sum of squared prediction errors when the least squares line $\hat{y} = 1.716 + 2.789x$, instead of $\bar{y} = 44.667$, is used to predict y.

e. To predict the amount of money that will be donated per year by an alumnus who has been out of school for $x = 20$ years, we calculate the 90% prediction interval

$$\hat{y} \pm t_{.05}\, s\sqrt{1 + \frac{1}{n} + \frac{(x_p - \bar{x})^2}{SS_{xx}}},$$

where $t_{.05} = 1.771$ (13 df) and

$$\hat{y} = 1.716 + 2.789(20) = 57.50.$$

Thus, the prediction interval is

$$57.50 \pm 1.771(32.139)\sqrt{1 + \frac{1}{15} + \frac{(20 - 15.4)^2}{995.6}} = 57.50 \pm 59.37$$

or (-1.87, 116.87).

This very wide prediction interval contains negative values which have no meaning in the context of this problem. We predict that the alumnus will not donate more than $116.87 per year to the college.

f. A 90% confidence interval for the mean amount contributed when $x_p = 20$ is computed as

$$\hat{y} \pm t_{.05}\, s\sqrt{\frac{1}{n} + \frac{(x_p - \bar{x})^2}{SS_{xx}}} = 57.50 \pm 1.771(32.139)\sqrt{\frac{1}{15} + \frac{(20 - 15.4)^2}{995.6}}$$

$$= 57.50 \pm 16.88 \quad \text{or} \quad (40.62,\ 74.38).$$

We estimate that the interval from $40.62 to $74.38 encloses the mean amount donated to the college when the number of years out of school is 20.

Exercise

11.14 In order to introduce consumers to a product, manufacturers often advertise with coupons that discount the store price of an item. Marketing executives for a frozen food processor have experimented to determine the relationship between the number of coupons that will be used by consumers within one month and the value of a coupon. The following recent data have been collected:

COUPON VALUE, x (Cents)	NUMBER OF COUPONS USED, y (Hundreds)
5	13.28
10	11.03
12	12.92
15	15.03
25	18.46
50	22.15

a. Hypothesize a simple linear model for the relationship between y and x.

b. Obtain the least squares prediction equation.

c. Test the null hypothesis (at $\alpha = .05$) that x contributes no information for the prediction of y against the alternative that the values of y tend to increase as x increases. State any assumptions required for the validity of the test procedure.

d. Calculate the values of r and r^2 for the data. Interpret their values.

e. Construct a 95% confidence interval for the mean number of coupons used when the value of the coupon is 20 cents.

12 MULTIPLE REGRESSION

SUMMARY

This chapter discussed the steps to be followed in a *multiple regression analysis*, a procedure for modeling a dependent variable y as a function of k independent variables, $x_1, x_2, \ldots, x_k$. The methodology is much the same as for simple straight-line models:

1. A probabilistic model is hypothesized.

2. The unknown parameters in the deterministic component of the model are estimated using the method of least squares.

3. The probability distribution of the random error component ε is specified.

4. Inferences are performed to assess the utility of the model.

5. If the model is judged to be satisfactory, it may be used for estimation and for prediction of y values to be observed in the future.

This chapter also discussed methods for checking the regression assumptions.

12.1 A MULTIPLE REGRESSION ANALYSIS: THE MODEL AND THE PROCEDURE

12.2 FITTING THE MODEL: THE METHOD OF LEAST SQUARES

12.3 MODEL ASSUMPTIONS

Example

12.1 Many people prefer to pay their electricity bills in equal monthly payments, rather than on the actual amount of electricity used each month. This reduces the high winter bills and increases the low summer bills.

A local electric company has proposed the following model to predict a customer's bill for next year:

$$y = \beta_0 + \beta_1 x_1 + \beta_2 x_2 + \varepsilon,$$

where y = total amount to be billed next year,
x_1 = total amount billed in current year,
and x_2 = inflation rate in current year.

Records from previous years yielded the following data for a set of 20 randomly selected residential customers:

AMOUNT BILLED IN FOLLOWING YEAR, y (\$)	AMOUNT BILLED IN PRIOR YEAR, x_1 (\$)	INFLATION RATE IN PRIOR YEAR, x_2 (%)
405	355	6.2
285	240	3.6
607	500	10.3
468	465	4.6
627	550	11.4
572	487	12.6
503	498	10.3
385	390	4.6
435	428	3.6
410	401	7.9
393	415	8.4
630	594	12.6
473	468	8.4
355	315	4.6
453	404	11.4
485	468	9.8
304	255	6.8
563	510	10.3
511	476	6.2
343	328	7.9

A portion of the output from the Statistical Analysis System (SAS) multiple regression routine for these data is shown below.

SOURCE	DF	SUM OF SQUARES	MEAN SQUARE	F VALUE	PR > F
MODEL	2	186699.0116	93349.51	98.29	0.0001
ERROR	17	16145.5384	949.74		
CORRECTED TOTAL	19	202844.5500		R-SQUARE	ROOT MSE
				.920	30.8178

PARAMETER	ESTIMATE	T FOR H0: PARAMETER = 0	PR > |T|	STD ERROR OF ESTIMATE
INTERCEPT	16.5901	0.50	0.6233	33.16066
X1	0.9197	9.17	0.0001	0.10034
X2	6.2820	1.98	0.0640	3.17090

a. Identify the least squares prediction equation.

b. Predict a customer's bill for next year if he was billed \$450 this year and the inflation rate is currently 11.8%.

Solution

a. The least squares estimates of β_0, β_1, and β_2 appear in the column labeled ESTIMATE:

$\hat{\beta}_0 = 16.59$, $\hat{\beta}_1 = 0.920$, and $\hat{\beta}_2 = 6.282$.

Thus, the least squares prediction equation is:

$\hat{y} = 16.59 + 0.920x_1 + 6.282x_2$.

b. For a customer with $x_1 = 450$ and $x_2 = 11.8$, the amount predicted for next year's bill is:

$\hat{y} = 16.59 + 0.920(450) + 6.282(11.8) = 504.7$.

We predict a bill of \$505 for this customer next year. (A measure of the reliability of such predictions is discussed in Section 12.6.)

12.2 State the assumptions made about the probability distribution of ε in a multiple regression model.

Solution

The random error component ε is assumed to have a normal distribution with mean zero and a variance σ^2 that is constant for all configurations of the independent variables $x_1, x_2, \ldots, x_k$. In addition, the errors associated with different observations of y are assumed to be independent.

12.3 Refer to Example 12.1.

a. Obtain the value of SSE for the electricity-bills example.

b. Estimate the variance of ε in the model.

Solution

a. The value for SSE appears in the printout as the SUM OF SQUARES for ERROR. Thus,

SSE = 16145.5384.

b. The estimator of σ^2, the variance of ε, is given by the mean square for error:

$$\text{MSE} = \frac{\text{SSE}}{n - (\text{number of estimated } \beta \text{ parameters})}.$$

In our example, $n = 20$ and three β parameters are estimated from the data. Thus,

$$\text{MSE} = \frac{16145.5384}{20 - 3} = 949.74.$$

Note that this value appears in the printout as the MEAN SQUARE for ERROR.

Exercises

12.1 Admission criteria at graduate schools of business are often based on a student's undergraduate grade point average (GPA) and the score on the Graduate Management Aptitude Test (GMAT). Recently, questions have been raised about the usefulness of these two variables in the prediction of a student's GPA in graduate school. Data from nine recent graduates with an MBA degree are shown below:

GPA IN GRADUATE SCHOOL, y	UNDERGRADUATE GPA, x_1	GMAT SCORE, x_2
3.83	3.90	680
3.72	3.89	660
3.61	3.35	710
3.50	3.20	530
3.46	3.78	490
3.41	3.90	520
3.30	3.10	560
3.26	2.93	610
3.07	3.21	550

The model $y = \beta_0 + \beta_1 x_1 + \beta_2 x_2 + \varepsilon$ was fit to the data; results from the SAS routine are shown below (values have been rounded):

SOURCE	DF	SUM OF SQUARES	MEAN SQUARE	F VALUE	PR > F
MODEL	2	.323	.161	7.68	.022
ERROR	6	.126	.021		
CORRECTED TOTAL	8	.449		R-SQUARE	ROOT MSE
				.7194	.1449

PARAMETER	ESTIMATE	T FOR H0: PARAMETER = 0	PR > |T|	STD ERROR OF ESTIMATE
INTERCEPT	1.2093	2.10	.081	.5771
X1	.3710	2.82	.030	.1310
X2	.0021	2.50	.048	.00084

a. Identify the least squares prediction equation.

b. What would be the predicted graduate school GPA for a student with an undergraduate GPA of 3.65 and a GMAT score of 640?

Exercise

12.2 Refer to Exercise 12.1.

a. Obtain the value of SSE from the printout for the graudate school GPA data.

b. Compute MSE, the estimate of σ^2 for the model.

12.4 ESTIMATING AND TESTING HYPOTHESES ABOUT THE β PARAMETERS

Examples

12.4 Refer to Examples 12.1-12.3. Is there evidence to indicate that the following year's bill increases as the current year's inflation rate increases? Use a significance level of $\alpha = .05$.

Solution

The hypotheses of interest concern the parameter β_2:

H_0: $\beta_2 = 0$
H_a: $\beta_2 > 0$

where β_2 is the mean increase in the following year's bill for a 1% increase in the current inflation rate, when the amount billed in the current year is held constant.

For $\alpha = .05$, the rejection region consists of values of t such that $t > t_{.05} = 1.740$, where the distribution of t has degrees of freedom equal to n - (number of β parameters estimated in model) = 20 - 3 = 17. (Note from Example 12.3 that this is exactly the number of degrees of freedom associated with the estimate of σ^2 for this model.)

The test statistic is $t = \hat{\beta}_2/s_{\hat{\beta}_2}$, where $s_{\hat{\beta}_2}$, the estimated standard deviation of the model coefficient $\hat{\beta}_2$, is found in the printout column labeled STD ERROR OF ESTIMATE. Then, for our example,

$$t = \frac{6.2820}{3.1709} = 1.98.$$

This computed value lies within the rejection region. We thus conclude that the mean amount of the following year's bill increases as the current inflation rate increases.

It should be noted that the t statistic for testing the null hypothesis that an individual β parameter is equal to zero is shown in the column of the printout labeled T FOR HO: PARAMETER = 0. The value in the column headed PR > |T| represents the two-tailed probability that

$t < -t_{computed}$ or $t > t_{computed}$.

In our example,

$P(t < -1.98 \text{ or } t > 1.98) = .0640,$

and thus,

$$P(t > 1.98) = \frac{.0640}{2} = .0320.$$

This implies that we would reject the null hypothesis in favor of our one-sided alternative for any value of α greater than .0320.

Note that the validity of this test procedure depends upon the following assumptions about the probability distribution of ε: the distribution of ε is normal with mean 0 and variance σ^2, which is constant for all values of x, and the errors are independent.

12.5 An applicance store has hypothesized the following quadratic model relating the number of air-conditioning units sold daily, y, to the daily high temperature, x:

$$y = \beta_0 + \beta_1 x + \beta_2 x^2 + \varepsilon.$$

Data collected from a random sample of 40 summer days were fit to the model, with the following results:

SOURCE	DF	SUM OF SQUARES
MODEL	2	9.2
ERROR	37	14.8
CORRECTED TOTAL	39	24.0

PARAMETER	ESTIMATE	STD ERROR OF ESTIMATE
INTERCEPT	-9.63	.371
X	0.19	.048
X * X	0.01	.0017

a. Give an interpretation of β_2 in the context of the problem.

b. Test to determine if the quadratic term makes a significant contribution to the model at $\alpha = .01$.

Solution

a. The parameter β_2, the coefficient of x^2, measures the curvature in the response curve relating y to x. The appliance store may believe, for example, that the number of air-conditioning units sold increases almost linearly as the daily high temperature increases through the lower range of temperatures. Then, in the upper range of daily temperatures, the increase in the number of units sold for a unit degree increase in temperature may begin to increase.

b. The parameter of interest is β_2, and the appliance store may wish to test its hypothesis, stated in part **a**.

H_0: $\beta_2 = 0$ (Response curve is linear through entire range of temperatures.)

H_a: $\beta_2 > 0$ (Upward curvature exists in the response curve.)

At $\alpha = .01$, the null hypothesis is rejected if

$t > t_{.01} \approx z_{.01} = 2.33$,

where t has $n - 3 = 37$ degrees of freedom, and thus is very similar to the standard normal (z) distribution.

From the computer printout, we obtain $\hat{\beta}_2 = .01$ and $s_{\hat{\beta}_2} = .0017$. Thus, the computed value of the test statistic is

$t = \hat{\beta}_2/s_{\hat{\beta}_2} = .01/.0017 = 5.88$.

The computed t value is within the rejection region and we conclude that there is significant upward curvature in the response curve relating y and x.

(This test, as will all inferential procedures in a multiple regression context, requires the assumptions about the probability distribution of ε as stated in the previous example.)

Exercises

12.3 Refer to Exercises 12.1-12.2.

a. Is there sufficient evidence (at $\alpha = .01$) that the mean graduate school GPA increases as undergraduate GPA increases, when the value of GMAT score is held constant?

b. State any assumptions required for the validity of the test procedure used in part **a**.

12.4 Data on 10 bank managers were collected for the following variables:

y = salary (in thousands of dollars),

x_1 = age,

and x_2 = number of years experience with this bank.

The following least squares equation was obtained:

$\hat{y} = 20 + .1x_1 + 1.2x_2$

with

$s_{\hat{\beta}_1} = .064$ and $s_{\hat{\beta}_2} = .45$.

a. State the probabilistic model that was fit to the data.

b. Use the results to determine whether there is evidence to indicate that the mean salary of bank managers depends on the length of experience with the bank.

12.5 CHECKING THE USEFULNESS OF A MODEL: R^2 AND THE ANALYSIS OF VARIANCE F TEST

Examples

12.6 Refer to Examples 12.1-12.3.

a. Obtain the value of R^2, the multiple coefficient of determination for the electricity-bills data. Interpret its value.

b. Is there evidence to indicate that the overall model is useful for predicting the following year's bill? Use $\alpha = .01$.

Solution

a. The SAS multiple regression routine gives the multiple coefficient of determination, R-SQUARE, in the output. For our example, $R^2 = .920$. Thus, 92% of the sample variation of the y values is accounted for by the regression model. In other words, the sum of squared prediction errors is reduced by 92% when the least squares prediction equation $\hat{y} = 16.59 + .92x_1 + 6.282x_2$ is used, instead of $\bar{y}$, to predict the value of y.

b. To test the global utility of the model, we test

H_0: $\beta_1 = \beta_2 = 0$

against

H_a: At least one of the coefficients differs from zero.

The test, which requires the standard assumptions about the probability distribution of ε, is based on an F statistic with k degrees of freedom in the numerator and $[n - (k + 1)]$ degrees of freedom in the denominator, where k is the number of independent variables in the model. For our example, $n = 20$, $k = 2$, and the null hypothesis will be rejected at $\alpha = .01$ if

$$F > F_{.01} = 6.11,$$

where F is based on 2 numerator df and 17 denominator df.

The test statistic is

$$F = \frac{R^2/k}{(1 - R^2)/[n - (k + 1)]} = \frac{.920/2}{(1 - .920)/[20 - (2 + 1)]} = 97.75.$$

This value exceeds the tabulated critical value of 6.11; thus, we conclude that at least one of the model coefficients β_1 and β_2 is significantly different from zero, and that the model

$$y = \beta_0 + \beta_1 x_1 + \beta_2 x_2 + \varepsilon$$

is useful for predicting the following year's electricity bill.

(Note that the computer routine provides the computed F for the test of the overall utility of the model. In the printout given in Example 12.1, we find $F = 98.29$; this differs from our computed value only because of rounding errors.)

12.7 Refer to Example 12.5.

a. Use the information given to compute the value of R^2 for the air-conditioning sales data.

b. Conduct the global F test of model utility at the $\alpha = .05$ level of significance.

Solution

a. The multiple coefficient of determination is defined as

$$R^2 = 1 - \frac{\text{SSE}}{\text{SS}_{yy}},$$

where SSE is referred to as SUM OF SQUARES for ERROR in the printout, and SS_{yy} is the CORRECTED TOTAL SUM OF SQUARES. For the air-conditioning sales data,

$$R^2 = 1 - \frac{14.8}{24.0} = 1 - .617 = .383.$$

b. The elements of the test are

H_0: $\beta_1 = \beta_2 = 0$
H_a: At least one of the coefficients is nonzero.

The test statistic is based on $k = 2$ numerator degrees of freedom and $n - (k + 1) = 40 - 3 = 37$ denominator degrees of freedom; thus, we will reject the null hypothesis at $\alpha = .05$ if $F > F_{.05} \approx 3.26$.

The computed value of the test statistic is

$$F = \frac{R^2/k}{(1 - R^2)/[n - (k + 1)]} = \frac{.383/2}{(1 - .383)/37} = 11.48.$$

We reject H_0 and conclude that the model is useful for predicting air-conditioning sales.

Exercises

12.5 Refer to Exercises 12.1-12.3. Compute the value of the multiple coefficient of determination, R^2, for the data on graduate school GPA. Interpret its value.

12.6 Refer to Exercises 12.1-12.3. Perform the global F test of the utility of the model. Use a significance level of $\alpha = .05$.

12.6 USING THE MODEL FOR ESTIMATION AND PREDICTION

Example

12.8 Refer to Example 12.1b, where we used the least squares equation to predict the amount of next year's electricity bill for a particular customer with $x_1 = 450$ and $x_2 = 11.8$. Suppose the corresponding 95% prediction interval were (253.9, 755.5). Would you expect a 95% confidence interval for $E(y)$, the mean electricity bill for all customers with $x_1 = 450$ and $x_2 = 11.8$ to be narrower or wider than this interval? Explain.

Solution

As was the case with the simple linear regression procedures of Chapter 11, the least squares equation yields the same value for both $E(y)$ and for the prediction of a future value of y for a specified configuration of values of the independent variables. (In this example, with $x_1 = 450$ and $x_2 = 11.8$, this common value was $\hat{y} = 504.7$, obtained in Example 12.1.) Furthermore, the confidence interval for the mean value will be narrower than the prediction interval for a particular value of y, because of the additional variability of ε in predicting a particular value of y.

Exercise

12.7 Refer to Exercises 12.1-12.3. Suppose that the 90% confidence interval for the mean graduate school GPA when $x_1 = 3.65$ and $x_2 = 640$ is given by (3.822, 3.992). Interpret this interval.

12.7 MULTIPLE REGRESSION: AN EXAMPLE

Example

12.9 A college administrator would like to be able to predict the number of credit hours students will take in a given quarter, so that he can plan the budget accordingly. He believes several factors influence the number of hours taken by each student, and proposed the following model to predict the number of credit hours taken:

$$y = \beta_0 + \beta_1 x_1 + \beta_2 x_2 + \beta_3 x_3 + \varepsilon,$$

where y = number of credit hours taken,

x_1 = total number of credit hours previously taken,

$$x_2 = \begin{cases} 1 & \text{if student is in upper division} \\ 0 & \text{if student is in lower division,} \end{cases}$$

and

$$x_3 = \begin{cases} 1 & \text{if fall or winter quarter} \\ 0 & \text{if summer or spring quarter.} \end{cases}$$

A random sample of 20 students produced the following data:

NUMBER OF CREDIT HOURS y	NUMBER OF CREDIT HOURS PREVIOUSLY TAKEN x_1	DUMMY VARIABLE FOR DIVISION x_2	DUMMY VARIABLE FOR QUARTER x_3
16	95	1	1
19	142	1	1
14	128	1	1
12	165	1	1
15	131	1	1
13	104	1	0
15	153	1	0
13	128	1	0
12	139	1	0
14	101	1	0
19	15	0	1
18	73	0	1
16	31	0	1
17	65	0	1
15	93	0	1
13	26	0	0
15	100	0	0
16	38	0	0
17	85	0	0
16	70	0	0

A portion of the SAS multiple regression analysis of these data is shown below:

SOURCE	DF	SUM OF SQUARES	MEAN SQUARE	F VALUE	PR > F
MODEL	3	33.0755	11.025	3.48	.0407
ERROR	16	50.6745	3.167		
CORRECTED TOTAL	19	83.7500		R-SQUARE	ROOT MSE
				.395	1.780

PARAMETER	ESTIMATE	T FOR HO: PARAMETER = 0	PR > |T|	STD ERROR OF ESTIMATE
INTERCEPT	15.751	13.50	0.0001	1.167
X1	-0.00670	-0.43	0.6756	0.0157
X2	-1.438	-1.07	0.3010	1.345
X3	1.696	2.13	0.0490	0.796

a. Identify the least squares model that was fit to the data.

b. What is the predicted number of credit hours an upper division student will take in spring quarter if he has already taken 100 credit hours?

c. Specify the probability distribution of ε.

d. Obtain an estimate of σ^2, the variance of ε.

e. Obtain the value of R^2 and interpret it.

f. Conduct the global F test of model utility. Use a significance level of .05.

g. Is there evidence that the number of credit hours taken tends to decrease as the number of credit hours previously taken increases? Use $\alpha = .05$.

Solution

a. The least squares model is:

$$\hat{y} = 15.751 - .00670x_1 - 1.438x_2 + 1.696x_3.$$

b. To predict the number of credit hours to be taken in spring quarter by an upper division student who has already taken 100 credit hours, we substitute $x_1 = 100$, $x_2 = 1$, and $x_3 = 0$ into the prediction equation:

$$\hat{y} = 15.751 - .00670(100) - 1.438(1) + 1.696(0) = 13.6.$$

c. We assume that the probability distribution of ε is normal, with a mean of zero and a constant variance of σ^2. In addition, the errors are assumed to be independent.

d. The estimate of σ^2, the variance of the random error component ε, is given in the SAS printout as MEAN SQUARE for ERROR:

MSE = 3.167.

Note that this quantity can be computed directly as

$$\text{MSE} = \frac{\text{SSE}}{n - (k + 1)} = \frac{50.6745}{20 - (3 + 1)} = 3.167.$$

e. The value of the multiple coefficient of determination is shown in the printout: $R^2 = .395$. Note that this quantity can also be computed as

$$R^2 = 1 - \frac{\text{SSE}}{\text{SS}_{yy}} = 1 - \frac{50.6745}{83.7500} = 1 - .605 = .395.$$

Thus, only 39.5% of the sample variation in the y values is accounted for by the least squares model.

f. The elements of the test are

H_0: $\beta_1 = \beta_2 = \beta_3 = 0$
H_a: At least one of the coefficients is nonzero.

The test is based on an F statistic with $k = 3$ numerator degrees of freedom and $n - (k + 1) = 20 - 4 = 16$ denominator degrees of freedom. For $\alpha = .05$, H_0 will be rejected for $F > F_{.05} = 3.24$.

The test statistic is

$$F = \frac{R^2/k}{(1 - R^2)/[n - (k + 1)]} = \frac{.395/3}{(1 - .395)/16} = 3.48.$$

(This value can be obtained directly from the printout.)

We reject H_0 and conclude that, at $\alpha = .05$, the model is useful for predicting the number of credit hours to be taken.

g. The parameter of interest is β_1, and we wish to test:

H_0: $\beta_1 = 0$

against

H_a: $\beta_1 < 0$

At significance level $\alpha = .05$, we will reject H_0 if $t < -t_{.05} = -1.746$, where t is based on $n - (k + 1) = 16$ df.

The test statistic is computed as

$$t = \hat{\beta}_1/s_{\hat{\beta}_1} = -.00670/.0157 = -.43.$$

This value, which can be obtained directly from the printout, does not lie within the rejection region. There is insufficient evidence to conclude that the number of credit hours taken decreases as the number of hours previously taken increases when the dummy variables for division and quarter are held constant.

12.9 RESIDUAL ANALYSIS: CHECKING THE REGRESSION ASSUMPTIONS

Examples

12.10 Refer to Example 12.1. The observed y values, the predicted y values, $\hat{y}$, and the corresponding residuals are shown below. The residuals are then plotted on the vertical axis against the independent variable, x_1, the amount billed in the current year, and against the independent variable x_2, the inflation rate in the current year.

a. Verify that each residual is equal to the difference between the observed y value and the estimated mean value $\hat{y}$.

b. Analyze the residual plots.

OBS.	ACTUAL y (\$)	PREDICTED y (\$)	RESIDUAL
1	405.	382.0312	22.96884
2	285.	259.9327	25.06726
3	607.	541.1435	65.85651
4	468.	473.1467	-5.146667
5	627.	594.0385	32.96149
6	572.	543.6360	28.36395
7	503.	539.3041	-36.30408
8	385.	404.1693	-19.16934
9	435.	432.8358	2.164154
10	410.	435.0166	-25.01663
11	393.	451.0334	-58.03339
12	630.	642.0437	-12.04370
13	473.	499.7774	-26.77737
14	355.	335.1920	19.80795
15	453.	459.7627	-6.762726
16	485.	508.5722	-23.57217
17	304.	293.8306	10.16940
18	563.	550.3405	12.65955
19	511.	493.3145	17.68546
20	343.	367.8787	-24.87872

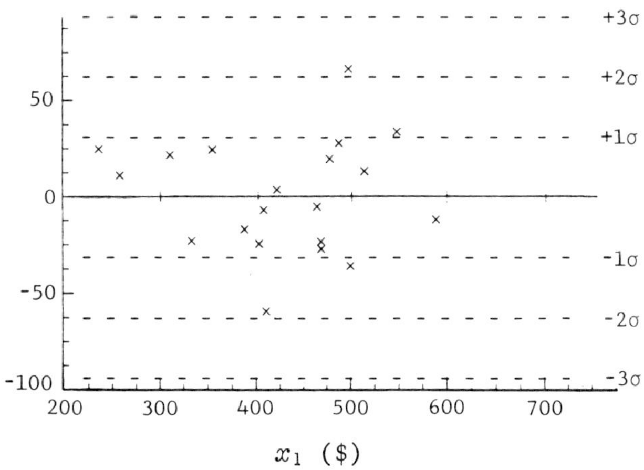

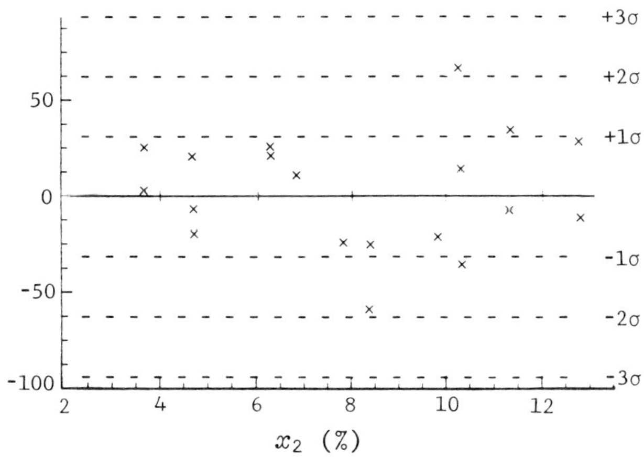

Solution

a. The residual for the first y value is calculated as follows:

$$\text{Residual} = \text{observed } y \text{ value} - \text{estimated mean}$$
$$= y - \hat{y} = 405 - 382.03 = 22.97$$

For the second y value the residual is:

$$\text{Residual} = \text{observed } y \text{ value} - \text{estimated mean}$$
$$= y - \hat{y} = 285 - 259.93 = 25.07$$

These residuals agree (after rounding) with the first two entries in the third column labeled Residuals in the accompanying table. Similar calculations produce the remaining residuals.

b. In both residual plots shown here, the residuals appear to be randomly distributed around the 0 line, as expected. If either of the plots had exhibited a mound shape or a bowl shape, this would have indicated that curvature should be added to the model.

12.11 The data for the electric bill prediction example used throughout this chapter are reproduced in the table with one important difference: The third value of the dependent variable, \$607, has been changed to \$407. The model

$$y = \beta_0 + \beta_1 x_1 + \beta_2 x_2 + \varepsilon$$

is then fit to these (modified) data, with the printout as shown below. The residuals are also shown and plotted against the independent variable x_1, the total amount billed in the current year. Analyze the residual plot.

NAME:	y(\$)	X1(\$)	X2(%)
1	405	355	6.2
2	285	240	3.6
3	407	500	10.3
4	468	465	4.6
5	627	550	11.4
6	572	487	12.6
7	503	498	10.3
8	385	390	4.6
9	435	428	3.6
10	410	401	7.9
11	393	415	8.4
12	630	594	12.6
13	473	468	8.4
14	355	315	4.6
15	453	404	11.4
16	485	468	9.8
17	304	255	6.8
18	563	510	10.3
19	511	476	6.2
20	343	328	7.9

VARIABLE	COEFFICIENT	STANDARD ERROR	t-TEST	.0500 SIGNIF	p-VALUE
a	42.8021	42.33377	1.011	N	.326
X1(\$)	.8635764	.1280934	6.742	Y	.000
X2(%)	4.767619	4.048048	1.178	N	.255

The critical t-value for d.f. = 17 and alpha = .0500 is 2.1098

Std dev of reg = 39.34283 R = .925 R-Sqrd = .856 Adj R-Sqrd = .839
F-test = 50.351 p-value = .0000
F value from table (alpha = .05) = 3.59
Observations = 20 Degrees of freedom for numerator = 2
Degrees of freedom for denominator = 17

OBS.	ACTUAL y (\$)	PREDICTED y (\$)	RESIDUALS
1	405.	378.9310	26.06903
2	285.	267.2239	17.77612
3	407.	523.6968	-116.6968
4	468.	466.2962	1.703796
5	627.	572.1199	54.88007
6	572.	523.4358	48.56421
7	503.	521.9697	-18.96967
8	385.	401.5280	-16.52795
9	435.	429.5762	5.423767
10	410.	426.7604	-16.76044
11	393.	441.2343	-48.23431
12	630.	615.8385	14.16150
13	473.	487.0039	-14.00388
14	355.	336.7597	18.24026
15	453.	446.0378	6.962158
16	485.	493.6785	-8.678528
17	304.	295.4339	8.566101
18	563.	532.3326	30.66742
19	511.	483.4237	27.57629
20	343.	363.7194	-20.71936

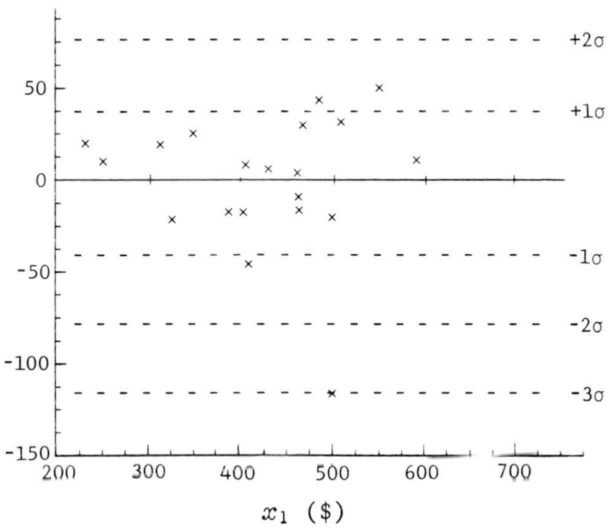

Solution

The residual plot readily indicates the altered measurement at x_1 = \$500. The residual at this value of x_1 lies almost 3 standard deviations below 0, while no other residual lies more than about 1.5 standard deviations from 0. There are several possible reasons for the presence of outliers. Data may have been entered incorrectly, or the measurement may not have been taken under the conditions you are attempting to model. For example, the lower than expected value of the dependent variable may be due to a one-time discount because the homeowner made improvements to make the structure more energy-efficient. In many instances there may be no obvious explanation for the presence of the outlier. You may want to rerun the regression analysis with the outlier omitted from the data to determine its effect on the analysis. Below is a new plot of the residuals (against x_1) when the regression is run without the outlier. Notice that only one residual is as much as 2 standard deviations away from 0 and that most are within 1 standard deviation of 0. Note that the standard deviation has decreased from 39.3 with the outlier to 26.68 without the outlier, indicating a model that will provide more precise estimates and predictions.

VARIABLE	COEFFICIENT	STANDARD ERROR	t-TEST	.0500 SIGNIF	p-VALUE
a	26.04615	28.94674	.900	N	.382
X1($)	.8994517	.08723658	10.310	Y	.000
X2(%)	5.735685	2.753861	2.083	N	.054

The critical t-value for d.f. = 16 and alpha = .0500 is 2.1199

Std dev of reg = 26.68562   R = .968   R-Sqrd = .937   Adj R-Sqrd = .929
F-test = 118.53   p-value = .0000
F value from table (alpha = .05) = 3.63
Observations = 19.   Degrees of freedom for numerator = 2
Degrees of freedom for denominator = 16

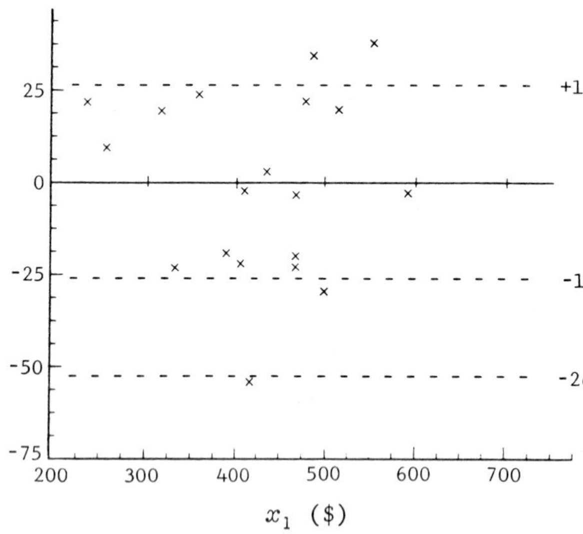

Exercises

12.8 Consider the executive salary and experience data in the table below. Log y is related to years of experience, x, using the second-order model

$$\log y = \beta_0 + \beta_1 x + \beta_2 x^2 + \varepsilon.$$

The regression output and a plot of the residuals [in terms of numbers of standard deviations (positive or negative)] from the mean 0 are shown below. Does the assumption of constant variance appear reasonable?

YEARS OF EXPERIENCE x	SALARY y	YEARS OF EXPERIENCE x	SALARY y	YEARS OF EXPERIENCE x	SALARY y
7	\$26,075	21	\$43,628	28	\$99,139
28	79,370	4	16,105	23	52,624
23	65,726	24	65,644	17	50,594
18	41,983	20	63,022	25	53,272
19	62,309	20	47,780	26	65,343
15	41,154	15	38,853	19	46,216
24	53,610	25	66,537	16	54,288
13	33,697	25	67,447	3	20,844
2	22,444	28	64,785	12	32,586
8	32,562	26	61,581	23	71,235
20	43,076	27	70,678	20	36,530
21	56,000	20	51,301	19	52,745
18	58,667	18	39,346	27	67,282
7	22,210	1	24,833	25	80,931
2	20,521	26	65,929	12	32,303
18	49,727	20	41,721	11	38,371
11	33,233	26	82,641		

```
The regression equation is
LOGY = 9.84 + 0.0497 X + 0.000009 XX

Predictor        Coef        Stdev    t-ratio
Constant      9.84289      0.08479     116.08
X             0.04969      0.01182       4.20
XX          0.0000093    0.0003753       0.02

s = 0.1557   R-sq = 86.4%   R-sq(adj) = 85.8%

Analysis of Variance

SOURCE        DF        SS         MS
Regression     2    7.2119     3.6059
Error         47    1.1400     0.0243
Total         49    8.3519
```

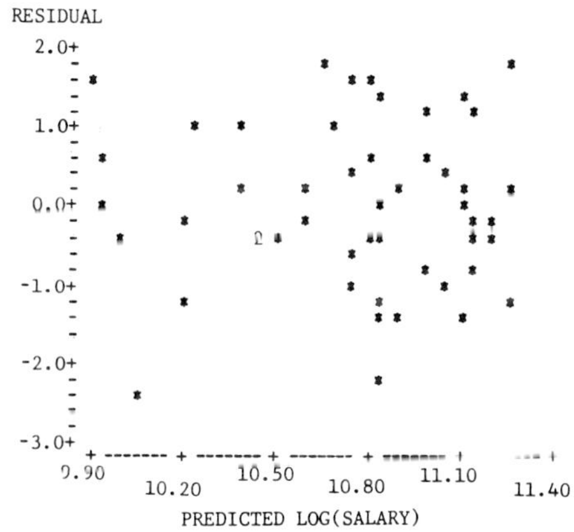

12.9 Refer to Exercise 12.8. A stem-and leaf display of the residuals is given here. Analyze the display, especially with regard to the normality assumption.

STEM	LEAF
-.3	3, 5
-.2	0, 1, 1
-.1	0, 1, 2, 5, 6, 6, 7, 8
-.0	0, 1, 2, 2, 3, 5, 5, 5, 5, 5, 6, 7, 7, 8
.0	1, 2, 3, 3, 4, 4, 5, 7, 8, 8
.1	0, 4, 5, 6, 8, 8
.2	1, 1, 3, 4, 5, 6, 6

13
INTRODUCTION TO MODEL BUILDING

SUMMARY

This chapter discussed the selection of an appropriate model for a given set of data. In a *model building* effort, the researcher will utilize knowledge of the process being modeled, in addition to formal statistical procedures.

The first step in the construction of a model for a response variable y is the identification of a set of independent variables, each of which is classified as either *qualitative* or *quantitative*. If the number of potentially important independent variables is very large, a *stepwise regression* procedure can be employed to reduce the set by screening out those variables which seem unimportant for the prediction of y.

The researcher is advised to consider at least *second-order models*, those which contain *quadratic terms* and *two-way interactions* among the quantitative variables. The model may be modified and improved by testing sets of β parameters for significance.

13.1 THE TWO TYPES OF INDEPENDENT VARIABLES: QUANTITATIVE AND QUALITATIVE

Example

13.1 Most automobile loan applications request biographical and demographic information on such variables as:

a. Sex
b. Marital status
c. Age
d. Monthly income
e. Amount of loan desired
f. Credit references.

For each of these variables, specify its type (qualitative or quantitative) and describe the nature of the levels that you might observe.

Solution

a. The variable for sex is qualitative, since its levels, "male" and "female," are not numerical, but instead are descriptive labels.

b. The levels of marital status (married, single, divorced, separated, widowed) are nonnumerical; hence, this is a qualitative variable.

c. Age is a quantitative variable with levels ranging from approximately 16 years to 100 years. (We assume that only those individuals of driving age would be applying for an automobile loan.)

d. This variable assumes numerical values within a very large range representing all possible values of an individual's monthly income, and thus is quantitative.

e. The amount of the loan requested is a quantitative variable which will assume a numerical values between $0 and $15,000, say.

f. The levels will be nonnumerical labels representing, for example, names of banks or major credit cards; thus, credit reference is a qualitative variable.

Exercise

13.1 For each of the following variables, state its type and describe the nature of the levels that may be observed.

a. Number of gasoline credit cards possessed.
b. Type of gasoline used in primary automobile.
c. Capacity of gasoline tank.
d. Mileage per gallon obtained by automobile.
e. Brand name of motor oil preferred.

13.2 MODELS WITH A SINGLE QUANTITATIVE INDEPENDENT VARIABLE

Examples

13.2 Records for nine individuals who have purchased term life insurance policies with a particular company yielded the following information on age (in years) and amount of monthly premium (in dollars):

AGE, x	MONTHLY PREMIUM, y
20	3.86
25	4.03
30	4.22
35	4.50
40	4.94
45	5.50
50	6.26
55	7.44
60	9.03

a. Plot the data on a scattergram.

b. Suggest a model to relate $E(y)$ and x.

Solution

a.

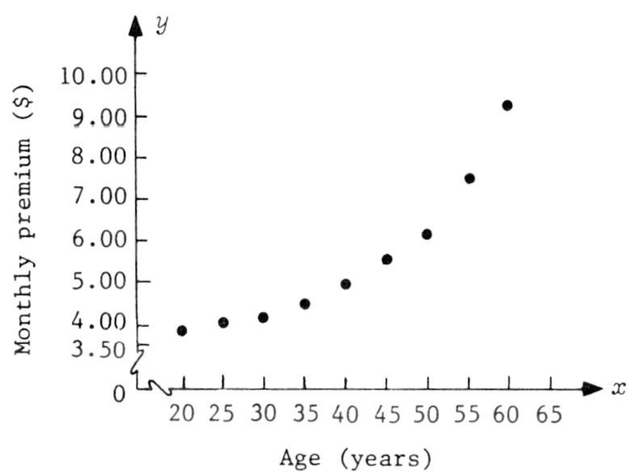

b. It is clear from the scattergram that the straight-line model $E(y) = \beta_0 + \beta_1 x$ is inappropriate, as the relationship between y and x appears to be linear only over the restricted age range from 20-40 years. In the upper age range, the amount of increase in the premium for a unit (one-year) increase in age increases. That is, the *rate* of increase in $E(y)$ is believed to increase as x increases. Thus, we may wish to fit a quadratic (second-order polynomial) model to the data:

$$E(y) = \beta_0 + \beta_1 x + \beta_2 x^2,$$

where β_2 is expected to be positive to reflect the upward curvature of the response curve.

13.3 Refer to Example 13.2. The least squares quadratic prediction equation was determined to be

$$\hat{y} = 6.49 - .2x + .004x^2, \text{ with } s_{\hat{\beta}_2} = .0006.$$

Test the hypothesis that the monthly premium increases at an increasing rate with age. Use a significance level of $\alpha = .05$.

Solution

The parameter of interest is β_2, and the test has the following elements:

H_0: $\beta_2 = 0$
H_a: $\beta_2 > 0$

At $\alpha = .05$, the null hypothesis will be rejected if $t > t_{.05} = 1.943$, where t is based on $n - (k + 1) = 9 - (2 + 1) = 6$ degrees of freedom.

The test statistic is

$$t = \hat{\beta}_2 / s_{\hat{\beta}_2} = .004/.0006 = 6.67.$$

This computed value lies within the rejection region. We thus conclude that β_2 is significantly larger than zero, i.e., that the amount of monthly premium increases at an increasing rate with age.

Exercise

13.2 A company which sells replacement computer parts advertises that it ships orders immediately upon receipt. The management is interested in modeling the relationship between time required for delivery of a customer's order, y, and the distance between shipping point and destination, x. It is believed that the model should allow for the average delivery time to increase as the distance increases to a certain value (say, 1000 miles), after which the amount of increase in delivery time for a unit increase in distance will decrease.

a. Write a model to relate $E(y)$ and x.

b. Sketch the shape of the response curve for the hypothesized model.

13.3 MODELS WITH TWO QUANTITATIVE INDEPENDENT VARIABLES

Example

13.4 Researchers for a consumer agency wish to investigate the relationship between mileage per gallon ratings (y) and the independent variables engine size (x_1, in cubic inches) and speed of automobile (x_2, in miles per hour).

a.

a. Write the first-order model for $E(y)$. What are the assumptions implied by the model?

b. Write the first-order model plus interaction for $E(y)$. Graph $E(y)$ versus x_2 as you would expect it to appear for $x_1 = 250$ and $x_1 = 400$, where x_2 ranges from 25 miles per hour to 60 miles per hour.

c. Write the complete second-order model for $E(y)$ as a function of x_1 and x_2.

Solution

a. The general first-order model for $k = 2$ quantitative independent variables is:

$$E(y) = \beta_0 + \beta_1 x_1 + \beta_2 x_2.$$

This model assumes that there is no curvature in the response curve and that the variables engine size (x_1) and speed of automobile (x_2) affect mileage per gallon ratings (y) independently of each other. All contour lines will be parallel.

b. The first-order model with interaction is given by

$$E(y) = \beta_0 + \beta_1 x_1 + \beta_2 x_2 + \beta_3 x_1 x_2.$$

The inclusion of the interaction term $\beta_3 x_1 x_2$ allows contour lines to be nonparallel.

For $x_1 = 250$,

$$\begin{aligned} E(y) &= \beta_0 + \beta_1(250) + \beta_2 x_2 + \beta_3(250)x_2 \\ &= (\beta_0 + 250\beta_1) + (\beta_2 + 250\beta_3)x_2, \end{aligned}$$

and for $x_1 = 400$,

$$E(y) = (\beta_0 + 400\beta_1) + (\beta_2 + 400\beta_3)x_2.$$

Note the differences in the slopes and y-intercepts of the contour lines as the size of the automobile engine changes.

Contour lines for $x_1 = 250$ and $x_1 = 400$ can be graphed as shown in the following diagram.

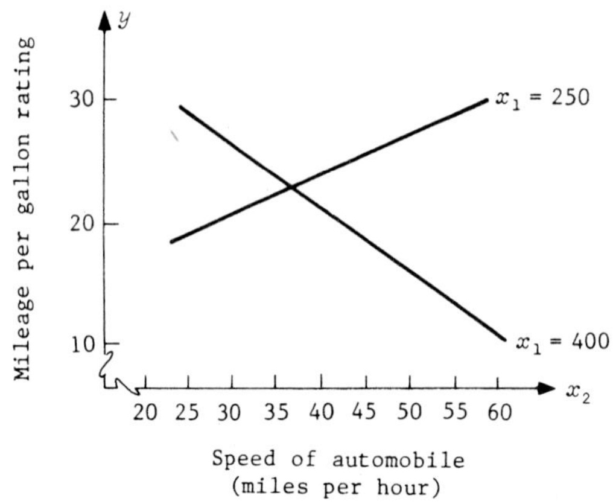

c. To allow for curvature in the contour lines, we may add quadratic terms to the model of part **b** to obtain the complete second-order model:

$$E(y) = \beta_0 + \beta_1 x_1 + \beta_2 x_2 + \beta_3 x_1 x_2 + \beta_4 x_1^2 + \beta_5 x_2^2.$$

Exercise

13.3 A large grocery store chain is interested in predicting a family's weekly food expenditure (y) based on weekly income (x_1) and the number of people in the family (x_2).

a. Write the first-order model for $E(y)$. Interpret the model in terms of the problem.

b. Do you think an interaction term would be appropriate for the model? Why or why not? Add an interaction term to the model of part **a**.

c. Write the complete second-order model for $E(y)$.

13.4 MODEL BUILDING: TESTING PORTIONS OF A MODEL

Examples

13.5 Refer to Example 13.4. The three models formulated to describe the relationship between mileage per gallon ratings (y) and the independent variables engine size (x_1) and speed of automobile (x_2) were fit to sample data for n = 50 automobiles with the following results:

1) First-order model:

$$E(y) = \beta_0 + \beta_1 x_1 + \beta_2 x_2$$
$$SSE_1 = 80.4$$

2) First-order model with interaction:

$$E(y) = \beta_0 + \beta_1 x_1 + \beta_2 x_2 + \beta_3 x_1 x_2$$
$$SSE_2 = 62.9$$

3) Second-order model:

$$E(y) = \beta_0 + \beta_1 x_1 + \beta_2 x_2 + \beta_3 x_1 x_2 + \beta_4 x_1^2 + \beta_5 x_2^2$$
$$SSE_3 = 55.8$$

Perform a test (at $\alpha = .05$) to determine whether the first-order model with interaction contributes more information than the first-order model for the prediction of y.

Solution

We wish to compare model (1) with model (2) and test whether the interaction term $\beta_3 x_1 x_2$ should be retained in model (2). The appropriate test is:

H_0: $\beta_3 = 0$
H : $\beta_3 \neq 0$

The F statistic is calculated as follows:

$$F = \frac{(SSE_1 - SSE_2)/1}{SSE_2/[n - \text{number of } \beta \text{ parameters in model (2)}]}$$

and is based on $\nu_1 = 1$ numerator and $\nu_2 = 50 - 4 = 46$ denominator degrees of freedom. At significance level $\alpha = .05$, we will reject H_0 if $F > F_{.05} \approx 4.06$. Substitution of the given values of SSE for the two models yields:

$$F = \frac{(80.4 - 62.9)/1}{62.9/(50 - 4)} = 12.80$$

This value of the test statistic lies within the rejection region. We thus conclude that the first-order model with interaction provides more information than the first-order model for predicting y; the interaction term $\beta_3 x_1 x_2$ makes an important contribution to the model.

13.6 Refer to Examples 13.4 and 13.5. Perform a test to determine whether the second-order model contributes more information than the first-order model with interaction for the prediction of y.

Solution

To determine whether the second-order terms are useful in the model, we will compare model (2) with model (3) and perform a test of

H_0: $\beta_4 = \beta_5 = 0$
H_a: At least one of the coefficients β_4 or β_5 is nonzero.

The test statistic is of the form

$$F = \frac{(SSE_2 - SSE_3)/2}{SSE_3/[n - \text{number of } \beta \text{ parameters in model (3)}]}$$

based on $\nu_1 = 2$ numerator degrees of freedom (because there are two parameters specified in H_0) and $\nu_2 = 50 - 6 = 44$ denominator degrees of freedom. Thus, we will reject H_0 (at $\alpha = .05$) if $F > F_{.05} \approx 3.21$.

The test statistic is computed as follows:

$$F = \frac{(62.9 - 55.8)/2}{55.8/(50 - 6)} = 2.80.$$

Since this value of the test statistic does not fall within the rejection region, we cannot reject H_0 at $\alpha = .05$. There is insufficient evidence to conclude that the second-order model is more useful than the first-order model with interaction for predicting mileage per gallon ratings.

Exercises

13.4 Refer to Exercise 13.3. The three models relating weekly food expenditure (y) to weekly income (x_1) and family size (x_2) were fit to $n = 80$ observations with the following results:

First-order model: SSE = 576.34
First-order model with interaction: SSE = 382.19
Second-order model: SSE = 104.65

Perform a test (at $\alpha = .05$) to determine whether the interaction term is a useful addition to the first-order model.

13.5 Refer to Exercises 13.3 and 13.4. Perform a test to determine whether the second-order model contributes more information than the first-order model with interaction for predicting weekly food expenditure. Use $\alpha = .05$.

13.5 MODELS WITH ONE QUALITATIVE INDEPENDENT VARIABLE

Examples

13.7 A management consulting firm is interested in constructing a model for the annual salary of bank managers, and believes that the manager's sex is an important independent variable to consider.

a. Write a model that will provide a single prediction equation for the mean salary of male and female managers, if sex is the only independent variable of interest.

b. Interpret the parameters of the model in part **a**.

Solution

a. Let μ_M be the mean annual salary of a male bank manager and μ_F the mean salary of a female manager. We can model $E(y)$, the mean annual salary, as follows:

$$E(y) = \beta_0 + \beta_1 x_1,$$

where

$$x_1 = \begin{cases} 1 & \text{if the manager is male} \\ 0 & \text{if the manager is female.} \end{cases}$$

b. To determine the mean annual salary for a male bank manager, we let the dummy variable x_1 assume the value 1. Then

$$\mu_M = E(y) = \beta_0 + \beta_1(1) = \beta_0 + \beta_1.$$

Similarly, for a female bank manager,

$$\mu_F = E(y) = \beta_0 + \beta_1(0) = \beta_0.$$

Thus, β_0 is the mean salary of a female bank manager and $\beta_1 = \mu_M - \mu_F$ is the difference in the mean salaries for male and female bank managers.

13.8 The owner of a fast-food chain with five locations (L_1, L_2, L_3, L_4, and L_5) wishes to model his daily sales as a function of location.

a. Write a model for mean daily sales, $E(y)$, as a function of location.

b. Interpret the parameters of the model in part **a**.

c. What is the difference (in terms of the model parameters) between the mean daily sales for locations L_3 and L_1?

d. What is the difference (in terms of the model parameters) between the mean daily sales for locations L_2 and L_5?

Solution

a. The model relating $E(y)$ to the qualitative variable location is

$$E(y) = \beta_0 + \beta_1 x_1 + \beta_2 x_2 + \beta_3 x_3 + \beta_4 x_4,$$

where

$$x_1 = \begin{cases} 1 & \text{if location } L_2 \\ 0 & \text{otherwise} \end{cases} \qquad x_2 = \begin{cases} 1 & \text{if location } L_3 \\ 0 & \text{otherwise} \end{cases}$$

$$x_3 = \begin{cases} 1 & \text{if location } L_4 \\ 0 & \text{otherwise} \end{cases} \qquad x_4 = \begin{cases} 1 & \text{if location } L_5 \\ 0 & \text{otherwise} \end{cases}$$

Note that four dummy variables are required to describe the five levels of the qualitative independent variable.

b. The parameter β_0 represents the mean daily sales at location L_1, the base level of the qualitative independent variable. The remaining parameters represent the differences between mean daily sales for the particular location and location L_1. Thus, for example, β_3 is the difference between the mean daily sales at location L_4 and location L_1. This can also be seen by substituting the appropriate values of the dummy variables into the model for $E(y)$.

For location L_4 (set $x_1 = 0$, $x_2 = 0$, $x_3 = 1$, $x_4 = 0$):

$$\mu_4 = E(y) = \beta_0 + \beta_1(0) + \beta_2(0) + \beta_3(1) + \beta_4(0) = \beta_0 + \beta_3.$$

For location L_1 (set $x_1 = x_2 = x_3 = x_4 = 0$):

$$\mu_1 = E(y) = \beta_0 + \beta_1(0) + \beta_2(0) + \beta_3(0) + \beta_4(0) = \beta_0.$$

Thus, $\mu_4 - \mu_1 = \beta_3$, as obtained above. The parameters β_1, β_2, and β_4 have analogous interpretations.

c. Location L_1 is the base level of the qualitative independent variable; thus, the difference between mean daily sales for locations L_3 and L_1 is the parameter representing level L_3, namely β_2:

$$\beta_2 = \mu_3 - \mu_1,$$

where μ_3 and μ_1 are the mean daily sales at locations L_3 and L_1, respectively.

d. To model the mean daily sales for location L_2, set $x_1 = 1$, $x_2 = x_3 = x_4 = 0$:

$$\mu_2 = \beta_0 + \beta_1(1) + \beta_2(0) + \beta_3(0) + \beta_4(0) = \beta_0 + \beta_1.$$

To model the mean daily sales for location L_5, set $x_1 = x_2 = x_3 = 0$, $x_4 = 1$:

$$\mu_5 = \beta_0 + \beta_1(0) + \beta_2(0) + \beta_3(0) + \beta_4(1) = \beta_0 + \beta_4.$$

The difference between the mean daily sales for locations L_2 and L_5 is

$$\mu_2 - \mu_5 = (\beta_0 + \beta_1) - (\beta_0 + \beta_4) = \beta_1 - \beta_4.$$

Exercise

13.6 A company wished to determine how well its management trainee program predicted an individual's success five years after completion of the program. For graduates of the training program, they chose to model the mean salary, $E(y)$, as a function of the qualitative independent variable preformance in the program (excellent, fair, or poor).

a. Define dummy variables to describe the levels of the qualitative independent variable.

b. Write the model relating $E(y)$ to performance in the training program.

c. Based on the model in part b, what is the mean salary for employees who were rated excellent?

d. In terms of the model parameters, what is the difference between the mean salaries for employees who were rated poor and those who were rated excellent?

13.6 COMPARING THE SLOPES OF TWO OR MORE LINES

13.7 COMPARING TWO OR MORE RESPONSE CURVES

Examples

Note: *In Examples 13.9–13.19 we will proceed to build a model in stages. Graphical interpretations will be provided at each stage.*

13.9 Suppose we wish to relate $E(y)$, the mean salary of a bank manager, to years of experience for bank managers in four cities (Chicago, New York, Miami, and St. Louis). Write a model for $E(y)$ that allows for a single straight-line relationship between mean salary and years of experience for all four cities. Graph a typical response curve.

Solution

The straight-line model $E(y) = \beta_0 + \beta_1 x_1$, where x = years of experience, is unable to detect a difference in mean salaries of bank managers among the four cities, if such differences exist. According to this model, a single straight line characterizes the relationship between mean salary and years of experience, as shown in the figure.

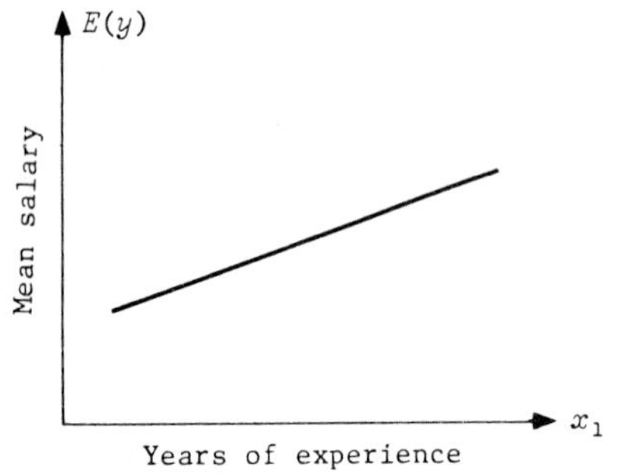

13.10 Refer to Example 13.9. Write a model that will allow the straight line relating mean salary $E(y)$ to years of experience x_1 to differ from one city to another, but in such a manner that the increase in mean salary per year increase in experience is the same for the four cities.

Solution

A model that allows the response lines to be parallel, but with different y-intercepts, is

$$E(y) = \beta_0 + \beta_1 x_1 + \beta_2 x_2 + \beta_3 x_3 + \beta_4 x_4,$$

where x_1 = years of experience,

$$x_2 = \begin{cases} 1 & \text{if New York} \\ 0 & \text{otherwise} \end{cases} \qquad x_3 = \begin{cases} 1 & \text{if Miami} \\ 0 & \text{otherwise} \end{cases}$$

$$x_4 = \begin{cases} 1 & \text{if St. Louis} \\ 0 & \text{otherwise} \end{cases}$$

Typical response curves are shown in the following figure:

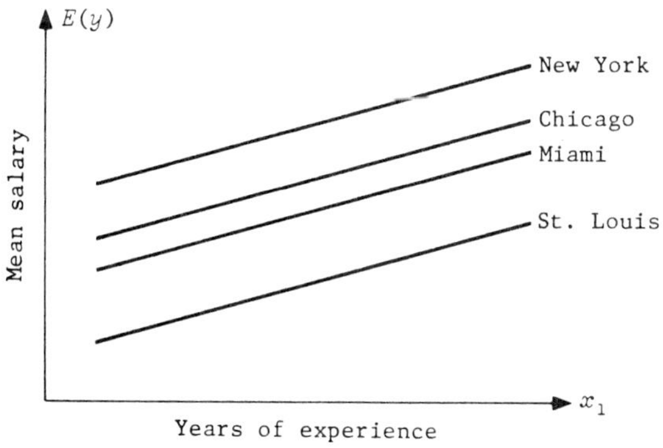

13.11 Refer to Examples 13.9 and 13.10. Write a model that allows the straight lines relating mean salary $E(y)$ to years of experience x_1 to differ for the four cities.

Solution

The model that allows the four straight lines to have different y-intercepts and slopes is obtained by adding interaction terms to the model developed in Example 13.10:

$$E(y) = \beta_0 + \beta_1 x_1 + \beta_2 x_2 + \beta_3 x_3 + \beta_4 x_4 + \beta_5 x_1 x_2 + \beta_6 x_1 x_3 + \beta_7 x_1 x_4.$$

The model permits nonparallel response lines, as shown in the figure:

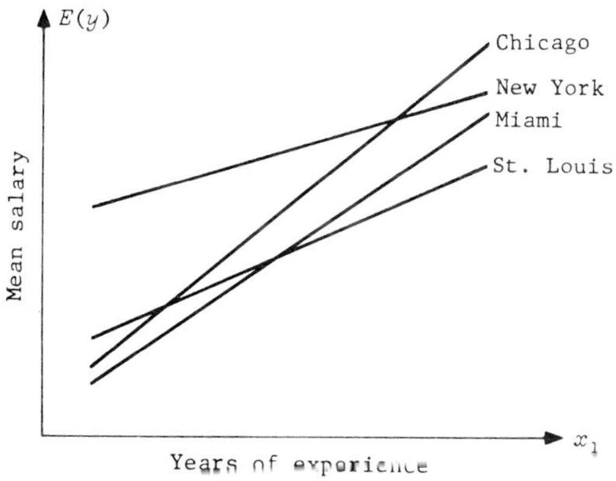

13.12 Refer to Example 13.11. Explain how you would perform a test to determine whether the four response lines differ (as in Example 13.11 figure) or whether a single line characterizes mean salary for all four cities (as in Example 13.9 figure).

Solution

We wish to compare the following models.

Model 1: $E(y) = \beta_0 + \beta_1 x_1$

Model 3: $E(y) = \beta_0 + \beta_1 x_1 + \beta_2 x_2 + \beta_3 x_3 + \beta_4 x_4 + \beta_5 x_1 x_2 + \beta_6 x_1 x_3 + \beta_7 x_1 x_4$

To determine whether Model 3 provides more information than Model 1 for predicting y, we perform the following test.

H_0: $\beta_2 = \beta_3 = \beta_4 = \beta_5 = \beta_6 = \beta_7 = 0$
H_a: At least one of the coefficients $\beta_2, \beta_3, \ldots, \beta_7$ is nonzero

If we let SSE_1 and SSE_3 denote the sum of squared errors for Model 1 and Model 3, respectively, then we write the test statistic as

$$F = \frac{(SSE_1 - SSE_3)/6}{SSE_3/(n - 8)}.$$

The test statistic is based on an F distribution with $\nu_1 = 6$ numerator degrees of freedom (because there are six parameters specified in H_0) and $\nu_2 = (n - 8)$ denominator degrees of freedom (because Model 3 contains eight β parameters).

Rejection of H_0 implies that Model 3 contributes more information than does Model 1 for the prediction of mean salary.

13.13 Refer to Example 13.11. Explain how you would perform a test to determine whether there is evidence that years of experience and city interact to affect mean salary.

Solution

It is required to fit the following two models, calculate the drop in the sum of squares for error, and conduct an F test.

Model 2: $E(y) = \beta_0 + \beta_1 x_1 + \beta_2 x_2 + \beta_3 x_3 + \beta_4 x_4$

Model 3: $E(y) = \beta_0 + \beta_1 x_1 + \beta_2 x_2 + \beta_3 x_3 + \beta_4 x_4 + \beta_5 x_1 x_2 + \beta_6 x_1 x_3 + \beta_7 x_1 x_4$

The relevant test is composed of the following elements.

H_0: $\beta_5 = \beta_6 = \beta_7 = 0$
H_a: At least one of the coefficients β_5, β_6, or β_7 is nonzero

The test statistic is $F = \dfrac{(SSE_2 - SSE_3)/3}{SSE_3/(n - 8)}$, where the distribution of F is based on $\nu_1 = 3$ numerator degrees of freedom and $\nu_2 = (n - 8)$ denominator degrees of freedom.

Rejection of the null hypothesis allows us to conclude that the independent variables, years of experience and city, interact to affect salary.

13.14 Suppose we believe that the relationship between mean salary $E(y)$ and years of experience x_1 is second-order. Write a model that allows for identical mean salary curves for all four cities.

Solution

The following model yields a single second-order curve to describe the relationship between $E(y)$ and x_1 for the four cities:

$$E(y) = \beta_0 + \beta_1 x_1 + \beta_2 x_1^2.$$

We would expect $E(y)$ to increase as the number of years of experience increases. However, the *rate* of increase would probably decrease as experience increases. A typical response curve might appear as in the following figure.

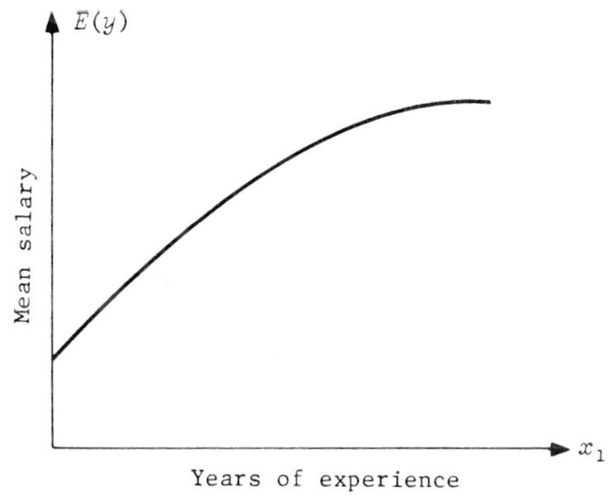

13.15 Add appropriate terms to the model of Example 13.14 to permit the response curves to have the same shapes, but different y-intercepts.

Solution

We now add three dummy variables to represent the four levels of the qualitative independent variable city.

$$E(y) = \beta_0 + \beta_1 x_1 + \beta_2 x_1^2 + \beta_3 x_2 + \beta_4 x_3 + \beta_5 x_4,$$

where x_2, x_3, and x_4 are as defined in Example 12.10. According to this model, the second-order response curves for the four cities have the same shape, but different y-intercepts, as shown in the figure:

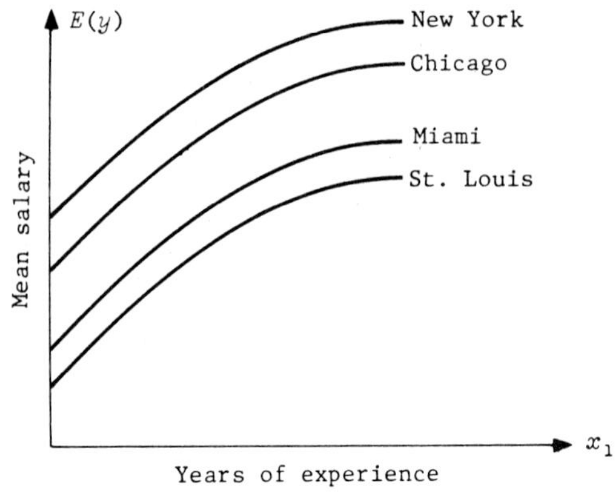

13.16 Add appropriate terms to the model of Example 13.15 to allow different response curves for the four cities.

Solution

We now add terms representing interaction between years of experience and city:

$$E(y) = \beta_0 + \beta_1 x_1 + \beta_2 x_1^2 + \beta_3 x_2 + \beta_4 x_3 + \beta_5 x_4 + \beta_6 x_1 x_2 + \beta_7 x_1 x_3 + \beta_8 x_1 x_4 + \beta_9 x_1^2 x_2 + \beta_{10} x_1^2 x_3 + \beta_{11} x_1^2 x_4$$

This model yields typical response curves as shown in the figure:

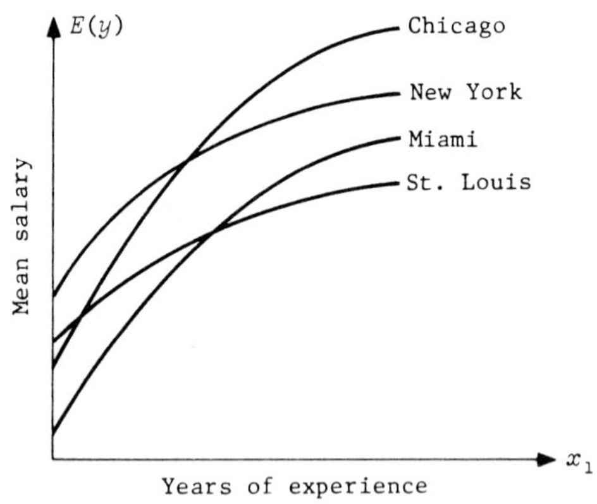

13.17 Refer to Example 13.16. Given the equation of the second-order model for the mean salary of bank managers in New York.

Solution

We substitute $x_2 = 1$, $x_3 = 0$, and $x_4 = 0$ into the second-order model:

$$E(y) = \beta_0 + \beta_1 x_1 + \beta_2 x_1^2 + \beta_3(1) + \beta_4(0) + \beta_5(0) + \beta_6 x_1(1) + \beta_7 x_1(0)$$
$$+ \beta_8 x_1(0) + \beta_9 x_1^2(1) + \beta_{10} x_1^2(0) + \beta_{11} x_1^2(0)$$
$$= (\beta_0 + \beta_3) + (\beta_1 + \beta_6)x_1 + (\beta_2 + \beta_9)x_1^2.$$

13.18 Specify the null hypothesis that would be tested to determine whether the second-order curves are identical for the four cities.

Solution

If the four response curves are in fact identical, it is not necessary to include the independent variable city in the model; thus, all terms involving x_2, x_3, or x_4 would be deleted, producing the model:

$$E(y) = \beta_0 + \beta_1 x_1 + \beta_2 x_1^2.$$

The appropriate null hypothesis would then be

$$H_0: \beta_3 = \beta_4 = \beta_5 = \cdots = \beta_{11} = 0.$$

13.19 Suppose it is known that the response curves differ for the four cities, but we wish to determine whether the second-order terms contribute useful information for the prediction of y. Specify the appropriate null hypothesis that would be tested.

Solution

If the second-order terms are not useful in the model, we would delete all terms involving x_1^2 and the null hypothesis would be

$$H_0: \beta_2 = \beta_9 = \beta_{10} = \beta_{11} = 0.$$

Exercises

13.7 The Internal Revenue Service (IRS) would like to construct a model for $E(y)$, the mean computation error on submitted income tax returns. Write a straight-line model for the relationship between mean computation error and annual gross income. Graph a typical response curve.

13.8 Refer to Exercise 13.7. Add terms to the model for $E(y)$ that represent the levels for type of return submitted ("long" form or "short" form). Assume the independent variables, annual gross income and type of form submitted, do not interact to affect the mean computation error. Graph the response curves.

13.9 Refer to Exercise 13.8.

a. Now add interaction terms to the model to allow the response curves to differ in slope and y-intercept. Graph typical response curves.

b. Specify the hypothesis you would test to determine whether there is a difference in the mean computation error for long forms and short forms.

13.10 Refer to Exercises 13.7-13.9. Suppose we believe that the relationship between mean computation error $E(y)$ and annual gross income is second-order. Write a model that allows for identical response curves for the two types of forms. Graph a typical response curve.

13.11 Refer to Exercise 13.10. Add appropriate terms to the model to permit the two response curves to have the same shape, but different y-intercepts. Graph typical response curves.

13.12 Add appropriate terms to the model of Exercise 13.11 to allow for interaction between annual gross income and type of form submitted. Graph typical response curves.

13.13 Refer to Exercise 13.12. Give the equation of the second-order model for the mean computation error on long forms.

13.14 Refer to Exercise 13.12. Specify the null hypothesis that would be tested to determine whether the second-order curves are identical for the two types of forms.

13.15 Refer to Exercise 13.12. Suppose it is known that the response curves differ for the two types of forms, but we wish to determine whether the second-order terms make a useful contribution to the model. Specify the null hypothesis that would be tested.

13.8 MODEL BUILDING: STEPWISE REGRESSION

Example

13.20 The rate of unemployment in the United States is often used to describe the state of the economy. Following is a list of variables that are thought to influence y = the monthly unemployment rate:

x_1 = inflation rate,

x_2 = price per ounce of gold,

x_3 = Dow Jones Industrial closing value (monthly average),

x_4 = prime interest rate,

$$x_5 = \begin{cases} 1 & \text{if month between October and March} \\ 0 & \text{if month between April and September} \end{cases}$$

Data for two previous years are shown below. Use a stepwise regression procedure to select from the above list the variables that should be included in a model for unemployment rate.

UNEMPLOYMENT RATE, y	INFLATION RATE, x_1	PRICE PER OUNCE OF GOLD, x_2	DOW JONES AVERAGE, x_3	PRIME INTEREST RATE, x_4	DUMMY VARIABLE FOR MONTH, x_5
5.9	13.0	250	870	12.0	1
6.0	12.1	250	840	12.1	1
6.0	14.0	250	880	12.1	1
5.7	12.5	245	830	12.1	1
5.6	12.0	245	840	12.0	0
5.6	12.0	240	840	12.0	0
5.5	11.1	245	830	12.0	0
5.6	11.0	250	820	11.9	0
5.7	10.5	250	830	11.9	0
5.7	10.5	255	860	11.9	0
6.0	13.0	260	880	11.9	1
5.9	12.0	255	870	11.8	1
5.9	12.0	255	850	11.8	1
5.8	11.0	250	840	11.8	1
5.7	15.0	265	810	11.8	1
5.7	13.0	260	860	11.8	1
5.8	14.1	260	855	11.8	0
5.8	14.0	285	820	11.8	0
5.6	13.0	300	842	11.6	0
5.7	12.9	315	848	11.8	0
6.0	14.1	335	890	12.3	0
5.8	14.0	400	880	13.3	0
6.0	12.8	430	878	15.0	1
5.8	12.8	415	820	15.6	1

Solution

The SAS stepwise regression printout is presented on the following page.

```
STEP 1   VARIABLE  X3  ENTERED          R-SQUARE = 0.406

                DF   SUM OF SQUARES   MEAN SQUARE    F    PROB > F

     REGRESSION   1       0.21657          0.217     15.04  0.0008
     ERROR       22       0.31676          0.0144
     TOTAL       23       0.53333

                     B VALUE   STD ERROR     F     PROB > F
     INTERCEPT        2.185
     X3               0.0042    0.00109   15.04    0.0008

STEP 2   VARIABLE  X5  ENTERED          R-SQUARE = 0.634

                DF   SUM OF SQUARES   MEAN SQUARE    F    PROB > F

     REGRESSION   2       0.33791          0.169     18.16  0.0001
     ERROR       21       0.19542          0.0093
     TOTAL       23       0.53333

                     B VALUE   STD ERROR     F     PROB > F
     INTERCEPT        2.482
     X3               0.0038     0.00089  18.40    0.0003
     X5               0.144      0.03975  13.04    0.0017

STEP 3    VARIABLE  X1  ENTERED         R-SQUARE = 0.661

                DF   SUM OF SQUARES   MEAN SQUARE    F    PROB > F

     REGRESSION   3       0.35268          0.118     13.02  0.0001
     ERROR       20       0.18065          0.0090
     TOTAL       23       0.53333

                     B VALUE   STD ERROR     F     PROB > F
     INTERCEPT        2.435
     X1               0.0213     0.01669   1.64    .2155
     X3               0.0035     0.00090  15.64    .0008
     X5               0.1380     0.0394   12.27    .0022

STEP 4    VARIABLE  X1  REMOVED         R-SQUARE = 0.634

                DF   SUM OF SQUARES   MEAN SQUARE    F     PROB > F

     REGRESSION   2       0.33791          0.169     18.16   0.0001
     ERROR       21       0.19542          0.0093
     TOTAL       23       0.53333

                     B VALUE   STD ERROR     F     PROB > F
     INTERCEPT        2.482
     X3               0.0038     0.00089  18.40    0.0003
     X5               0.144      0.03975  13.04    0.0017
```

The first variable included in the model is x_3, the Dow Jones average monthly closing. At the second step, the variable x_5, a dummy variable for month, enters the model. In the third step, x_1, the inflation rate, is selected for the model. However, the F statistic for x_1 (F = 1.64) is not statistically significant at the preassigned level of α = .10; thus, x_1 is removed from the model in the next step. Since none of the other independent variables can meet the α = .10 criterion for admission into the model, the stepwise procedure is terminated. We would then concentrate on the variables x_3 and x_5 in the effort to construct a model for $E(y)$. It remains to be decided how the variables should be entered into the prediction equation; the techniques described in Chapter 13 may be applied. (Note that the assumption of independent random errors is debatable for time series data such as these. One should be cautious in making inferences from the model.)

Exercise

13.16 Describe in detail a stepwise regression procedure; explain its importance as a method of choosing which of a large set of potential independent variables should be included in a model-building effort.

13.9 MODEL BUILDING: RESIDUAL ANALYSIS AND TRANSFORMATIONS

Examples

13.21 Identify the problem(s) in each of the following residual plots.

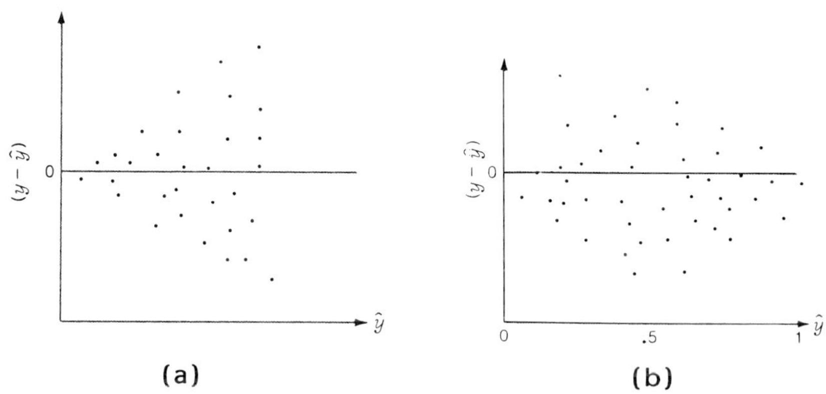

Solution

a. For small values of the predicted value $\hat{y}$, the residuals are close to their expected value of 0; for larger values of the predicted value, the residuals still appear to be centered at 0 but the residuals have a greater spread. The residuals exhibit an increase in variability proportional to the increase in the mean level of the response. If these residuals result from an additive model, this indicates a multiplicative model may be appropriate.

b. The scale on the $\hat{y}$-axis indicates that the response is a proportion or percentage. In this case the binomial distribution is often appropriate. Recall that the standard deviation of the binomial distribution is proportional to $\sqrt{pq}$, where p is the true proportion of the binomial random variable. Since pq is maximized at $p = .5$, we obtain the "football" shape as shown in Figure (b); near .5 the residuals have high variability, while near 0 and 1 the residuals have low variability. The assumption of constant variance of the error component appears to be violated.

13.22 Breakdowns of machines that produce steel cans are very costly. The more breakdowns, the fewer cans produced, and the smaller the company's profits. To help anticipate profit loss, the owners of a can company would like to find a model that will predict the number of breakdowns on the assembly line. The model proposed by the company's statisticians is the following:

$$y = \beta_0 + \beta_1 x_1 + \beta_2 x_2 + \beta_3 x_3 + \beta_4 x_4 + \varepsilon$$

where

y = Number of breakdowns per 8-hour shift

$$x_1 = \begin{cases} 1 & \text{if afternoon shift} \\ 0 & \text{otherwise} \end{cases}$$

$$x_2 = \begin{cases} 1 & \text{if midnight shift} \\ 0 & \text{otherwise} \end{cases}$$

x_3 = Temperature of the plant (°F)

x_4 = Number of inexperienced personnel working on the assembly line

After the model is fit using the least squares procedure, the residuals are plotted against $\hat{y}$, as shown in the accompanying figure.

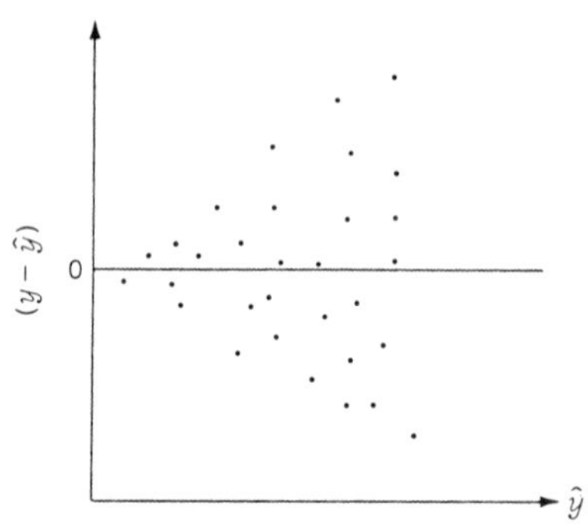

a. Do you detect a pattern in the residual plot? What does this suggest about the least squares assumptions?

b. Given the nature of the response variable, y, and the pattern detected in part a, what model adjustments would you recommend?

Solution

a. The residuals appear to be randomly distributed about the assumed mean of 0, but the funnel-shaped appearance indicates that the variance of the random error becomes larger as $\hat{y}$ increases in value. Therefore, the assumption of constant variance appears to be violated.

b. Since the response variable represents counts per unit of time (number of breakdowns per 8-hour shift) and since the range of the residuals (and hence, σ_y) increases as $E(y)$, which is estimated by $\hat{y}$, increases, the transformation $y^* = \sqrt{y}$ can be tried to stabilize the variance.

Exercise

13.17 In Hawaii condemnation proceedings are underway to enable private citizens to own the property that their homes are built on. Prior to 1980, only estates were permitted to own land, and homeowners leased the land from the estate (a law that dates back to the feudal period in Hawaii). To comply with the new law, a large Hawaiian estate wants to use regression analysis to estimate the fair market value of its land. A first proposal is the quadratic model

$$E(y) = \beta_0 + \beta_1 x + \beta_2 x^2$$

where

y = Leased fee value (i.e., sale price of property)
x = Size of property in square feet

Data collected for 20 property sales in a particular neighborhood, given in the accompanying table, were used to fit the model. The least squares prediction equation is

$$\hat{y} = -44.0947 + 11.5339x - .06378x^2$$

PROPERTY	LEASED FEE VALUE y, thousands of dollars	SIZE x, thousands
1	70.7	13.5
2	52.7	9.6
3	87.6	17.6
4	43.2	7.9
5	103.8	11.5
6	45.1	8.2
7	86.8	15.2
8	73.3	12.0
9	144.3	13.8
10	61.3	10.0
11	148.0	14.5
12	85.0	10.2
13	171.2	18.7
14	97.5	13.2
15	158.1	16.3
16	74.2	12.3
17	47.0	7.7
18	54.7	9.9
19	68.0	11.2
20	75.2	12.4

a. Calculate the predicted values and corresponding residuals for the model.

b. Plot the residuals versus $\hat{y}$. Do you detect any trends? If so, what does the pattern suggest about the model?

c. Based on your results, how should the estate proceed?

14
METHODS FOR QUALITY IMPROVEMENT

SUMMARY

The key to quality improvement is to control as much as possible the variation in the process that produces a product or delivers a service.

There are common causes and special causes of variation. Processes that are in control reflect only common causes of variation; processes that are not in control exhibit both common and special causes of variation.

The $\bar{x}$-chart is used to monitor the mean of a process; the R-chart is used to monitor the variation of a process; the p-chart is used to monitor the proportion of defectives resulting from a process. The six pattern-analysis rules are used to interpret the control charts.

14.7 A CONTROL CHART FOR MONITORING THE MEAN OF A PROCESS: THE $\bar{x}$-CHART

Example

14.1 Suppose a process for manufacturing shafts for an electric motor is in control. At the end of each hour, for a period of 20 hours, the manufacturer selected a random sample of four shafts and measured the diameter of each. The measurements (in inches) for the 20 samples are recorded in the table on the next page. Construct a control chart for the sample means and interpret the results.

Solution

The first step in constructing an $\bar{x}$-chart is to compute the sample mean, $\bar{x}$, and range, R, for each of the 20 samples. These values are shown in the last two columns of the table.

SAMPLE NUMBER	SAMPLE MEASUREMENTS (inches)				SAMPLE MEAN $\bar{x}$	RANGE R
1	1.505	1.499	1.501	1.488	1.4983	.017
2	1.496	1.513	1.512	1.501	1.5055	.017
3	1.516	1.485	1.492	1.503	1.4990	.031
4	1.507	1.492	1.511	1.491	1.5003	.020
5	1.502	1.491	1.501	1.502	1.4990	.011
6	1.502	1.488	1.506	1.483	1.4948	.023
7	1.489	1.512	1.496	1.501	1.4995	.023
8	1.485	1.518	1.494	1.513	1.5025	.033
9	1.503	1.495	1.503	1.496	1.4993	.008
10	1.485	1.519	1.503	1.507	1.5035	.034
11	1.491	1.516	1.497	1.493	1.4993	.025
12	1.486	1.505	1.487	1.492	1.4925	.019
13	1.510	1.502	1.515	1.499	1.5065	.016
14	1.495	1.485	1.493	1.503	1.4940	.018
15	1.504	1.499	1.504	1.500	1.5018	.005
16	1.499	1.503	1.508	1.497	1.5018	.011
17	1.501	1.493	1.509	1.491	1.4985	.018
18	1.497	1.510	1.496	1.500	1.5008	.014
19	1.503	1.526	1.497	1.500	1.5065	.029
20	1.494	1.501	1.508	1.519	1.5055	.025

Next, we calculate $\bar{\bar{x}}$, the average of the 20 sample means, and $\bar{R}$, the average of the 20 sample ranges:

$$\bar{\bar{x}} = \frac{\sum_{i=1}^{20} \bar{x}_i}{20} = \frac{(1.4983 + 1.5055 + 1.4990 + \cdots + 1.5055)}{20} = 1.50045$$

$$\bar{R} = \frac{\sum_{i=1}^{20} \bar{R}_i}{20} = \frac{(.017 + .017 + .031 + \cdots + .025)}{20} = .01985$$

The value of $\bar{\bar{x}} = 1.50045$ locates the center line on the control chart. To find upper and lower control limits, we need the value of the control limit factor A_2, found in Table XVII of Appendix B. For $n = 4$ measurements in each sample, $A_2 = .729$. Then

$$\text{UCL} = \bar{\bar{x}} + A_2\bar{R} = 1.50045 + (.729)(.01985) = 1.51492$$

$$\text{LCL} = \bar{\bar{x}} - A_2\bar{R} = 1.50045 - (.729)(.01985) = 1.48598$$

Using these limits, we construct the control chart for the sample means shown below. Note that all 20 sample means fall within the control limits.

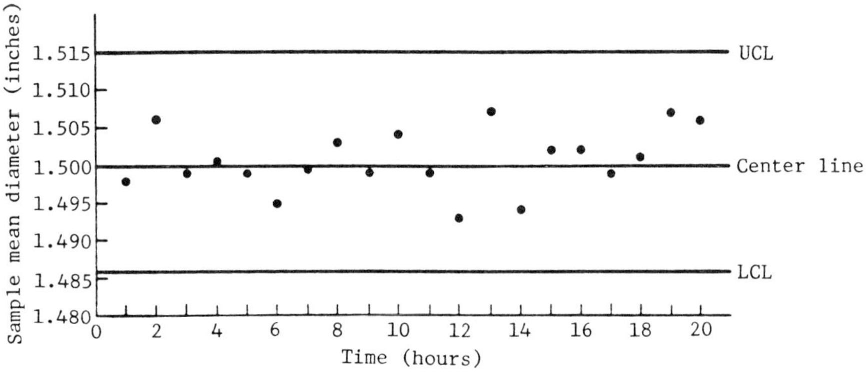

Exercise

14.1 A corporation that manufactures field rifles for the Department of Defense operates a production line that turns out finished firing pins. In order to monitor the process, an inspector randomly selects five firing pins from the production line, measures their lengths (in inches), and repeats this process at 30-minute intervals over a 5-hour period.

30-MINUTE INTERVAL	FIRING PIN LENGTHS				
1	1.05	1.03	.99	1.00	1.03
2	.93	.96	1.01	.98	.97
3	1.02	.99	.99	1.00	.98
4	.98	1.01	1.02	.99	.97
5	1.02	.99	1.04	1.07	.98
6	1.05	.98	.96	.91	1.02
7	.92	.95	1.00	.99	1.01
8	1.06	.98	.98	1.04	1.00
9	.97	.99	.99	.98	1.01
10	1.00	.96	1.02	1.03	.99

a. Use the data for the ten time periods listed in the table to calculate the center line for an $\bar{x}$-chart.

b. Compute upper and lower control limits.

c. Calculate and plot the ten sample means to form an $\bar{x}$ chart for the firing pin lengths.

d. Suppose the Defense Department's specification for the firing pins is that they be 1.00 inch plus or minus .08 inch in length. Does the manufacturing process appear to be in control?

14.8 A CONTROL CHART FOR MONITORING THE VARIATION OF A PROCESS: THE R-CHART

Example

14.2 Refer to Example 14.1. Recall that the manufacturer selected a sample of 4 shafts each hour, for a period of 20 hours, and measured the diameter of each. Assuming the process is "is control," construct and interpret an R-chart for process variation.

Solution

In Example 14.1, we calculated the mean of the 20 sample ranges to be $\bar{R} = .01985$. This value is the center line. For $n = 4$, the values of D_3 and D_4 given in Table XVII of Appendix B are $D_3 = 0$ and $D_4 = 2.282$. Then the upper and lower control limits for the R-chart are:

$$\text{UCL} = \bar{R}D_4 = (.01985)(2.282) = .045298$$

$$\text{LCL} = \bar{R}D_3 = (.01985)(0) = 0$$

The chart is shown below.

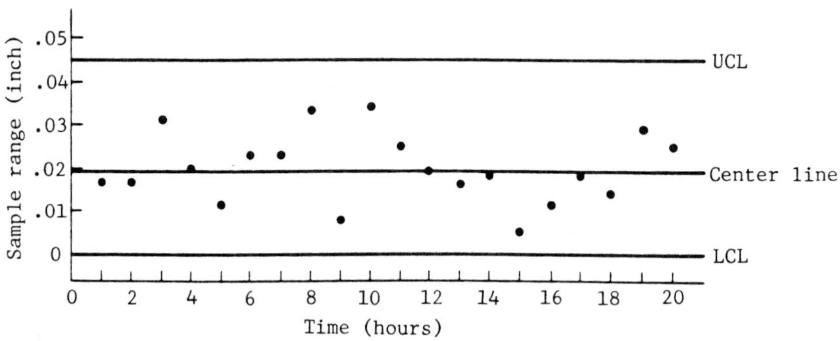

To monitor the variation in shaft diameters produced by the manufacturing process, a quality control engineer would check to determine that the sample range does not exceed the UCL of .045298 inch. (Since the LCL is 0, no diameter can fall below this value.)

Exercise

14.2 Refer to Exercise 14.1. Suppose the inspector wants to monitor the variation in firing pin lengths with an R-chart.

a. Locate the center line for the R-chart.

b. Locate upper and lower control limits for the R-chart.

c. Calculate and plot the ten sample ranges in an R-chart. Does the process variation appear to be in control?

14.9 A CONTROL CHART FOR MONITORING THE PROPORTION OF DEFECTIVES GENERATED BY A PROCESS: THE p-CHART

Example

14.3 To monitor the manufacturing process of rubber support bearings used in the superstructure and foundation pads of nuclear power plants, an industrial engineer randomly samples 100 bearings from the production line each day during a 15-day period. The bearings were inspected for defects and the number of defectives found each day are recorded in the table below. Construct a p-chart for the fraction of defective bearings.

DAY	1	2	3	4	5	6	7	8	9	10	11	12	13	14	15
Number of Defectives	2	12	3	4	4	1	3	5	3	2	10	3	3	2	3
Proportion of Defectives	.02	.12	.03	.04	.04	.01	.03	.05	.03	.02	.10	.03	.03	.02	.03

Solution

The center line for the p-chart is the proportion of defective bearings in the combined sample of $k = 1{,}500$ bearings:

$$\bar{p} = \frac{\text{Total number of defective bearings}}{\text{Total number inspected}} = \frac{60}{1{,}500} = .04$$

Upper and lower control limits are then computed as follows:

$$\text{UCL} = \bar{p} + 3\sqrt{\frac{\bar{p}(1 - \bar{p})}{n}} = .04 + 3\sqrt{\frac{(.04)(.96)}{100}} = .04 + .059 = .099$$

$$\text{LCL} = \bar{p} - 3\sqrt{\frac{\bar{p}(1 - \bar{p})}{n}} = .04 - 3\sqrt{\frac{(.04)(.96)}{100}} = .04 - .059 = -.019$$

Thus, if the process is in control, we expect the sample proportion of defective rubber bearings to fall between 0 (since no sample proportion can be negative) and .099 with a high probability.

A control chart for the percentage of defective bearings is shown in the figure below. Note that on days 2 and 11, the sample proportion fell outside the control limits. This suggests possible problems with the manufacturing process and warrants further investigation.

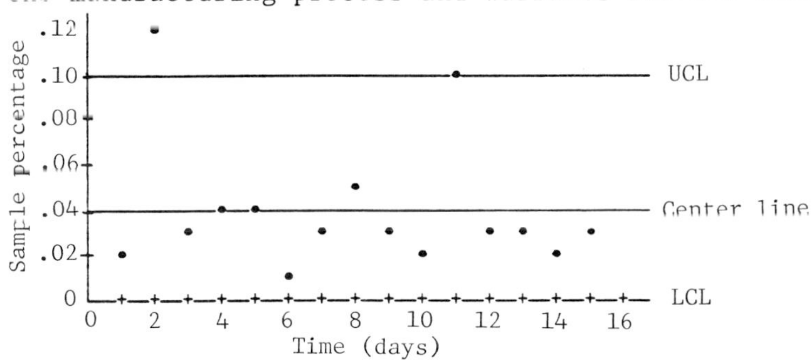

Once the problem that caused the two unusually large percentages of defectives has been identified and corrected, the control limits should be modified so that they can be applied to future data. One method of adjusting is to recalculate their values based on only the sample points that fall within the control limits of the above figure. Omitting the data for days 2 and 11, we obtain the modified values:

$$\bar{p} = \frac{\text{Total number of defective bearings (excluding days 2 and 11)}}{\text{Total number inspected (excluding days 2 and 11)}}$$

$$= \frac{38}{1,300} = .029$$

$$\text{UCL} = \bar{p} + 3\sqrt{\frac{\bar{p}(1 - \bar{p})}{n}} = .029 + 3\sqrt{\frac{(.029)(.971)}{100}} = .029 + .051 = .080$$

$$\text{LCL} = \bar{p} - 3\sqrt{\frac{\bar{p}(1 - \bar{p})}{n}} = .029 - 3\sqrt{\frac{(.029)(.971)}{100}} = .029 - .051 = -.022$$

Now a control chart with center line $\bar{p} = .029$, UCL = .08, and LCL = 0 can be used to monitor the percentage defective produced in future days of the process.

Exercise

14.3 A manufacturer of computer terminal fuses wants to establish a control chart to monitor the production process. Each hour, for a period of 25 hours, during a time when the process is known to be in control, a quality control engineer randomly selected and tested 100 fuses from the production line. The number of defective fuses found each hour is recorded in the table.

Hour	1	2	3	4	5	6	7	8	9	10	11	12	13
Number Defective	6	4	9	3	0	6	4	2	1	2	1	3	4

Hour	14	15	16	17	18	19	20	21	22	23	24	25
Number Defective	5	5	2	1	1	0	3	7	9	2	10	3

a. Construct a p-chart for the sample percentage of defective terminal fuses.

b. Locate the center line on the p-chart.

c. Locate upper and lower control limits on the p-chart. Does the process appear to be in control?

15
TIME SERIES: INDEX NUMBERS AND DESCRIPTIVE ANALYSES

SUMMARY

Data on business phenomena are often collected sequentially over time. *Time series models* are then constructed to describe these data and to make forecasts (predictions of future values).

Descriptive techniques for time series include *index numbers*, *moving averages*, and *exponential smoothing*; when descriptive models are used to forecast future values, no measure of the reliability of the forecast is possible.

15.1 INDEX NUMBERS: AN INTRODUCTION

15.2 SIMPLE INDEX NUMBERS

Example

15.1 The following table shows the annual oil production of the thirteen-nation Organization of Petroleum Exporting Countries (OPEC) cartel expressed as a percentage of world total for the years 1973-1982.

OPEC PRODUCTION
(Percentage of World Total)

Year	%	Year	%
1973	67.8	1978	64.3
1974	67.9	1979	63.2
1975	65.6	1980	59.8
1976	68.0	1981	48.9
1977	66.5	1982	43.9

a. Calculate the simple index for OPEC production of oil during this period, using 1973 as the base year.

b. Recompute the index, using 1980 as the base year.

Solution

a. First define Y_t = OPEC production as a percentage of world total in year t. With 1973 as the base year, we have

$t_0 = 1973$ and $Y_0 = 67.8$.

Now we calculate:

$$I_{1973} = \left(\frac{Y_{1973}}{Y_{1973}}\right)100 = \left(\frac{67.8}{67.8}\right)100 = 100.00$$

$$I_{1974} = \left(\frac{Y_{1974}}{Y_{1973}}\right)100 = \left(\frac{67.9}{67.8}\right)100 = 100.15$$

$$I_{1975} = \left(\frac{Y_{1975}}{Y_{1973}}\right)100 = \left(\frac{65.6}{67.8}\right)100 = 96.76$$

Similar calculations for the years 1976-1982 yield the complete index shown below.

YEAR	INDEX	YEAR	INDEX
1973	100.00	1978	94.84
1974	100.15	1979	93.22
1975	96.76	1980	88.20
1976	100.29	1981	72.12
1977	98.08	1982	64.75

b. To use 1980 as the base year, we set $t_0 = 1980$ and $Y_0 = 59.8$. Then

$$I_{1973} = \left(\frac{Y_{1973}}{Y_{1980}}\right)100 = \left(\frac{67.8}{59.8}\right)100 = 113.38$$

$$I_{1974} = \left(\frac{Y_{1974}}{Y_{1980}}\right)100 = \left(\frac{67.9}{59.8}\right)100 = 113.55$$

and so forth. The completed calculations are shown below:

YEAR	INDEX	YEAR	INDEX	YEAR	INDEX
1973	113.38	1977	111.20	1980	100.00
1974	113.55	1978	107.53	1981	81.77
1975	109.70	1979	105.69	1982	73.41
1976	113.71				

Note that the index numbers using 1980 as the base period may be derived from the index numbers using 1973 as the base period (computed in part a), without referring to the original data, by means of the following relation:

$$I_{t(\text{base }1980)} = I_{t(\text{base }1973)}\left(\frac{Y_{1973}}{Y_{1980}}\right) = I_{t(\text{base }1973)}\left(\frac{67.8}{59.8}\right) = I_{t(\text{base }1973)}(1.1338)$$

Thus, for example,

$$I_{1978(\text{base }1980)} = I_{1978(\text{base }1973)}(1.1338)$$

$$= (94.84)(1.1338) = 107.53,$$

as was computed in part b.

Exercise

15.1 The price of silver (dollars per ounce) for the years 1970-1982 is shown in the table.

PRICE PER OUNCE OF SILVER

Year	Price	Year	Price
1970	$1.771	1977	$ 4.623
1971	1.546	1978	5.401
1972	1.684	1979	11.109
1973	2.558	1980	20.633
1974	4.708	1981	10.481
1975	4.419	1982	7.950
1976	4.353		

a. Construct and graph a simple index for the price per ounce of silver for the period 1970-1982, using 1974 as the base period.

b. Recompute the index, using 1970 as the base period.

15.3 COMPOSITE INDEX NUMBERS

Examples

15.2 The annual expenditures for new plant and equipment (in billions of dollars) of all manufacturing and mining, transportation, and other U.S. enterprises (including electrical and gas utilities, trade, and construction) for the period 1974-1981 are given in the following table. Calculate the simple composite index for total annual expenditures for new plant and equipment in the United States, using 1975 as the base period.

EXPENDITURES FOR NEW PLANT AND EQUIPMENT

Year	Manufacturing and Mining	Transportation	All Other	Total
1974	57,830	8,230	90,920	156,980
1975	61,020	8,680	88,010	157,710
1976	67,390	8,890	95,170	171,450
1977	78,460	9,400	110,220	198,080
1978	89,930	10,680	130,630	231,240
1979	110,060	12,350	148,050	270,460
1980	129,320	12,090	154,220	295,630
1981	143,650	12,050	165,790	321,490

Solution

To compute a simple composite index, we first need to sum the values of the respective time series variables—in this example, the sum of the annual expenditures for new plant and equipment for manufacturing and mining, transportation, and other United States enterprises. The sum of these annual expenditures is shown in the column labeled "Total" in the table above. This column of numbers is used to compute the simple composite index.

If we let Y_t represent the total annual expenditures during year t and use 1975 as the base period, then

$$I_{1974} = \left(\frac{Y_{1974}}{Y_{1975}}\right)100 = \left(\frac{156{,}980}{157{,}710}\right)100 = 99.5$$

$$I_{1975} = \left(\frac{Y_{1975}}{Y_{1975}}\right)100 = \left(\frac{157{,}710}{157{,}710}\right)100 = 100.0$$

$$I_{1976} = \left(\frac{Y_{1976}}{Y_{1975}}\right)100 = \left(\frac{171{,}450}{157{,}710}\right)100 = 108.7$$

and so forth. The complete simple composite index for total annual expenditures for new plant and equipment during 1974-1981 is given below.

YEAR	INDEX	YEAR	INDEX	YEAR	INDEX
1974	99.5	1977	125.6	1980	187.5
1975	100.0	1978	146.6	1981	203.8
1976	108.7	1979	171.5		

15.3 Consider the information on the prices of dairy products for the years 1976-1981, as provided in the table. Using 1976 as the base period, calculate the Laspeyres weighted composite index for the dairy products. The weights are the total quantities of the products consumed in 1976.

YEAR	AVERAGE PRICE PER UNIT		
	Cheese (pounds)	Milk (gallons)	Butter (pounds)
1976	\$1.45	\$1.60	\$ .70
1977	1.49	1.61	.80
1978	1.55	1.67	.83
1979	1.63	1.72	.91
1980	1.75	1.80	1.03
1981	1.67	1.94	1.54
	Total Quantity Consumed (Billions)		
1976	2.6	47.6	3.1

Solution

The first step in calculating a Laspeyres weighted composite price index is to multiply the commodity prices P_{it} at time t by the corresponding base period quantities Q_{it_0}. In this example, we need to multiply the average price per unit of cheese, milk, and butter for each year by the corresponding quantity of the commodity consumed during 1976. The three products are then summed to give the value of the composite time series which is to be indexed. These preliminary calculations are shown in the following table.

YEAR	WEIGHTED PRICE = $Q_{i,\,1976}P_{it}$			SUM OF WEIGHTED PRICES
	Cheese	Milk	Butter	$\Sigma Q_{i,\,1976}P_{it}$
1976	(2.6)(1.45) = 3.77	(47.6)(1.60) = 76.16	(3.1)(.70) = 2.17	3.77 + 76.16 + 2.17 = 82.10
1977	(2.6)(1.49) = 3.87	(47.6)(1.61) = 76.64	(3.1)(.80) = 2.48	3.87 + 76.64 + 2.48 = 82.99
1978	(2.6)(1.55) = 4.03	(47.6)(1.67) = 79.49	(3.1)(.83) = 2.57	4.03 + 79.49 + 2.57 = 86.09
1979	(2.6)(1.63) = 4.24	(47.6)(1.72) = 81.87	(3.1)(.91) = 2.82	4.24 + 81.87 + 2.82 = 88.93
1980	(2.6)(1.75) = 4.55	(47.6)(1.80) = 85.68	(3.1)(1.03) = 3.19	4.55 + 85.68 + 3.19 = 93.42
1981	(2.6)(1.67) = 4.34	(47.6)(1.94) = 92.34	(3.1)(1.54) = 4.77	4.34 + 92.34 + 4.77 = 101.45

After computing the weighted sums in the rightmost column of the table, we calculate the index as follows:

$$I_{1976} = \frac{\Sigma Q_{i,\,1976}P_{i,\,1976}}{\Sigma Q_{i,\,1976}P_{i,\,1976}} \times 100 = \frac{82.10}{82.10} \times 100 = 100.0$$

$$I_{1977} = \frac{\Sigma Q_{i,\,1976} P_{i,\,1977}}{\Sigma Q_{i,\,1976} P_{i,\,1976}} \times 100 = \frac{82.99}{82.10} \times 100 = 101.1$$

$$I_{1978} = \frac{\Sigma Q_{i,\,1976} P_{i,\,1978}}{\Sigma Q_{i,\,1976} P_{i,\,1976}} \times 100 = \frac{86.09}{82.10} \times 100 = 104.9$$

and so forth. The complete Laspeyres index is given below:

YEAR	INDEX
1976	100.0
1977	101.1
1978	104.9
1979	108.3
1980	113.8
1981	123.6

15.4 The prices and quantities consumed for commodities X and Y during the years 1975 and 1985 are as shown in the table.

	COMMODITY X		COMMODITY Y	
YEAR	Unit Price	Quantity Consumed	Unit Price	Quantity Consumed
1975	\$2.00	200	\$4.50	50
1985	\$3.00	500	\$8.00	100

Compute the Paasche price index for the commodities using 1975 as the base period.

Solution

Recall that a Paasche index is calculated by using for each period the purchase quantities of that period. For this example, we have:

$$I_{1975} = \frac{\Sigma Q_{i,\,1975} P_{i,\,1975}}{\Sigma Q_{i,\,1975} P_{i,\,1975}} \times 100 = \left[\frac{200(2.00) + 50(4.50)}{200(2.00) + 50(4.50)}\right] \times 100$$

$$= \frac{625}{625} \times 100 = 100.0$$

$$I_{1985} = \frac{\Sigma Q_{i,\,1985} P_{i,\,1985}}{\Sigma Q_{i,\,1985} P_{i,\,1975}} \times 100 = \left[\frac{500(3.00) + 100(8.00)}{500(2.00) + 100(4.50)}\right] \times 100$$

$$= \frac{2300}{1450} \times 100 = 158.6$$

Exercises

15.2 The prices of coffee, gasoline, and sugar for each month of 1983 are shown in the table. Using May 1983 as the base period, compute the simple composite price index of the three items for January through December 1983.

MONTH 1983	PRICE OF COFFEE (Per Pound)	PRICE OF GASOLINE (Per Gallon)	PRICE OF SUGAR (Per Pound)
January	$1.47	$1.15	$.32
February	1.47	1.10	.33
March	1.47	1.06	.32
April	1.39	1.13	.33
May	1.36	1.18	.33
June	1.36	1.20	.34
July	1.36	1.21	.34
August	1.36	1.20	.34
September	1.36	1.19	.34
October	1.36	1.17	.34
November	1.36	1.16	.33
December	1.36	1.15	.33

15.3 The numbers of transactions (in thousands) per quarter at a New York City bank are recorded for the years 1983 and 1984 in the table. Using Quarter I, 1983 as the base period, construct a simple composite index for the quarterly number of transactions at the New York City bank from 1983 to 1984.

		WITHDRAWALS		DEPOSITS	
YEAR	QUARTER	Savings	Checking	Savings	Checking
1983	I	41.2	561.8	86.7	392.1
	II	50.8	490.0	71.1	424.0
	III	33.9	733.7	75.3	630.5
	IV	27.5	811.9	66.5	557.6
1984	I	20.8	852.5	70.9	610.4
	II	32.0	814.0	89.2	731.1
	III	39.4	966.1	107.5	500.3
	IV	18.5	1045.5	93.4	872.2

15.4 Consider the information on the annual amount of life insurance in force in the United States, as provided in the table. Calculate the Laspeyres weighted composite index for total life insurance in force for the years 1972-1982, with 1972 as the base period.

YEAR	ORDINARY POLICIES	GROUP CERTIFICATES	INDUSTRIAL POLICIES
1972	853.9	640.7	40.0
1973	928.2	708.3	40.6
1974	1009.0	827.0	39.4
1975	1083.4	904.7	39.4
1976	1177.7	1002.6	39.2
1977	1289.3	1115.0	39.0
1978	1425.1	1244.0	38.1
1979	1586.0	1419.0	37.8
1980	1761.0	1579.0	36.0
1981	1978.0	1889.0	34.5
1982	2217.0	2066.0	32.8
	Total Number of Purchases (Millions)		
1972	11.8	6.7	8.1

15.5 The accompanying table shows the prices (in dollars per gallon) and quantities consumed (in millions of gallons) of three types of gasoline in a particular region.

	REGULAR GAS		PREMIUM GAS		UNLEADED GAS	
YEAR	Price	Quantity	Price	Quantity	Price	Quantity
1970	$ .30	800	$ .35	1500	$ .32	500
1975	1.10	600	1.25	1200	1.18	450
1985	1.19	900	1.30	1500	1.28	600

Construct the Paasche price index for gasoline, using 1970 as the base year.

15.4 SMOOTHING WITH MOVING AVERAGES

Example

15.5 The quarterly power loads (in megawatts) for a utility company located in the southern part of the United States are given in the following table. Construct a 4-point moving average to smooth the time series.

YEAR	QUARTER	TIME, t	POWER LOAD, Y_t
1981	I	1	103.5
	II	2	94.7
	III	3	118.6
	IV	4	109.3
1982	I	5	126.1
	II	6	116.0
	III	7	141.2
	IV	8	131.6
1983	I	9	144.5
	II	10	137.1
	III	11	159.0
	IV	12	149.5
1984	I	13	166.1
	II	14	152.5
	III	15	178.2
	IV	16	169.0

Solution

We first calculate the 4-point uncentered moving average as the mean of $N = 4$ consecutive values of the time series:

$$M_{2.5} = \frac{Y_1 + Y_2 + Y_3 + Y_4}{4} = \frac{103.5 + 94.7 + 118.6 + 109.3}{4}$$

$$= \frac{426.1}{4} = 106.525$$

$$M_{3.5} = \frac{Y_2 + Y_3 + Y_4 + Y_5}{4} = \frac{94.7 + 118.6 + 109.3 + 126.1}{4}$$

$$= \frac{448.7}{4} = 112.175$$

$$M_{4.5} = \frac{Y_3 + Y_4 + Y_5 + Y_6}{4} = \frac{470}{4} = 117.5$$

and so forth. The complete uncentered 4-point moving average for the power load data is shown in the next table.

TIME	UNCENTERED 4-POINT MOVING AVERAGE
1	
2	
	106.525
3	
	112.175
4	
	117.500
5	
	123.150
6	
	128.725
7	
	133.325
8	
	138.600
9	
	143.050
10	
	147.525
11	
	152.925
12	
	156.775
13	
	161.575
14	
	166.450
15	
16	

We now obtain the centered moving average by computing the mean of each adjacent pair in the uncentered moving average:

$$M_3 = \frac{M_{2.5} + M_{3.5}}{2} = \frac{106.525 + 112.175}{2} = 109.35$$

$$M_4 = \frac{M_{3.5} + M_{4.5}}{2} = \frac{112.175 + 117.500}{2} = 114.84$$

$$M_5 = \frac{M_{4.5} + M_{5.5}}{2} = \frac{117.500 + 123.150}{2} = 120.33$$

and so forth. The complete centered 4-point moving average is presented in the following table. Note that $N/2 = 4/2 = 2$ values are lost at each end of the time series.

TIME	CENTERED 4-POINT MOVING AVERAGE
1	
2	
3	109.35
4	114.84
5	120.33
6	125.94
7	131.03
8	135.96
9	140.83
10	145.29
11	150.23
12	154.85
13	159.18
14	164.01
15	
16	

Exercises

15.6 The accompanying table shows the price of gold (in dollars per troy ounce) over the period 1970-1983. Construct a 3-point moving average to smooth the time series.

YEAR	PRICE OF GOLD
1970	36.41
1971	41.25
1972	58.61
1973	97.81
1974	159.70
1975	161.40
1976	124.80
1977	148.30
1978	193.50
1979	307.80
1980	606.01
1981	450.63
1982	374.18
1983	449.03

15.7 Refer to the gold price time series given in Exercise 15.6. Compute a centered 4-point moving average for the data.

15.5 EXPONENTIAL SMOOTHING

Example

15.6 The accompanying table shows data on a country's imports (in millions of metric tons) of crude oil and natural gas over a 16-year period. Compute exponentially smoothed values of the time series, using the smoothing constant $w = .6$.

YEAR	IMPORTS	YEAR	IMPORTS
1	19.3	9	15.3
2	18.4	10	14.8
3	16.4	11	14.9
4	16.6	12	15.4
5	17.5	13	13.4
6	16.4	14	12.3
7	16.0	15	10.1
8	18.2	16	10.9

Solution

We compute the exponentially smoothed series as follows:

$$E_1 = Y_1$$

$$E_t = wY_t + (1 - w)E_{t-1} = .6Y_t + .4E_{t-1}$$

Thus,

$$E_1 = 19.30$$

$$E_2 = .6Y_2 + .4E_1 = .6(18.4) + .4E_1 = 18.76$$

$$E_3 = .6Y_3 + .4E_2 = .6(16.4) + .4E_2 = 17.34$$

$$E_4 = .6Y_4 + .4E_3 = .6(16.6) + .4E_3 = 16.90$$

The complete exponentially smoothed series is presented in the following table.

YEAR	EXPONENTIALLY SMOOTHED SERIES	YEAR	EXPONENTIALLY SMOOTHED SERIES
1	19.30	9	16.16
2	18.76	10	15.34
3	17.34	11	15.08
4	16.90	12	15.27
5	17.26	13	14.15
6	16.74	14	13.04
7	16.30	15	11.28
8	17.44	16	11.05

Exercises

15.8 The following table shows beer production (in millions of barrels) in the United States for the period 1973-1982. Construct an exponentially smoothed series for the data, using a smoothing constant of $w = .3$.

YEAR	BEER PRODUCTION	YEAR	BEER PRODUCTION
1973	148.6	1978	179.1
1974	156.2	1979	184.2
1975	160.6	1980	194.1
1976	163.7	1981	193.7
1977	170.5	1982	196.2

15.9 Refer to Exercise 15.8. Construct an exponentially smoothed series for the beer production data, using a smoothing constant of $w = .7$.

16
TIME SERIES: MODELS AND FORECASTING

SUMMARY

This chapter describes how to model a time series as a combination of *secular*, *seasonal*, *cyclical*, and *residual components*. The *exponential smoothing* and *Holt-Winters* methods for forecasting future values of a time series are developed. Simple linear and multiple regression models can also be used to forecast long-term trends. The chapter concludes with discussions of *autoregressive* time series models and testing for *autocorrelation* with the *Durbin-Watson* statistic.

16.1 TIME SERIES COMPONENTS

Example

16.1 The following table gives the net income (in units of \$100,000) of a major department store, by calendar quarters, over a period of three years.

QUARTER	INCOME	QUARTER	INCOME
III (1981)	1.2	I (1983)	1.7
IV	2.1	II	2.1
I (1982)	1.3	III	2.4
II	1.6	IV	3.1
III	1.8	I (1984)	2.6
IV	2.6	II	2.8

Plot the time series data. Which components of a time series can you observe from the graph?

Solution

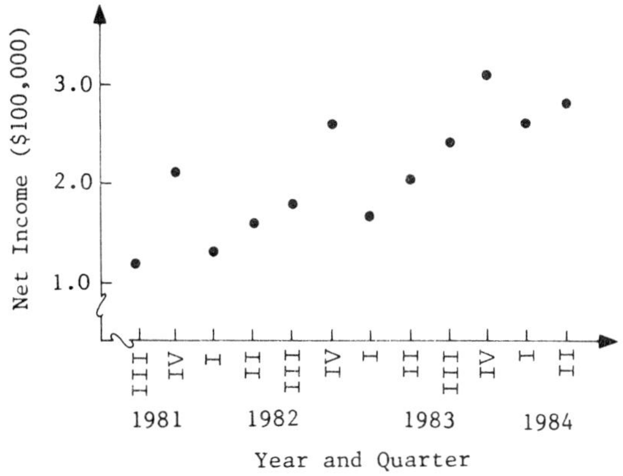

The *secular trend* component describes the long-term behavior of the time series. In this example, the plot shows that net income appears to increase fairly steadily with time. The three data points that represent the fourth quarters of each year are fluctuations (*seasonal effects*) that occur during specific portions of the year. In this instance, the peaks may be attributable to Christmas sales. *Cyclical effects*, which may generally be attributed to economic conditions at a particular time, and *residual effects*, which reflect the randomness of the phenomenon, are not easily observed from this plot.

16.2 FORECASTING: EXPONENTIAL SMOOTHING

16.3 FORECASTING TRENDS: THE HOLT-WINTERS FORECASTING MODEL

Examples

16.2 Refer to Example 15.6.

a. Use $w = .8$ to smooth the series for years 1-14. Then forecast the country's crude oil and natural gas imports for years 15 and 16.

b. Compute the forecast errors for years 15 and 16.

Solution

a. The exponentially smoothed series is computed using the method of Example 15.6, but here we use a smoothing constant of $w = .8$. The results are shown in the following table, with the original values of the time series.

YEAR	ORIGINAL VALUE OF TIME SERIES	EXPONENTIALLY SMOOTHED SERIES
1	19.3	19.30
2	18.4	18.58
3	16.4	16.84
4	16.6	16.65
5	17.5	17.33
6	16.4	16.59
7	16.0	16.12
8	18.2	17.78
9	15.3	15.80
10	14.8	15.00
11	14.9	14.92
12	15.4	15.30
13	13.4	13.78
14	12.3	12.60

The forecast for year 15 is computed as follows:

$$F_{15} = wY_{14} + (1 - w)E_{14} = .8(12.3) + .2(12.60) = 12.36$$

With the exponential smoothing model, the forecast F_{15} is used to forecast not only Y_{15}, but also all future values of Y_t. Thus,

$$F_{16} = F_{15} = 12.36.$$

b. The calculation of the forecast errors is illustrated in the next table.

YEAR	ACTUAL VALUE OF TIME SERIES	FORECAST VALUE	FORECAST ERROR
15	10.1	12.36	-2.26
16	10.9	12.36	-1.46

16.3 Refer to Examples 15.6 and 16.2.

a. Calculate the Holt-Winters exponential smoothing and trend components for the import series using $w = .8$ and $v = .5$.

b. Use the Holt-Winters forecasting technique to forecast the country's crude oil and natural gas imports for years 15 and 16.

Solution

a. Beginning with year $t = 2$, we calculate the two components according to the formulas:

$$E_2 = Y_2$$
$$T_2 = Y_2 - Y_1$$
$$E_t = wY_t + (1 - w)(E_{t-1} + T_{t-1})$$
$$T_t = v(E_t - E_{t-1}) + (1 - v)T_{t-1}$$

Substituting $w = .8$ and $v = .5$ yields:

$$E_2 = Y_2 = 18.4$$
$$T_2 = Y_2 - Y_1 = 18.4 - 19.3 = -0.9$$
$$E_3 = .8Y_3 + .2(E_2 + T_2) = .8(16.4) + .2(18.4 - 0.9) = 16.62$$
$$T_3 = .5(E_3 - E_2) + .5T_2 = .5(16.62 - 18.4) + .5(-0.9) = -1.34$$

The entire set of E_t and T_t values is given in the following table, with the original values of the time series.

YEAR	Y_t	E_t	T_t	YEAR	Y_t	E_t	T_t
1	19.3	-	-	8	18.2	17.69	0.62
2	18.4	18.40	-0.90	9	15.3	15.90	-0.59
3	16.4	16.62	-1.34	10	14.8	14.90	-0.80
4	16.6	16.34	-0.81	11	14.9	14.74	-0.48
5	17.5	17.11	-0.02	12	15.4	15.17	-0.03
6	16.4	16.54	-0.30	13	13.4	13.75	-0.73
7	16.0	16.05	-0.40	14	12.3	12.44	-1.02

b. For year 15, we have

$$F_{15} = E_{14} + T_{14} = 12.44 + (-1.02) = 11.42,$$

and for year 16, the forecast is

$$F_{16} = E_{14} + 2T_{14} = 12.44 + 2(-1.02) = 10.40.$$

Exercises

10.1 The Federal Reserve Board (FRB) Index of Quarterly Output is an industrial production index often used as a leading indicator of business activity. The values of this index for 10 recent years are given in the following table.

YEAR	INDEX	YEAR	INDEX
1	106.8	6	129.8
2	115.2	7	138.2
3	125.6	8	146.1
4	124.8	9	152.2
5	117.8	10	138.8

a. Construct an exponentially smoothed series, using a smoothing constant of $w = .5$. Then forecast the values of the index for years 11 and 12.

b. Repeat part a using a smoothing constant of $w = .7$.

16.2 Refer to Exercise 16.1.

a. Calculate the Holt-Winters exponential smoothing and trend components for the FRB index using $w = .6$ and $v = .5$.

b. Use the Holt-Winters forecasting methodology to forecast the values of the FRB index in years 11 and 12.

16.4 FORECASTING TRENDS: SIMPLE LINEAR REGRESSION

16.5 SEASONAL REGRESSION MODELS

Examples

16.4 A large department store chain has observed a steady increase in the demand for a particular item of women's apparel. The data shown in the table represent the sales (in thousands of items) of the product over the past 10 months.

MONTH	NUMBER OF ITEMS SOLD	MONTH	NUMBER OF ITEMS SOLD
1	33	6	43
2	35	7	45
3	37	8	47
4	40	9	49
5	42	10	54

Plot the data and suggest an appropriate model for the data.

Solution

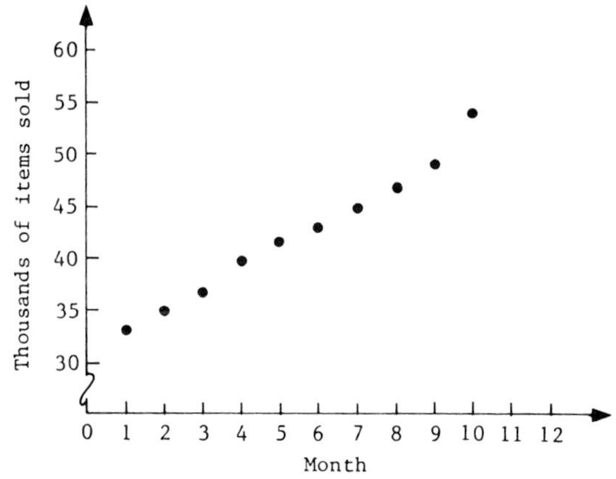

The plot shown in the scattergram suggests a linear trend. Thus, the model $E(Y_t) = \beta_0 + \beta_1 t$ may be appropriate, where Y_t is the number of items (in thousands) sold in month t.

16.5 Refer to Example 16.4. The least squares model was fit, and a portion of the SAS regression analysis is shown below.

SOURCE	DF	SUM OF SQUARES	MEAN SQUARE	F
MODEL	1	377.6	377.6	437.80
ERROR	8	6.9	.8625	
CORRECTED TOTAL	9	384.5	R-SQUARE	ROOT MSE
			.98206	.9287

PARAMETER	ESTIMATE	T FOR H0: PARAMETER = 0	STD ERROR OF ESTIMATE
INTERCEPT	30.7333	48.45	.6343
T	2.1394	20.93	.1022

T	PREDICTED VALUE	LOWER 95% CL INDIVIDUAL	UPPER 95% CL INDIVIDUAL
11	54.267	51.674	56.860
12	56.406	53.687	59.125
13	58.545	55.687	61.403

a. Plot the least squares prediction equation on your scattergram.

b. Note the predicted values (forecasts) and associated prediction intervals for sales in months 11, 12, and 13. Comment on the problems associated with using this model for long-term forecasts.

Solution

a.

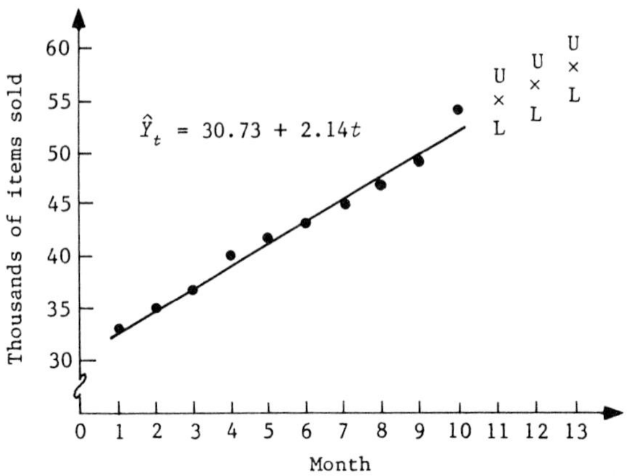

b. The 95% prediction intervals for sales in months 11, 12, and 13 are shown on the scattergram. For example, for month 12 we have $\hat{Y}_{12}$ = 54.267 and a 95% prediction interval of (51.674, 56.860).

There are two problems associated with the use of a least squares model for forecasting time series:

1) We are attempting to forecast the future value of a time series, which requires a prediction outside the range of the independent variable(s) upon which the model was based. The danger of this type of prediction is clear: If the experimental conditions change substantially after the model is developed, the forecasts of future values will be meaningless.

2) The least squares model forecasts only the secular trend, and does not account for cyclical effects.

Exercise

16.3 The following table shows the values of an index of industrial production for a particular country over the last eight years. Construct a scattergram and suggest an appropriate model for the data.

YEAR	INDEX	YEAR	INDEX
1	112.3	5	122.9
2	100.0	6	133.1
3	111.1	7	142.4
4	115.7	8	146.8

16.4 Refer to Exercise 16.3.

a. Fit a least squares model to the data.

b. Obtain 95% prediction intervals for the value of the industrial production index in years 9 and 10.

16.6 AUTOCORRELATION AND THE DURBIN-WATSON TEST

Example

16.6 A leading pharmaceutical company that produces a new hypertension pill would like to model annual revenue generated by this product. Company researchers utilized data collected over the past 15 years to fit the model

$$E(Y_t) = \beta_0 + \beta_1 X_t + \beta_2 t$$

where Y_t = revenue in year t (in millions of dollars),

X_t = cost per pill in year t,

t = year (1, 2, ..., 15).

A portion of the SAS regression analysis is shown on the following page. A company statistician suspects that the residuals are positively autocorrelated. Test this claim using $\alpha = .05$.

SOURCE	DF	SUM OF SQUARES	MEAN SQUARE	F VALUE
MODEL	2	48.8233	24.4116	206.19
ERROR	12	1.4207	.1184	
CORRECTED TOTAL	14	50.2440		

R-SQUARE	ROOT MSE
.97172	.3441

PARAMETER	ESTIMATE	T FOR HO: PARAMETER = 0	STD ERROR OF ESTIMATE
INTERCEPT	3.26119	1.74	1.879
T	0.39159	5.56	0.070
X	1.58761	0.38	4.129

SUM OF RESIDUALS	0.00000
SUM OF SQUARED RESIDUALS	1.42075
SUM OF SQUARED RESIDUALS - ERROR SS	-0.00000
FIRST-ORDER AUTOCORRELATION	0.48473
DURBIN-WATSON D	0.77615

Solution

We will use the Durbin-Watson test to check for first-order autocorrelation of the residuals:

H_0: No first-order autocorrelation of residuals
H_a: Positive first-order autocorrelation of residuals

Test statistic: $d = 0.776$ (from printout)

Rejection region: From the table of critical values of the Durbin-Watson statistic, with significance level $\alpha = .05$, $k = 2$ independent variables, and $n = 15$, we obtain $d_L = 0.95$. Thus, for this one-tailed test, we will reject H_0 if $d < d_L = 0.95$.

Conclusion: Since the computed value of the test statistic lies within the rejection region ($0.776 < 0.95$), there is sufficient evidence to conclude that the residuals are positively autocorrelated. Thus, the least squares model may be inappropriate and doubt is cast on any inferences derived from it.

Exercise

16.5 Time series data for a period of 30 years were used to fit a multiple regression model relating the U.S. birth rate (Y_t) to $k = 3$ independent variables:

X_{1t} = percentage of women in labor force

X_{2t} = unemployment rate

X_{3t} = divorce rate

The results of the analysis are summarized as follows:

$\hat{Y}_t = 4.30 - 0.048X_{1t} - 0.039X_{2t} - 0.009X_{3t}$

$R^2 = 0.71$

Durbin-Watson $d = 0.56$

Is there sufficient evidence to conclude that the regression residuals are autocorrelated?

16.7 FORECASTING WITH AUTOREGRESSIVE MODELS

Example

16.7 In recent years, the United States dollar has declined on foreign money markets. One currency the dollar is often compared to is the West German mark. Data on the number of marks to the dollar have been collected over a 25-month period. (Month 1 was used as the base time period; thus, the data shown below are the index values.)

DOLLAR DECLINE DATA

MONTH, t	INDEX NUMBER, Y_t	MONTH, t	INDEX NUMBER, Y_t
1	100.0	14	86.0
2	98.5	15	86.3
3	96.5	16	86.4
4	94.3	17	88.2
5	95.0	18	88.8
6	98.0	19	87.9
7	96.9	20	84.5
8	95.8	21	85.5
9	92.7	22	83.3
10	91.6	23	83.2
11	85.1	24	82.6
12	88.8	25	80.7
13	87.5		

The following model was proposed for the secular component:

$Y_t = \beta_0 + \beta_1 t + R_t;$

the autoregressive model for the random component, which allows for cyclical effects, is:

$R_t = \phi R_{t-1} + \epsilon_t.$

A portion of the SAS printout is given below.

ESTIMATES OF THE AUTOREGRESSIVE PARAMETERS

LAG	COEFFICIENT	STD DEVIATION	T RATIO
1	-0.5124	0.172	-2.98

	DF	SUM OF SQUARES	MEAN SQUARE	F RATIO	APPROX PROB
REGRESS	1	212.871	212.871	61.12	0.0001
ERROR	23	80.10375	3.483		
TOTAL	24	292.9748		R-SQUARE = .7266	

VARIABLE	B VALUE	STD DEVIATION	T RATIO	APPROX PROB
INTERCEPT	99.37234	1.427	69.632	0.0001
T	-0.73561	0.094	-7.818	0.0001

a. What are the estimated models?

b. Use the models to forecast the index numbers for the next six months (Months 26-31). Compute approximate 95% prediction bounds for the forecasts.

Solution

a. The estimated models, from the printout, are:

$$\hat{Y}_t = 99.3723 - .7356t + \hat{R}_t,$$

$$\hat{R}_t = .5124\hat{R}_{t-1}.$$

b. For Month 26, we have $t = 26$. Now,

$$\hat{R}_t = Y_t - (99.3723 - .7356t);$$

Thus,

$$\hat{R}_{25} = Y_{25} - [99.3723 - .7356(25)] = 80.7 - 80.9823 = -.2823.$$

Therefore,

$$\hat{R}_{26} = \hat{\phi}\hat{R}_{25} = .5124(-.2823) = -.1447$$

and

$$\hat{Y}_{26} = \hat{\beta}_0 + \hat{\beta}_1(26) + \hat{R}_{26} = 99.3723 - .7356(26) - .1447 = 80.1020.$$

We predict an index number of 80.1020 for Month 26. Approximate 95% prediction bounds on this forecast are given by:

$$80.1020 \pm 2\sqrt{\text{MSE}} = 80.1020 \pm 2\sqrt{3.483}$$
$$= 80.1020 \pm 2(1.8663) \quad \text{or} \quad (76.3694,\ 85.8346).$$

For $t = 27$ (Month 27), we have

$$\hat{R}_{27} = \hat{\phi}\hat{R}_{26} = .5124(-.1447) = -.0741$$

and

$$\hat{Y}_{27} = \hat{\beta}_0 + \hat{\beta}_1(27) + \hat{R}_{27} = 99.3723 - .7356(27) - .0741 = 79.4370.$$

Approximate 95% prediction bounds are computed by

$$79.4370 \pm 2\sqrt{\text{MSE}} = 79.4370 \pm 2(1.8663) \quad \text{or} \quad (75.7044,\ 83.1696).$$

The calculations required for the forecasts and prediction intervals are shown in the following table.

t	$\hat{R}_t = \hat{\phi}\hat{R}_{t-1} = .5124\hat{R}_{t-1}$	$\hat{Y}_t = 99.3723 - .7356t + \hat{R}_t$	$\hat{Y}_t \pm 2\sqrt{\text{MSE}} = \hat{Y}_t \pm 3.7326$
26	-.1447	80.1020	(76.3694, 85.8346)
27	.5124(-.1447) = -.0741	79.4370	(75.7044, 83.1696)
28	.5124(-.0741) = -.0380	78.7375	(75.0049, 82.4701)
29	.5124(-.0380) = -.0195	78.0204	(74.2878, 81.7530)
30	.5124(-.0195) = -.0100	77.2943	(73.5617, 81.0269)
31	.5124(-.0100) = -.0051	76.5636	(72.8310, 80.2962)

17
DESIGN OF EXPERIMENTS AND ANALYSIS OF VARIANCE

SUMMARY

This chapter presented experimental designs useful for comparing more than two means. The *completely randomized design* (*independent sampling design*) uses p independent random samples to compare the means of p populations. The *randomized block design* is an extension of the paired difference design which uses relatively *homogeneous blocks* of experimental units. Each of p *treatments* is randomly assigned to one experimental unit in each block to compare the treatment means.

The method of analysis for either design involves a comparison of the variation among the treatment means (measured by MST, the mean square for treatments) to the variation among experimental units (measured by MSE, the mean square for error). If the ratio MST/MSE is large, we conclude that the means of at least two of the populations differ.

The analysis of variance procedure can also be used to analyze data from a *two-factor factorial experiment*. Such an analysis allows us to test for *interaction* among factors.

The chapter included examples of the use of *Bonferroni's procedure*, which can be used to compare all pairs of treatment means.

17.1 ELEMENTS OF A DESIGNED EXPERIMENT

17.2 THE COMPLETELY RANDOMIZED DESIGN

Examples

17.1 A major appliance dealer wishes to compare his mean television sales during three different periods of the week: Beginning (Monday, Tuesday); Middle (Wednesday, Thursday); and End (Friday, Saturday). His plan is to select random samples of sales records from each period and record the number of television sets sold. What type of experimental design is this?

Solution

The appliance dealer is employing a completely randomized design (independent sampling design). In this example, the means of $p = 3$ populations (television sales at the Beginning, Middle, and End of the week) are to be compared by selecting independent random samples from each of the populations.

17.2 Refer to Example 17.1. Set up the test to compare the mean sales for the three periods. (Data will be provided in the next example.)

Solution

We wish to test the null hypothesis that the mean number of television sets sold is the same for each of the three periods, against the alternative hypothesis that at least two of the means are different:

H_0: $\mu_1 = \mu_2 = \mu_3$
H_a: At least two of the means differ

where μ_1, μ_2, and μ_3 are the true mean number of television sets sold at the Beginning, Middle, and End of the week, respectively.

The test is based on the following assumptions:

1) The television sales during each of the three periods have approximately normal distributions.

2) The variance of the number of television sets sold is the same in each of the three periods.

The test statistic is

$$F = \frac{\text{MST}}{\text{MSE}}$$

and the null hypothesis is rejected (at significance level α) if $F > F_\alpha$, where the distribution of F is based on $p - 1 = 3 - 1 = 2$ numerator degrees of freedom and $n - p = n - 3$ denominator degrees of freedom.

17.3 Refer to Examples 17.1-17.2. The data for the experiment are shown in the following table.

TELEVISION SALES
(Number of Sets Sold)

	BEGINNING	MIDDLE	END
	9	8	15
	9	11	14
	11	6	10
	9	8	11
	12	9	10
		12	12
TOTAL	50	54	72

Perform the test to compare the mean sales for the three periods. Use $\alpha = .05$.

Solution [Note: In the examples of this chapter, we use the calculation formulas for analysis of variance presented in Appendix D of the text.]

The following calculations are required:

$$n = n_1 + n_2 + n_3 = 5 + 6 + 6 = 17,$$

$$\Sigma y_i = T_1 + T_2 + T_3 = 50 + 54 + 72 = 176,$$

and $$\Sigma y_i^2 = 9^2 + 9^2 + 11^2 + \cdots + 11^2 + 10^2 + 12^2 = 1904.$$

Thus,

$$\text{CM} = \frac{(\Sigma y_i)^2}{n} = \frac{(176)^2}{17} = 1822.12,$$

$$\text{SS(Total)} = \Sigma y_i^2 - \text{CM} = 1904 - 1822.12 = 81.88,$$

$$\text{SST} = \frac{T_1^2}{n_1} + \frac{T_2^2}{n_2} + \frac{T_3^2}{n_3} - \text{CM} = \frac{50^2}{5} + \frac{54^2}{6} + \frac{72^2}{6} - 1822.12$$

$$= 1850 - 1822.12 = 27.88,$$

$$\text{SSE} = \text{SS(Total)} - \text{SST} = 81.88 - 27.88 = 54.00,$$

$$\text{MST} = \frac{\text{SST}}{p - 1} = \frac{27.88}{2} = 13.94,$$

$$\text{MSE} = \frac{\text{SSE}}{n - p} = \frac{54.00}{17 - 3} = \frac{54.00}{14} = 3.86.$$

Then the computed value of the test statistic is

$$F = \frac{\text{MST}}{\text{MSE}} = \frac{13.94}{3.86} = 3.61.$$

The critical value of F is based on $p - 1 = 2$ numerator df and $n - p = 14$ denominator df. Thus, for $\alpha = .05$, the rejection region consists of values of F such that $F > F_{.05} = 3.74$.

Since the value of the test statistic does not lie within the rejection region, there is insufficient evidence to conclude that a significant difference exists among the mean sales during the different periods of the week.

17.4 Refer to Examples 17.1-17.3. Summarize the results of the analysis of variance in an ANOVA table.

Solution

The ANOVA summary table for this completely randomized design is as follows:

SOURCE	df	SS	MS	F
Period of week	2	27.88	13.94	3.61
Error	14	54.00	3.86	
Totals	16	81.88		

17.5 Refer to Example 17.3. Construct a 90% confidence interval for μ_1, the mean number of television sets sold at the beginning of a week.

Solution

The general form of a 90% confidence interval for μ_1 is

$$\bar{y}_1 \pm t_{\alpha/2}(s/\sqrt{n_1}),$$

where the distribution of t is based on $(n - p)$ degrees of freedom and $s = \sqrt{\text{MSE}}$ is the estimate of σ^2, the common variance of the p populations. In the television sales example, we have

$$\bar{y}_1 = T_1/n_1 = 50/5 = 10,$$

$$s = \sqrt{\text{MSE}} = \sqrt{3.86} \approx 1.96,$$

and $t_{\alpha/2} = t_{.05} = 1.761$ (with $n - p = 17 - 3 = 14$ df). Thus, the required confidence interval is

$$\bar{y}_1 \pm t_{.05}\frac{s}{\sqrt{n_1}} = 10.0 \pm 1.761\left(\frac{1.96}{\sqrt{5}}\right) = 10.0 \pm 1.5,$$

or (8.5, 11.5). We are 90% confident that the mean number of television sets sold at the beginning of a week lies within this interval.

17.6 Refer to Example 17.3.

a. Construct a 95% confidence interval for the difference in the mean numbers of television sets sold at the end and beginning of the week.

b. Interpret the interval.

<u>Solution</u>

a. We wish to obtain a 95% confidence interval for $\mu_3 - \mu_1$; the general form is

$$(\bar{y}_3 - \bar{y}_1) \pm t_{\alpha/2}s\sqrt{\frac{1}{n_3} + \frac{1}{n_1}}$$

where $s = \sqrt{\text{MSE}}$ and t is based on $(n - p)$ degrees of freedom. For the data given in Example 15.3,

$$\bar{y}_3 = \frac{T_3}{n_3} = \frac{72}{6} = 12.0, \quad \bar{y}_1 = \frac{T_1}{n_1} = \frac{50}{5} = 10.0,$$

$$s = \sqrt{\text{MSE}} = \sqrt{3.86} \approx 1.96,$$

and $t_{\alpha/2} = t_{.025} = 2.145$ (14 df).

Thus, a 95% confidence interval for $\mu_3 - \mu_1$ is given by

$$(\bar{y}_3 - \bar{y}_1) \pm t_{.025}\,s\sqrt{\frac{1}{n_3} + \frac{1}{n_1}} = (12.0 - 10.0) \pm 2.145(1.96)\sqrt{\frac{1}{6} + \frac{1}{5}}$$

$$= 2.0 \pm 2.5 \quad \text{or} \quad (-.5, 4.5).$$

b. We estimate, with 95% confidence, that μ_1, the mean television sales at the beginning of a week, could be larger than μ_3, the mean television sales at the end of a week, by as much as .5 set, or it could be less than μ_3 by 4.5 sets. Note that the confidence interval contains zero; this is not surprising since (in Example 17.3) we failed to reject the hypothesis of equality of the mean television sales for the three periods of the week.

17.7 A durability test was performed on three of the most heavily advertised brands of flashlight batteries. Six batteries of each brand were tested and the time (in hours) was recorded at which a point less than 90% of full power was reached. The results are shown in the following table.

	BRAND 1	BRAND 2	BRAND 3
	59	61	38
	43	63	42
	47	57	38
	45	49	43
	51	48	40
	53	60	46
TOTALS	298	338	247

a. Is there evidence (at $\alpha = .05$) of a difference in the mean durabilities of the three brands of batteries?

b. Estimate the mean durability of Brand 2 batteries with a 90% confidence interval.

c. Estimate the difference between the mean durabilities of Brands 2 and 3 with a 95% confidence interval.

d. What assumptions are required for the validity of the procedures used in parts a-c?

Solution

a. The elements of the hypothesis test are the following:

H_0: $\mu_1 = \mu_2 = \mu_3$
H_a: At least two of the means are different

where μ_1, μ_2, and μ_3 are the mean durabilities of all batteries of Brands 1, 2, and 3, respectively.

At $\alpha = .05$, the null hypothesis will be rejected for all values of the test statistic F such that $F > F_{.05} = 3.68$, where the distribution of F is based on $p - 1 = 3 - 1 = 2$ numerator df and $n - p = 18 - 3 = 15$ denominator df.

The following computations are required:

$$\Sigma y_i = 883, \quad \Sigma y_i^2 = 44435$$

$$\text{CM} = \frac{(\Sigma y_i)^2}{n} = \frac{(883)^2}{18} = 43316.056$$

$$\text{SS(Total)} = \Sigma y_i^2 - \text{CM} = 44435 - 43316.056 = 1118.944$$

(continued)

$$SST = \frac{T_1^2}{n_1} + \frac{T_2^2}{n_2} + \frac{T_3^2}{n_3} - CM$$

$$= \frac{(298)^2}{6} + \frac{(338)^2}{6} + \frac{(247)^2}{6} - 43316.056 = 693.444$$

$$SSE = SS(\text{Total}) - SST = 1118.944 - 693.444 = 425.5$$

$$MST = \frac{SST}{p - 1} = \frac{693.444}{3 - 1} = 346.722$$

$$MSE = \frac{SSE}{n - p} = \frac{425.5}{18 - 3} = 28.367$$

Now, the test statistic is

$$F = \frac{MST}{MSE} = \frac{346.722}{28.367} = 12.22.$$

This value lies within the rejection region; we thus conclude (at $\alpha = .05$) that the mean durabilities for at least two of the brands of batteries differ.

b. A 90% confidence interval for μ_2 is given by

$$\bar{y}_2 \pm t_{.05}(s/\sqrt{n_2}),$$

where t is based on $n - p = 15$ degrees of freedom and $s = \sqrt{MSE} = \sqrt{28.367} \approx 5.326$. Thus, we have

$$\frac{338}{6} \pm 1.753\left(\frac{5.326}{\sqrt{6}}\right) = 56.33 \pm 3.81 \quad \text{or} \quad (52.52,\ 60.14).$$

We estimate, with 90% confidence, that the mean durability of all Brand 2 flashlight batteries lies within the interval from 52.52 to 60.14 hours.

c. The general form of a 95% confidence interval for $\mu_2 - \mu_3$ is

$$(\bar{y}_2 - \bar{y}_3) \pm t_{.025}\, s\sqrt{\frac{1}{n_2} + \frac{1}{n_3}},$$

where $t_{.025} = 2.131$ is based on $n - p = 15$ degrees of freedom.

Substitution yields:

$$\left(\frac{338}{6} - \frac{247}{6}\right) \pm 2.131(5.326)\sqrt{\frac{1}{6} + \frac{1}{6}} = 15.17 \pm 6.55 \quad \text{or} \quad (8.62,\ 21.72).$$

We are 95% confident that the mean durability of Brand 2 batteries exceeds the mean durability of Brand 3 batteries by between 8.62 hours and 21.72 hours.

d. The hypothesis test and confidence interval procedures require the following assumptions:

1) The durabilities of the flashlight batteries have approximately normal distributions for Brands 1, 2, and 3.

2) The variance of the durability distribution is the same for the three brands of batteries.

17.8 Refer to Example 17.7. Use the Bonferroni technique to compare the pairs of means corresponding to the three brands. Use $\alpha = .05$ as the overall significance level for the comparisons.

Solution

The general form of the Bonferroni confidence intervals is

$$\bar{y}_i - \bar{y}_j \pm t_{\alpha/(2c)} s \sqrt{\frac{1}{n_i} + \frac{1}{n_j}}$$

where there are $c = p(p - 1)/2 = 3(3 - 2)/2 = 3$ pairs of treatment means to be compared, $t_{\alpha/(2c)} = t_{.05/6} = t_{.0083} \approx t_{.005} = 2.947$ with $(n - p) - 18 - 3 = 15$ degrees of freedom, and $s = \sqrt{\text{MSE}} \approx 5.326$. Substituting the values of the sample means and respective sample sizes into the general formula yields:

(i) $$\bar{y}_1 - \bar{y}_2 \pm (2.947)(5.326)\sqrt{\frac{1}{n_1} + \frac{1}{n_2}}$$

$$\frac{298}{6} - \frac{338}{6} \pm 15.6957\sqrt{\frac{1}{6} + \frac{1}{6}}$$

$$-6.6667 \pm 9.0619 \quad \text{or} \quad (-15.73, 2.40)$$

The mean durability for brand 1 does not differ significantly from the mean durability for brand 2, since the interval contains 0.

(ii) $$\bar{y}_1 - \bar{y}_3 \pm (2.947)(5.326)\sqrt{\frac{1}{n_1} + \frac{1}{n_3}}$$

$$\frac{298}{6} - \frac{247}{6} \pm 15.6957\sqrt{\frac{1}{6} + \frac{1}{6}}$$

$$8.5 \pm 9.0619 \quad \text{or} \quad (-.56, 17.56)$$

The mean durability for brand 1 is not significantly different from that for brand 3.

(iii) $$\bar{y}_2 - \bar{y}_3 \pm (2.947)(5.326)\sqrt{\frac{1}{n_2} + \frac{1}{n_3}}$$

$$\frac{338}{6} - \frac{247}{6} \pm 15.6957\sqrt{\frac{1}{6} + \frac{1}{6}}$$

$$15.1667 \pm 9.0619 \quad \text{or} \quad (6.10, 24.23)$$

Since both endpoints of the interval are positive, the implication is that the mean durability for brand 2 is significantly greater than the mean durability for brand 3.

Exercises

17.1 A tire company wished to investigate the effect of different types of advertising on the sales of its most popular tire. Each of three methods—(1) newspaper advertisement with the regular tire price, (2) newspaper advertisement listing a "special" price for the tire, and (3) no newspaper advertising—was used for a period of two months, with one week intervals between the different methods. The data below give the sales (number of tires sold) for randomly selected days from each period.

METHOD OF ADVERTISING		
1	2	3
29	30	18
26	72	17
18	47	20
35	48	18
42	28	26
19	36	14
		16
		18

a. What type of experimental design is represented here?

b. Test to see whether there are differences in the mean numbers of tires sold daily for each method of advertising. Use $\alpha = .05$.

c. Estimate the mean number of tires sold daily when no newspaper advertising is used. Use a 90% confidence interval.

d. Estimate the difference in the mean numbers of tires sold daily between Methods 1 and 2 of advertising. Use a 95% confidence interval.

e. What assumptions are required for the validity of the procedure used in parts b-d?

17.2 Refer to Exercise 17.1. Use the Bonferroni technique to compare all pairs of means. Use $\alpha = .10$ as the overall level of significance.

17.3 A company is considering the implementation of a new training program for its salesmen. They have recently conducted an experiment in which five new salesmen were randomly assigned to receive the new training method and five were randomly assigned to receive the old method. The commissions for each salesman during the week following completion of the program are shown below.

OLD TRAINING PROGRAM	NEW TRAINING PROGRAM
\$413	\$513
387	372
293	402
227	294
193	257

a. Is there evidence (at $\alpha = .025$) of a difference in the mean commissions for the two training programs? Use the methods of Chapter 9 to perform an independent samples t test.

b. Now use the same data to conduct an analysis of variance F test (at $\alpha = .05$) of the null hypothesis that there is no difference in the mean commissions for the two programs.

c. Square the values of the test statistic and critical value from part **a** and compare them to the respective values from part **b**. (Note that for $p = 2$, the ANOVA F test is equivalent to the independent samples t test.)

17.3 THE RANDOMIZED BLOCK DESIGN

Examples

17.9 Due to periodic gasoline shortages on the world market, scientists have been experimenting to find alternative fuels for automobiles. A study was recently performed to compare the mileage obtained with regular gasoline to the mileages obtained with two alternative fuels, gasohol and methanol. The following experimental design was used: Five cars, with a wide range of expected mileage ratings, were selected. Each car was tested with each type of fuel, under identical experimental conditions. The fuels were assigned to the cars in a random order. What type of experimental design is this?

Solution

This is a randomized block design in which the cars represent $b = 5$ blocks of relatively homogeneous experimental units. There are $p = 3$ treatments (fuels), each of which is randomly assigned once to each block.

17.10 Refer to Example 17.9.

a. Set up the test to compare the mean mileage ratings for the three types of fuel. (Data will be provided in the following example.)

b. Set up the test to determine if blocking is important in this experiment, i.e., if the mean mileage ratings differ for the five automobiles.

Solution

a. It is desired to test the null hypothesis that the mean mileage rating is the same for the three types of fuel against the alternative that at least two of the means are different.

H_0: $\mu_1 = \mu_2 = \mu_3$
H_a: At least two of the means are different

where μ_1, μ_2, and μ_3 are the population mean mileage (per gallon) ratings obtained with regular gasoline, gasohol, and methanol, respectively.

The test is based on the following assumptions:

1) The probability distributions of mileage ratings corresponding to all the automobile-fuel combinations are approximately normal.

2) The variances of all the probability distributions are equal.

The test statistic is F = MST/MSE and the null hypothesis will be rejected (at significance level α) if $F > F_\alpha$, where the distribution of F is based on $p - 1 = 3 - 1 = 2$ numerator df and $(n - b - p + 1) = (n - 5 - 3 + 1) = (n - 7)$ denominator df.

b. To compare the block means, we perform a test of

H_0: The population mean mileage ratings for the five automobiles are equal (i.e., the five block means are equal)

against

H_a: At least two of the mean mileage ratings for the five automobiles are different (i.e., at least two of the block means differ).

The test requires the same assumptions as the test in part a, and is based on the test statistic F = MSB/MSE.

The null hypothesis is rejected for all values of F such that $F > F_\alpha$, where F has $(b - 1) = 5 - 1 = 4$ numerator df and $(n - p - b + 1) = (n - 3 - 5 + 1) = (n - 7)$ denominator df.

17.11 Refer to Examples 17.9–17.10. The data for the experiment are shown in the table below (values shown are miles per gallon).

	FUEL			
AUTOMOBILE	Regular Gasoline	Gasohol	Methanol	TOTALS
1	32	30	25	87
2	25	26	21	72
3	19	17	14	50
4	15	12	10	37
5	12	10	8	30
TOTALS	103	95	78	276

a. Perform the test to compare the mean mileage ratings for the three types of fuel. Use $\alpha = .05$.

b. Perform the test to determine if blocking is important in this experiment. Use $\alpha = .05$.

Solution

a. The following calculations are required:

$$\Sigma y_i^2 = 32^2 + 25^2 + 19^2 + \cdots + 14^2 + 10^2 + 8^2 = 5914$$

$$\text{CM} = \frac{(\Sigma y_i)^2}{n} = \frac{(276)^2}{15} = 5078.4$$

$$\text{SS(Total)} = \Sigma y_i^2 - \text{CM} = 5914 - 5078.4 = 835.6$$

$$\text{SST} = \frac{T_1^2}{b} + \frac{T_2^2}{b} + \frac{T_3^2}{b} - \text{CM}$$

$$= \frac{(103)^2}{5} + \frac{(95)^2}{5} + \frac{(78)^2}{5} - 5078.4 = 65.2$$

$$\text{SSB} = \frac{B_1^2}{p} + \frac{B_2^2}{p} + \frac{B_3^2}{p} + \frac{B_4^2}{p} + \frac{B_5^2}{p} - \text{CM}$$

$$= \frac{(87)^2}{3} + \frac{(72)^2}{3} + \frac{(50)^2}{3} + \frac{(37)^2}{3} + \frac{(30)^2}{3} - 5078.4$$

$$- 762.27$$

$$\text{SSE} = \text{SS(Total)} - \text{SST} - \text{SSB} = 835.6 - 65.2 - 762.27 = 8.13$$

$$\text{MST} = \frac{\text{SST}}{p - 1} = \frac{65.2}{2} = 32.6$$

$$\text{MSB} = \frac{\text{SSB}}{b - 1} = \frac{762.27}{4} = 190.57$$

$$\text{MSE} = \frac{\text{SSE}}{n - p - b + 1} = \frac{8.13}{15 - 3 - 5 + 1} = \frac{8.13}{8} = 1.02$$

Then the computed value of the test statistic is

$$F = \frac{\text{MST}}{\text{MSE}} = \frac{32.60}{1.02} = 31.96.$$

The critical value of F is based on $p - 1 = 2$ numerator df and $n - p - b + 1 = 8$ denominator df. Thus, for $\alpha = .05$, the rejection region consists of values of F such that $F > F_{.05} = 4.46$.

Since the value of the test statistic lies within the rejection region, we conclude that the population mean mileage ratings for at least two of the fuels differ.

b. The test statistic is

$$F = \frac{\text{MSB}}{\text{MSE}} = \frac{190.57}{1.02} = 186.83.$$

Since the calculated $F = 186.83$ greatly exceeds the critical value of $F_{.05} = 3.84$ ($b - 1 = 4$ numerator df and $n - p - b + 1 = 8$ denominator df), we have strong evidence that the mean mileage ratings differ among the five automobiles. Thus, the decision to use a randomized block design was wise.

17.12 Refer to Examples 17.9–17.11. Summarize the results of the analysis of variance in an ANOVA table.

Solution

The ANOVA summary table for this randomized block design is as follows:

SOURCE	*df*	SS	MS	*F*
Fuel (Treatments)	2	65.20	32.60	31.96
Automobiles (Blocks)	4	762.27	190.57	186.83
Error	8	8.13	1.02	
Totals	14	835.60		

17.13 Refer to Example 17.11. Construct a 95% confidence interval for $\mu_1 - \mu_3$, the difference in mean mileage ratings obtained between regular gasoline and methanol.

Solution

The general form of a 95% confidence interval for $\mu_1 - \mu_3$ is

$$(\bar{y}_1 - \bar{y}_3) \pm t_{.025}\, s\sqrt{\frac{1}{b} + \frac{1}{b}},$$

where $b = 5$ is the number of blocks, $s = \sqrt{\text{MSE}}$, and the distribution of t is based on $n - p - b + 1 = 8$ degrees of freedom. For this example, we have

$$\bar{y}_1 = \frac{103}{5} = 20.6, \quad \bar{y}_3 = \frac{78}{5} = 15.6, \quad t_{.025} = 2.306,$$

and $\quad s = \sqrt{\text{MSE}} = \sqrt{1.02} \approx 1.01.$

Substitution yields the desired confidence interval:

$$(20.6 - 15.6) \pm 2.306(1.01)\sqrt{\frac{1}{5} + \frac{1}{5}} = 5.0 \pm 1.47 \quad \text{or} \quad (3.53,\ 6.47)$$

We estimate, with 95% confidence, that the population mean mileage rating obtained with regular gasoline is between 3.53 and 6.47 miles per gallon greater than the population mean rating obtained with methanol.

17.14 Three of the currently most popular television shows produced the following ratings (percentage of the television audience tuned in to the show) over a period of four weeks:

	SHOW			
WEEK	A	B	C	TOTALS
1	33.7	27.4	22.8	83.9
2	37.1	31.2	19.7	88.0
3	34.1	31.4	24.8	90.3
4	29.4	27.2	27.9	84.5
TOTALS	134.3	117.2	95.2	346.7

a. Is there evidence (at $\alpha = .01$) that the mean ratings differ for the three shows?

b. Is there evidence (at $\alpha = .01$) that the use of weeks as blocks is justified in this experiment?

c. Construct a 95% confidence interval for the difference in mean ratings between Shows B and C.

d. State the assumptions necessary for the validity of the procedures used in parts a–c.

Solution

a. The hypothesis test has the following elements:

H_0: $\mu_1 = \mu_2 = \mu_3$
H_a: At least two of the means differ

where μ_1, μ_2, and μ_3 are the population mean ratings for Shows A, B, and C, respectively.

At $\alpha = .01$, the null hypothesis will be rejected for all values of the test statistic F such that $F > F_{.01} = 10.92$, where F is based on $p - 1 = 3 - 1 = 2$ numerator degrees of freedom and $n - p - b + 1 = 12 - 3 - 4 + 1 = 6$ denominator degrees of freedom.

The following computations are required:

$$\Sigma y_i^2 = (33.7)^2 + (37.1)^2 + \cdots + (24.8)^2 + (27.9)^2 = 10{,}290.65$$

$$\text{CM} = \frac{(\Sigma y_i)^2}{n} = \frac{(346.7)^2}{12} = 10{,}016.74$$

$$\text{SS(Total)} = \Sigma y_i^2 - \text{CM} = 10{,}290.65 - 10{,}016.74 = 273.91$$

$$\text{SST} = \frac{T_1^2}{b} + \frac{T_2^2}{b} + \frac{T_3^2}{b} - \text{CM}$$

$$= \frac{(134.3)^2}{4} + \frac{(117.2)^2}{4} + \frac{(95.2)^2}{4} - 10{,}016.74 = 192.10$$

$$\text{SSB} = \frac{B_1^2}{p} + \frac{B_2^2}{p} + \frac{B_3^2}{p} + \frac{B_4^2}{p} - \text{CM}$$

$$= \frac{(83.9)^2}{3} + \frac{(88.0)^2}{3} + \frac{(90.3)^2}{3} + \frac{(84.5)^2}{3} - 10.016.74$$

$$= 9.11$$

$$\text{SSE} = \text{SS(Total)} - \text{SST} - \text{SSB} = 273.91 - 192.10 - 9.11 = 72.70$$

$$\text{MST} = \frac{\text{SST}}{p - 1} = \frac{192.10}{2} = 96.05$$

$$\text{MSB} = \frac{\text{SSB}}{b - 1} = \frac{9.11}{3} = 3.04$$

$$\text{MSE} = \frac{\text{SSE}}{n - p - b + 1} = \frac{72.70}{12 - 3 - 4 + 1} = \frac{72.70}{6} = 12.12$$

Now the test statistic is

$$F = \frac{\text{MST}}{\text{MSE}} = \frac{96.05}{12.12} = 7.92.$$

This values does not lie within the rejection region. There is insufficient evidence (at $\alpha = .01$) to conclude that there are differences in the mean ratings for the three shows.

b. The test statistic is

$$F = \frac{\text{MSB}}{\text{MSE}} = \frac{3.04}{12.12} = 0.25,$$

and the rejection region consists of values of F such that $F > F_{.01} = 9.78$, based on $(b - 1) = 3$ numerator df and $(n - p - b + 1) = 6$ denominator df. The sample does not provide strong enough evidence to indicate that blocking is important in this experiment.

c. The general form of a 95% confidence interval for $\mu_2 - \mu_3$ is

$$(\bar{y}_2 - \bar{y}_3) \pm t_{.025}\, s\sqrt{\frac{1}{b} + \frac{1}{b}},$$

where

$$\bar{y}_2 = \frac{117.2}{4} = 29.3, \quad \bar{y}_3 = \frac{95.2}{4} = 23.8, \quad t_{.025} = 2.447 \ (6\ df)$$

and $s = \sqrt{\text{MSE}} = \sqrt{12.12} = 3.48.$

Substitution yields:

$$(29.3 - 23.8) \pm 2.447(3.48)\sqrt{\frac{1}{4} + \frac{1}{4}} = 5.5 \pm 6.02 \quad \text{or} \quad (-.52,\ 11.52)$$

This interval is very wide and includes the value zero. Thus, we cannot conclude that the population mean ratings for Shows B and C are different. This is consistent with the F test of part **a**, in which we failed to reject the null hypothesis of the equality of the population means.

d. The hypothesis test and confidence interval procedures require the following assumptions:

1) The probability distributions of television ratings corresponding to all the show-week combinations are approximately normal.

2) The variances of all the probability distributions are equal.

Exercises

17.4 A restaurant owner operates three restaurants within a city: one in a major shopping center (A), one near the college campus (B), and one at the beach area (C). The management has collected the following data on daily sales (in hundreds of dollars):

DAY	RESTAURANT A	B	C
Wednesday	9.5	7.4	4.9
Thursday	7.4	8.3	6.1
Friday	11.6	10.4	5.7
Saturday	17.3	6.9	13.2
Sunday	9.8	5.3	12.7

a. What type of experimental design is represented here?

b. Construct an ANOVA summary table for this experiment.

c. Is there evidence of a difference in the mean sales among the restaurants? Use $\alpha = .05$.

d. Is there evidence (at $\alpha = .05$) of a difference in the mean sales for the five days?

e. Estimate the difference in mean sales between the restaurants located at the shopping center and near the college campus. Use a 90% confidence interval.

f. State the assumptions required for the validity of the procedures used in parts b–e.

17.5 A comparison of tire prices (in dollars) for three different brands of tires (size C78-13 whitewall) produced the following data:

TYPE OF TIRE	BRAND A	B	C
4-ply polester	45	48	43
Glass-belted	58	57	54
Steel-belted	71	75	68

a. Set up the ANOVA summary table.

b. Is there evidence of a difference in mean prices among the three brands? Use $\alpha = .05$.

c. Estimate the difference in the mean prices between Brands A and C with a 95% confidence interval.

17.4 FACTORIAL EXPERIMENTS

Examples

17.15 A graphic design company employs four typesetters, each of whom is trained to work at each of three machines. In an effort to investigate the possibility of interaction between typesetter and machine, each typesetter was assigned to each machine for two 1-week periods. The average number of errors per page produced during the trials were recorded. What type of experimental design does this represent?

Solution

The design is a two-factor factorial experiment where factor A (typesetter) is at $a = 4$ levels and factor B (machine) is at $b = 3$ levels. The complete 4×3 factorial experiment is replicated $r = 2$ times.

17.16 Refer to Example 17.15. The data for the experiment are shown in the table.

	MACHINE					
TYPESETTER	1		2		3	
1	5	5	15	20	10	10
2	10	16	6	6	14	18
3	24	16	12	6	12	8
4	8	6	6	9	4	4

a. Perform an analysis of variance for the data and construct an ANOVA table.

b. Do the data present sufficient evidence to indicate an interaction between typesetter and type of machine? Use $\alpha = .05$.

Solution

a. The following preliminary calculations are required:

$$\text{CM} = \frac{(\Sigma y_i)^2}{n} = \frac{(5 + 5 + \cdots + 4 + 4)^2}{24} = \frac{(250)^2}{24} = 2604.16667$$

$$\begin{aligned}\text{SS(Total)} &= \Sigma y_i^2 - \text{CM} = 5^2 + 5^2 + \cdots + 4^2 + 4^2 - \text{CM} \\ &= 3292 - 2604.16667 = 687.83333\end{aligned}$$

$$\begin{aligned}\text{SS}(A) &= \frac{\Sigma A_i^2}{br} - \text{CM} = \frac{65^2 + 70^2 + 78^2 + 37^2}{3(2)} - \text{CM} \\ &= \frac{16{,}578}{6} - 2604.16667 = 158.83333\end{aligned}$$

$$\begin{aligned}\text{SS}(B) &= \frac{\Sigma B_i^2}{ar} - \text{CM} = \frac{90^2 + 80^2 + 80^2}{4(2)} - \text{CM} \\ &= \frac{20{,}900}{8} - 2604.16667 = 8.33333\end{aligned}$$

$$\begin{aligned}\text{SS}(AB) &= \frac{\Sigma\Sigma AB_{ij}^2}{r} - \text{SS}(A) - \text{SS}(B) - \text{CM} \\ &= \frac{10^2 + 35^2 + \cdots + 15^2 + 8^2}{2} - \text{SS}(A) - \text{SS}(B) - \text{CM} \\ &= \frac{6378}{2} - 158.83333 - 8.33333 - 2604.16667 = 417.66667\end{aligned}$$

$$\begin{aligned}\text{SSE} &= \text{SS(Total)} - \text{SS}(A) - \text{SS}(B) - \text{SS}(AB) \\ &= 687.83333 - 158.83333 - 8.33333 - 417.66667 \\ &= 103.00000\end{aligned}$$

$$\text{MS}(A) = \frac{\text{SS}(A)}{a - 1} = \frac{158.83333}{3} = 52.94444$$

$$\text{MS}(B) = \frac{\text{SS}(B)}{b - 1} = \frac{8.33333}{2} = 4.16667$$

$$\text{MS}(AB) = \frac{\text{SS}(AB)}{(a - 1)(b - 1)} = \frac{417.66667}{3(2)} = 69.61111$$

$$\text{MSE} = \frac{\text{SSE}}{ab(r - 1)} = \frac{103.00000}{4(3)(1)} = 8.58333$$

The results are summarized in the following ANOVA table.

SOURCE	df	SS	MS
Typesetter (A)	3	158.83333	52.94444
Machine (B)	2	8.33333	4.16667
Typesetter-Machine Interaction	6	417.66667	69.61111
Error	12	103.00000	8.58333
Total	23	687.83333	

b. The hypotheses of interest are:

H_0: Typesetter and Machine do not interact in their effect on average number of errors per page

H_a: There is interaction between the factors Typesetter and Machine

The test statistic is the ratio of the mean squares for interaction and error:

$$F = \frac{\text{MS}(AB)}{\text{MSE}} = \frac{69.61111}{8.58333} = 8.11$$

From the ANOVA table constructed in part a, we see that the degrees of freedom for the numerator and denominator of the F statistic are 6 and 12, respectively. Thus, at significance level .05, we will reject H_0 if $F > 3.00$.

Since the computed value of the test statistic falls within the rejection region ($8.11 > 3.00$), we reject H_0. There is sufficient evidence to conclude that Typesetter and Machine interact. We will consider pairwise comparisons of the sample means in the next section.

17.17 Refer to Examples 17.15 and 17.16.

a. Construct a 95% confidence interval for the average number of errors per page made by Typesetter 2 using Machine 3.

b. Construct a 90% confidence interval for the difference between the mean number of errors per page for Typesetters 2 and 3 working at Machine 3.

Solution

a. A 95% confidence interval for the mean $E(y)$ associated with Typesetter 2 using Machine 3 is

$$\bar{y}_{2,3} \pm t_{.025}(s/\sqrt{r})$$

where $\bar{y}_{2,3}$ is the mean of the $r = 2$ values given for the factor level combination of Typesetter 2 and Machine 3, $s = \sqrt{\text{MSE}} = \sqrt{8.58333} = 2.930$, and $t_{.025} = 2.179$ based on 12 degrees of freedom. Substitution of these values into the confidence interval formula yields:

$$\frac{32}{2} \pm 2.179\left(\frac{2.930}{\sqrt{2}}\right) = 16 \pm 4.51 \quad \text{or} \quad (11.49, 20.51)$$

We are 95% confident that the mean number of errors per page made by Typesetter 2 working at Machine 3 is between 11.49 and 20.51.

b. A 90% confidence interval for the difference between the mean numbers of errors per page for Typesetters 2 and 3 working at Machine 3 is given by

$$(\bar{y}_{2,3} - \bar{y}_{3,3}) \pm t_{.05}\, s\sqrt{2/r}$$

where $\bar{y}_{2,3}$ and $\bar{y}_{3,3}$ are the means of the values of y obtained by Typesetters 2 and 3, respectively, at Machine 3, $t_{.05} = 1.782$ based on 12 df, and $s = 2.930$ as in part **a**. Substitution yields the interval

$$\left(\frac{32}{2} - \frac{20}{2}\right) \pm 1.782(2.930)\sqrt{2/2} = 6 \pm 5.22 \quad \text{or} \quad (.78, 11.22).$$

Since all the values in the interval are positive, we are 90% confident that, when working on Machine 3, Typesetter 2 makes more errors per page, on average, than does Typesetter 3.

Exercises

17.6 A company conducted an experiment to determine the effects of three types of incentive pay plans on worker productivity for both union and nonunion workers. The company used plants in adjacent towns; one was unionized and the other was not. One-third of the production workers in each plant were assigned to each incentive plan. Then six workers were randomly selected from each group and their productivity (in numbers of items produced) was measured for a one-week period. The six productivity measures for the factor level combinations are listed in the table following part **b** of this exercise.

a. Perform an analysis of variance for the data given in the table and construct an ANOVA table.

b. Do the data present sufficient evidence to indicate an interaction between union affiliation and incentive plan? Test using $\alpha = .05$.

WORKERS	INCENTIVE PLAN A		B		C	
Union	337	328	346	373	317	341
	362	319	351	338	335	329
	305	344	355	365	310	315
Nonunion	359	346	371	377	350	336
	345	396	352	401	349	351
	381	373	399	378	374	340

17.7 Refer to Exercise 17.6.

a. Construct a 90% confidence interval for the mean productivity for a unionized worker on incentive plan B.

b. Find a 90% confidence interval for the difference in mean productivity between union and nonunion workers on incentive plan B.

17.5 USING REGRESSION ANALYSIS FOR ANOVA

Examples

17.18 Suppose a large chain of department stores wants to compare the mean dollar amounts owed by its delinquent credit card customers in three different annual income groups: under $12,000, $12,000-$25,000, and over $25,000. Samples of ten customers with delinquent accounts are randomly selected from each group and the amount owed by each customer is recorded. The data are shown in the table below. The experiment is a completely randomized design with three treatments: under $12,000, $12,000-$25,000, and over $25,000. Analyze the data shown using a regression analysis. Use $\alpha = .05$.

	UNDER $12,000	$12,000-$25,000	OVER $25,000
	$148	$513	$335
	76	264	643
	393	433	216
	520	94	536
	236	535	128
	134	327	723
	55	214	258
	166	135	380
	415	280	594
	153	304	465
Totals	$2,296	$3,099	$4,278

Solution

The appropriate linear model for $p = 3$ treatments is

Complete model: $y = \beta_0 + \beta_1 x_1 + \beta_2 x_2 + \varepsilon$

where

$$x_1 = \begin{cases} 1 & \text{if income class 2} \\ 0 & \text{if not} \end{cases}$$

$$x_2 = \begin{cases} 1 & \text{if income class 3} \\ 0 & \text{if not} \end{cases}$$

The Minitab regression analysis for the complete model is shown below.

```
The regression equation is
Y = 230 + 80.3 X1 + 198 X2

Predictor       Coef      Stdev     t-ratio
Constant      229.60      53.43        4.30
X1             80.30      75.56        1.06
X2            198.20      75.56        2.62

s = 168.9    R-sq = 20.5%    R-sq(adj) = 14.6%

SOURCE        DF        SS         MS
Regression     2    198772      99386
Error         27    770671      28543
Total         29    969443
```

The reduced model, obtained by omitting the two treatment parameters, is

Reduced model: $y = \beta_0 + \varepsilon$

Since we know that the least squares estimate of β_0 for this model is $\bar{y}$, it follows that the sum of squares for error for the reduced model is:

$$\text{SSE}_1 = \text{SS(Total)} = \sum_{i=1}^{n} (y_i - \bar{y})^2 = \sum_{i=1}^{n} y_i^2 - \frac{\left(\sum_{i=1}^{n} y_i\right)^2}{n}$$

This quantity is shown above as

$\text{SS(Total)} = 969{,}443$

Then the drop in the sum of squares for error that is attributable to a difference in treatment means is

$$\begin{aligned} \text{SST} &= \text{SSE}_1 - \text{SSE}_2 \\ &= 969{,}443 - 770{,}671 = 198{,}772 \end{aligned}$$

To test the null hypothesis $H_0\colon \beta_1 = \beta_2 = 0$ or, equivalently, $H_0\colon \mu_1 = \mu_2 = \mu_3$, we form the test statistic

$$F = \frac{(\text{SSE}_1 - \text{SSE}_2)/(p - 1)}{\text{SSE}_2/(n - p)} = \frac{198{,}772/2}{770{,}671/27} = 3.48$$

For $\nu_1 = p - 1 = 3 - 1 = 2$ and $\nu_2 = n - p = 30 - 3 = 27$ *df*, $F_{.05} = 3.35$. Since the computed value of F, 3.48, exceeds the critical value, there is sufficient evidence (at $\alpha = .05$) to indicate that the means for the three groups of delinquent creditors differ.

17.19 A manufacturer, whose daily supply of raw materials is variable and limited, can use the material to produce two different products in various proportions. The profit per unit of raw material obtained by producing each of the two products depends on the length of a product's manufacturing run and, hence, on the amount of raw material assigned to it. Other factors, such as worker productivity and machine breakdown, affect the profit per unit as well, but their net effect on profit is random and uncontrollable. The manufacturer has conducted an experiment to investigate the effect of the level of supply of raw materials, S, and the ratio of its assignment, R, to the two product manufacturing lines on the profit y per unit of raw material. The ultimate goal would be to be able to choose the best ratio, R, to match each day's supply of raw materials, S. The levels of supply of the raw material chosen for the experiment were 15, 18, and 21 tons; the levels of the ratio of allocation to the two product lines were $\frac{1}{2}$, 1, and 2. The response was the profit (in dollars) per unit of raw material supply obtained from a single day's production. Three replications of a complete 3×3 factorial experiment were conducted in a random sequence (i.e., a completely randomized design). The data for the 27 days are shown in the table below.

		RAW MATERIAL SUPPLY, TONS (S) 15	18	21
RATIO OF RAW MATERIAL ALLOCATION (R)	$\frac{1}{2}$	23, 20, 21	22, 19, 20	19, 18, 21
	1	22, 20, 19	24, 25, 22	20, 19, 22
	2	18, 18, 16	21, 23, 20	20, 22, 24

a. Write the complete model for the experiment.

b. What hypothesis would you test to determine whether supply and ratio interact?

Solution

a. Both factors, supply and ratio, are quantitative. According to the relevant box, when the factors in a factorial experiment are quantitative, the main effects are represented by terms such as x, x^2, x^3, and so forth. Since each factor has three levels, we require two main effects, x and x^2, for each factor. (In general, the number of main effect terms will be one less than the number of levels for a factor.) Consequently, the complete factorial model for this 3×3 factorial experiment is

$$y = \beta_0 + \underbrace{\beta_1 x_1 + \beta_2 x_1^2}_{\text{Supply main effects}} + \underbrace{\beta_3 x_2 + \beta_4 x_2^2}_{\text{Ratio main effects}}$$

$$+ \underbrace{\beta_5 x_1 x_2 + \beta_6 x_1 x_2^2 + \beta_7 x_1^2 x_2 + \beta_8 x_1^2 x_2^2}_{\text{Supply-Ratio interaction}} + \varepsilon$$

where

x_1 = Supply of raw material (in tons)

x_2 = Ratio of allocation

Note that the interaction terms for the model are constructed by taking the products of the various main effect terms, one from each factor. For example, we included terms involving the products of x_1 with x_2 and x_2^2. The remaining interaction terms were formed by multiplying x_1^2 by x_2 and by x_2^2.

b. To test the null hypothesis that supply and ratio do not interact, we must test the null hypothesis that the interaction terms are not needed in the linear model of part **a**.

H_0: $\beta_5 = \beta_6 = \beta_7 = \beta_8 = 0$

This requires that we fit the reduced model

$$y = \beta_0 + \beta_1 x_1 + \beta_2 x_1^2 + \beta_3 x_2 + \beta_4 x_2^2$$

and perform the partial F-test outlined in Section 13.4. The test statistic is

$$F = \frac{(\text{SSE}_1 - \text{SSE}_2)/4}{s^2}$$

where

SSE_1 = SSE for reduced model

SSE_2 = SSE for complete model

s^2 = MSE for complete model

17.20 Use the SAS computer software package to fit a second-order model to the data of the factorial experiment in Example 17.19.

Solution

An analysis of variance for a complete two-variable factorial experiment *always* yields results, including an SSE, that would be obtained by fitting a complete factorial model of the type indicated in part **a** of Example 17.19. However, we would not expect the third- and fourth-order terms to contribute much to the model and would recommend a second-order model to fit the response surface. The second-order model in two independent variables is

$$y = \beta_0 + \beta_1 x_1 + \beta_2 x_1^2 + \beta_3 x_2 + \beta_4 x_2^2 + \beta_5 x_1 x_2 + \varepsilon$$

where

x_1 = Supply of raw material (in tons)

x_2 = Ratio of allocation

The SAS regression analysis printout obtained by fitting this model to the data of Example 17.19 is shown below. The estimates $\hat{\beta}_0 = -27.815$, $\hat{\beta}_1 = 5.944$, ..., $\hat{\beta}_5 = .746$ can be obtained from the printout. Hence, the second-order prediction equation relating supply of raw materials, S, and ratio of allocation, R, to profit per unit of raw material supply, y, is

$$\hat{y} = -27.815 + 5.944x_1 - .185x_1^2 - 7.762x_2 - 2.296x_2^2 + .746x_1 x_2$$

ANALYSIS OF VARIANCE

SOURCE	DF	SUM OF SQUARES	MEAN SQUARE	F VALUE	PROB > F
MODEL	5	63.50793651	12.70158730	4.895	0.0040
ERROR	21	54.49206349	2.59486017		
C TOTAL	26	118.00000			

ROOT MSE	1.610857	R-AQUARE	0.5382
DEP MEAN	20.66667	ADJ R-SQ	0.4283
C.V.	7.794469		

PARAMETER ESTIMATES

VARIABLE	DF	PARAMETER ESTIMATE	STANDARD ERROR	T FOR H0: PARAMETER = 0	PROB > |T|
INTERCEP	1	-27.81481481	23.80152168	-1.169	0.2557
S	1	5.94444444	2.64418353	2.248	0.0354
SS	1	-0.18518519	0.07306996	-2.534	0.0193
R	1	-7.76190476	5.04522969	-1.538	0.1389
RR	1	-2.29629630	1.33939441	-1.714	0.1012
SR	1	0.74603175	0.20294890	3.676	0.0014

17.21 Refer to Examples 17.19 and 17.20. Do the data provide sufficient information to indicate that the complete factorial model given in Example 17.19 contributes more information for the prediction of y than the second-order model in Example 17.20? The ANOVA table for the complete model is given below.

SOURCE	*df*	SS	MS
Supply	2	20.22	10.11
Ratio	2	8.22	4.11
Supply-Ratio interaction	4	46.22	11.56
Error	18	43.33	2.41
Total	26	118.00	

Solution

If the response to the question is "yes," then at least one of the parameters, β_6, β_7, or β_8, of the complete factorial model differs from 0 (i.e., they are needed in the model). Consequently, the null hypothesis, "The complete factorial model contributes no more information about y than that contributed by a second-order model" is equivalent to the hypothesis

$$H_0: \quad \beta_6 = \beta_7 = \beta_8 = 0$$

You will recall (from Section 13.4) that to test this hypothesis, we need to determine the drop in the sum of squares for error between the reduced model (i.e., the second-order model) and the complete model (i.e., the complete factorial model). From the ANOVA table above, SSE for the complete model is $SSE_2 = 43.33$. From Example 17.20, the reduced (second-order) model gives $SSE_1 = 54.492$. Therefore, the drop in SSE associated with β_6, β_7, and β_8, based on 3 df, is

$$\text{Drop} = SSE_1 - SSE_2 = 54.492 - 43.33 = 11.16$$

The F-statistic needed for the test is

$$F = \frac{\text{MS(Drop)}}{\text{MSE(Complete model)}} = \frac{11.16/3}{2.41} = 1.54$$

Since MS(Drop) is based on 3 df and MSE(Complete model) is based on 18 df, we compare the computed value of F with $F_{.05} = 3.16$, where $F_{.05}$ is the tabulated value of F for 3 and 18 df. Since the computed value of F (1.54) is less than the critical value, $F_{.05} = 3.16$, we cannot reject the null hypothesis that $\beta_6 = \beta_7 = \beta_8 = 0$. That is, there is insufficient evidence to indicate that the third- and fourth-order terms associated with β_6, β_7, and β_8 contribute information for the prediction of y.

Exercises

17.8 A production manager who supervises an assembly operation wants to investigate the effect of the incoming rate (parts per minute) x_1 of components and room temperature x_2 on the productivity (number of items produced per minute) y. The component parts approach the worker on a belt and return to the worker if not selected on the first trip past the assembly point. It is thought that an increase in the arrival rate of components has a positive effect on the assembly rate, up to a point, after which increases may annoy the assembler and reduce productivity. Similarly, it is suspected that lowering the room temperature is beneficial to a point, after which reductions may reduce productivity. The experimenter used the same assembly position for each worker. Thirty-two workers were used for the experiment, two each assigned to the 16 independent variable level combinations of a 4×4 factorial experiment. The data, in parts per minute averaged over a 5-minute period, are shown in the table.

		RATE OF INCOMING COMPONENTS, PARTS PER MINUTE (x_1)			
		40	50	60	70
ROOM TEMPERATURE, °F (x_2)	65	24.0, 23.8	25.6, 25.4	29.2, 29.4	28.4, 27.6
	70	25.0, 26.0	28.8, 28.8	31.6, 32.0	30.2, 30.0
	75	25.6, 25.0	27.6, 28.0	29.8, 28.6	28.0, 27.0
	80	24.0, 24.6	27.6, 26.2	27.6, 28.6	26.0, 24.4

a. Perform an analysis of variance for the data. Display the computed quantities in an ANOVA table.

b. Write the linear model implied by the analysis of variance. [HINT: For a quantitative variable recorded at four levels, main effects include terms for x, x^2, and x^3.]

c. Do the data provide sufficient evidence to indicate differences among the mean responses for the 16 treatments of the 4×4 factorial experiment? Test using $\alpha = .05$.

d. Do the data provide sufficient evidence to indicate an interaction between arrival rate x_1, and room temperature x_2 on worker productivity? Test using $\alpha = .05$.

e. Find the value of R^2 that would be obtained if you were to fit the linear model in part b to the data.

f. Explain why a regression analysis would be a useful addition to the inferential methods used in parts a-e.

17.9 A second-order model would be a reasonable choice to model the data of Exercise 17.8. To simplify the analysis, we will code the arrival rate and temperature values as follows:

$$x_1 = \frac{\text{Arrival rate} - 55}{5} \qquad x_2 = \frac{\text{Temperature} - 72.5}{2.5}$$

A printout of the SAS regression analysis is shown on the following page.

a. Write the second-order linear model for the response. Note the difference between this model and the ANOVA model in Exercise 17.8, part a.

b. Give the prediction relating the response y to the coded independent variables x_1 and x_2.

c. Why does the SSE given in the computer printout differ from the SSE obtained in Exercise 17.8?

d. Find the value of R^2 appropriate for your second-order model and interpret its value.

e. Do the data provide sufficient evidence to indicate that the complete factorial model provides more information for predicting y than a second-order model?

ANALYSIS OF VARIANCE

SOURCE	DF	SUM OF SQUARES	MEAN SQUARE	F VALUE	PROB > F
MODEL	5	130.80680	26.16136000	27.726	0.0001
ERROR	26	24.53320000	0.94358462		
C TOTAL	31	155.34000			

ROOT MSE	0.9713828	R-SQUARE	0.8421
DEP MEAN	27.325	ADJ R-SQ	0.8117
C.V.	3.554923		

PARAMETER ESTIMATES

VARIABLE	DF	PARAMETER ESTIMATE	STANDARD ERROR	T FOR H0: PARAMETER = 0	PROB > |T|
INTERCEP	1	29.85625000	0.34876060	85.607	0.0001
X1	1	0.56000000	0.07679456	7.292	0.0001
X2	1	-0.16250000	0.07679456	-2.116	0.0441
X1X2	1	-0.11350000	0.03434357	-3.305	0.0028
X1X1	1	-0.27500000	0.04292946	-6.406	0.0001
X1X2	1	-0.23125000	0.04292946	-5.387	0.0001

18
NONPARAMETRIC STATISTICS

SUMMARY

This chapter presented several *nonparametric techniques* for comparing one, two, or more populations. Such methods have wide applicability and are particularly useful when observations cannot be assigned specific values, but can be ranked. The techniques require fewer restrictive assumptions than their parametric counterparts, and allow for a comparison of the probability distributions, rather than specific parameters, of the populations of interest.

The *Wilcoxon rank sum test* may be used to compare two populations when the data arise from an independent sampling design; the *Wilcoxon signed rank test* is used to analyze data from a paired difference experiment. The *Kruskal-Wallis H test* uses data from a completely randomized design to compare p populations. The *Friedman F_r test* is appropriate for comparing p populations based on a randomized block design. *Spearman's rank correlation coefficient* provides a nonparametric measure of correlation between two variables.

18.1 SINGLE-POPULATION INFERENCES: THE SIGN TEST

Example

18.1 The Environmental Protection Agency (EPA) sets certain pollution guidelines for major industries. The EPA criterion for a particular company that discharges waste into a nearby river is that the median amount of pollution in water samples collected from the river may not exceed 5 parts per million (ppm). Responding to numerous complaints, the EPA takes 10 water samples from the river at the discharge point and measures the pollution level in each sample. The results (in ppm) are given below:

5.1   4.3   5.3   6.2   5.6   4.7   8.4   5.9   6.8   3.0

Do the data provide sufficient evidence to indicate that the median pollution level in water discharged at the plant exceeds 5 ppm? Test using $\alpha = .05$.

Solution

We want to test

H_0: $M = 5$
H_a: $M > 5$

using the sign test. The test statistic is

S = Number of sample observations that exceed 5
= 7

where S has a binomial distribution with parameters $n = 10$ and $p = .5$.

From Section 9.3, we know that the observed significance level (p-value) of the test is the probability that we observe a value of the test statistic S that is at least as contradictory to the null hypothesis as the computed value. For this one-sided case, the p-value is the probability that we observe a value of S greater than or equal to 7. We find the probability using the binomial table for $n = 10$ and $p = .5$ in Table II of Appendix B:

$$p\text{-Value} = P(S \geq 7) = 1 - P(S \leq 6)$$
$$= 1 - .8281$$
$$= .1719$$

Since the p-value, .1719, is larger than $\alpha = .05$, we cannot reject the null hypothesis. That is, there is insufficient evidence to indicate that the median pollution level of water discharged from the plant exceeds 5.

Exercise

18.1 *Scram* is the term used by nuclear engineers to describe a rapid emergency shutdown of a nuclear reactor. The nuclear industry has made a concerted effort to reduce significantly the number of unplanned scrams each year. The number of unplanned scrams at each of a random sample of 20 nuclear reactor units in a recent year are given below.

1	8	0	3	3	9	1	2	4	5
4	3	1	2	7	10	2	6	3	0

Test the hypothesis that the median number of unplanned scrams at nuclear reactor plants is less than 5. Use $\alpha = .10$.

18.2 COMPARING TWO POPULATIONS: WILCOXON RANK SUM TEST FOR INDEPENDENT SAMPLES

Examples

18.2 A savings and loan corporation is considering two possible locations for a new branch bank in a particular city. It is desired to determine whether a difference exists between the annual incomes for families in the two locations. Nine families from location A and seven families from location B were randomly selected, and their annual incomes (in thousands of dollars) were recorded as shown in the following table.

LOCATION A	LOCATION B
14.3	19.3
15.5	25.5
12.1	30.2
8.3	52.1
20.5	28.6
16.2	22.2
14.3	18.5
17.3	
24.3	

a. What assumptions would be required for the valid application of the independent samples t test to compare the population mean annual incomes of the two locations? Do you think the assumptions are reasonable in this situation?

b. Use the Wilcoxon rank sum test to see if there is a difference in the probability distributions of annual income in the two locations. Use $\alpha = .05$.

Solution

a. The independent samples t test for the difference between two population means requires the assumptions of independent samples selected from normal populations with equal variances. In this case, the assumption of normality of the population distributions may not be reasonable, since distributions of annual income are often markedly skewed to the right. It may thus be advisable to perform the nonparametric counterpart of the t test.

b. The Wilcoxon rank sum test for independent samples is a test of

H_0: The probability distributions corresponding to the annual incomes for families in both locations are identical

against

H_a: The probability distribution of annual incomes for location A is shifted to the right or to the left of the probability distribution of annual incomes for location B.

For $\alpha = .05$, the null hypothesis will be rejected if

$T_B \leqslant 41$ or $T_B \geqslant 78$,

where T_B is the rank sum of the incomes from the smaller sample (location B), and the critical values are obtained from part (a) of Table XI in the text.

To compute the value of the test statistic, T_B, we first rank all the sample observations as though they were selected from the same population:

LOCATION A		LOCATION B	
Observation	Rank	Observation	Rank
14.3	3.5	19.3	9
15.5	5	25.5	13
12.1	2	30.2	15
8.3	1	52.1	16
20.5	10	28.6	14
16.2	6	22.2	11
14.3	3.5	18.5	8
17.3	7		
24.3	12		

[Note that the two observations of 14.3 would have received ranks 3 and 4; thus, each is assigned their average rank of (3 + 4)/2 = 3.5.]

Now, the rank sum corresponding to the smaller sample is

$T_B = 9 + 13 + 15 + 16 + 14 + 11 + 8 = 86.$

This value of the test statistic lies in the rejection region; thus, we conclude that the distributions of annual income for the two locations are different.

18.3 Use the following data to test the hypothesis that the population distributions corresponding to A and B are identical, against the alternative that observations from population A tend to be smaller than the observations from population B. Use $\alpha = .05$.

A	B
2	12
8	7
7	6
12	7
5	9
0	4
3	4
	1

Solution

We will perform a Wilcoxon rank sum test of

H_0: The probability distributions corresponding to populations A and B are identical

against

H_a: The probability distribution for population A is shifted to the left of that for population B.

At $\alpha = .05$, we will reject the null hypothesis if $T_A \leqslant 41$, where T_A is the rank sum for the smaller sample, and the critical value for this one-sided test is obtained from part (b) of Table XI in the text.

We now pool the measurements from both samples and rank the measurements from smallest to largest.

A		B	
Observation	Rank	Observation	Rank
2	3	12	14.5
8	12	7	10
7	10	6	8
12	14.5	7	10
5	7	9	13
0	1	4	5.5
3	4	4	5.5
		1	2

Note that the tied observations are treated as follows: The two observations of 4 would have received ranks 5 and 6; thus, each is assigned the average rank of $(5 + 6)/2 = 5.5$. Similarly, the three observations tied at 7 would have received ranks 9, 10, and 11; thus, each observation receives the average rank of $(9 + 10 + 11)/3 = 10$.

The test statistic is the rank sum associated with the smaller sample:

$$T_A = 3 + 12 + 10 + 14.5 + 7 + 1 + 4 = 51.5$$

Since this value does not fall within the rejection region, there is insufficient evidence at the $\alpha = .05$ level to support the alternative hypothesis. We cannot conclude, on the basis of this sample information, that the distribution for population A lies to the left of the distribution for population B.

Exercise

18.2 A large banking institution has established management trainee programs in two different cities, A and B. Before the trainees are given their final bank assignments, they must take a final examination, which has 100 possible points. Seven trainees from City A and six trainees from City B were randomly selected, and their scores on the final examination were recorded:

CITY A	CITY B
93	92
57	90
68	68
45	57
79	68
77	80
63	

The banking institution wishes to compare the final examination scores for trainees in the two cities.

a. What assumptions are necessary in order to perform an independent samples t test for a difference in the mean final examination score attained by trainees in the two cities? Are the assumptions reasonable?

b. Use the Wilcoxon rank sum test to determine if there is a difference (at $\alpha = .10$) in the probability distributions of final examination scores for trainees in the two cities.

18.3 COMPARING TWO POPULATIONS: WILCOXON SIGNED RANK TEST FOR THE PAIRED DIFFERENCE EXPERIMENT

Example

18.4 Many large supermarket chains now produce their own goods for sale under a house label. They advertise that, although the house brands are of the same quality as the national brands, they can be sold at lower prices because of lower production costs. A comparison of the daily sales (number of units sold) of eleven products at a local supermarket produced the following data:

ITEM		NATIONAL BRAND	HOUSE BRAND
1.	Catsup	303	237
2.	Corn (canned)	504	428
3.	Bread	205	127
4.	Margarine	157	136
5.	Dog food	205	49
6.	Peaches (canned)	273	302
7.	Cola	394	147
8.	Green beans (frozen)	93	248
9.	Ice cream	188	188
10.	Cheese	126	147
11.	Beer	303	29

It is desired to compare the sales of the national brand and house brand products.

a. What type of experimental design is represented here?

b. Perform the (nonparametric) Wilcoxon signed rank test of the hypothesis that the probability distributions of the sales of national and house brands are identical. The alternative hypothesis of interest is that the sales of national brands tend to exceed those of house brands. Use $\alpha = .01$.

Solution

a. This is a paired difference experiment, and the analysis will be based on the differences between the pairs of measurements.

b. The Wilcoxon signed rank test for the paired difference design provides a test of

H_0: The probability distributions of the sales for national and house brand products are identical

against

H_a: The sales for national brands tend to exceed those for house brands.

To compute the value of the test statistic, we first obtain the ranks of the absolute values of the differences between the measurements; the calculations are shown in the following table.

PRODUCT	SALES: NATIONAL BRAND	SALES: HOUSE BRAND	DIFFERENCE (NATIONAL-HOUSE)	ABSOLUTE VALUE OF DIFFERENCE	RANK OF ABSOLUTE VALUE
1	303	237	66	66	4
2	504	428	76	76	5
3	205	127	78	78	6
4	157	136	21	21	1.5
5	205	49	156	156	8
6	273	302	-29	29	3
7	394	147	247	247	9
8	93	248	-155	155	7
9	188	188	0	0	(Eliminated)
10	126	147	-21	21	1.5
11	303	29	274	274	10

[Observe that the differences of zero are eliminated, since they do not contribute to the rank sums. In addition, ties in absolute differences receive the average of the ranks they would be assigned if they were unequal but successive measurements. Thus, the absolute differences tied at 21, which would have received ranks 1 and 2, are each assigned the average rank of $(1 + 2)/2 = 1.5$.]

For this one-sided test, the test statistic is T_-, the negative rank sum. This is because, if the alternative hypothesis is true, we expect most of the national minus house brand sale differences to be positive; thus, we would expect the *negative* rank sum T_- to be small if the alternative hypothesis is true. The critical value will be based on $n = 10$ paired observations and is obtained from Table XII of the text. Thus, at significance level $\alpha = .01$, the null hypothesis will be rejected if $T_- \leqslant 5$.

We now compute the negative rank sum, the sum of the ranks of the negative differences:

$T_- = 3 + 7 + 1.5 = 11.5.$

This value does not lie within the rejection region; there is insufficient evidence (at $\alpha = .01$) to conclude that the sales of national brands significantly exceed sales of the house brands.

Exercise

18.3 Refer to the following data, in which the costs of textbooks at a campus bookstore and an off-campus bookstore are compared.

	PRICE	
TEXTBOOK	Campus Bookstore	Off-Campus Bookstore
1	$27.95	$25.95
2	23.00	22.00
3	20.50	21.00
4	26.00	24.95
5	31.00	29.95
6	23.00	22.50
7	28.50	27.00
8	19.95	18.50
9	22.95	20.75
10	27.00	25.50

Perform an appropriate nonparametric statistical test of

H_0: The probability distributions of textbook prices are identical for the two bookstores

against

H_a: Textbook prices at the off-campus bookstore tend to be lower than the prices at the campus bookstore.

Use a significance level of $\alpha = .05$.

18.4 KRUSKAL-WALLIS *H* TEST FOR A COMPLETELY RANDOMIZED DESIGN

Examples

18.5 Use the table of critical values of the χ^2 distribution to find the following values of χ^2_α:

a. $\chi^2_{.05}$ with 8 degrees of freedom.

b. $\chi^2_{.01}$ with 15 degrees of freedom.

Solution

a. We first observe that the table of critical values of the χ^2 distribution in the text (Table XIII) gives values χ^2_α such that $P(\chi^2 > \chi^2_\alpha) = \alpha$. Now, at the intersection of the column labeled $\chi^2_{.05}$ and the row corresponding to 8 degrees of freedom, we find the entry 15.5073; thus, $P(\chi^2 > 15.5073) = .05$ when $df = 8$ (see figure on the next page).

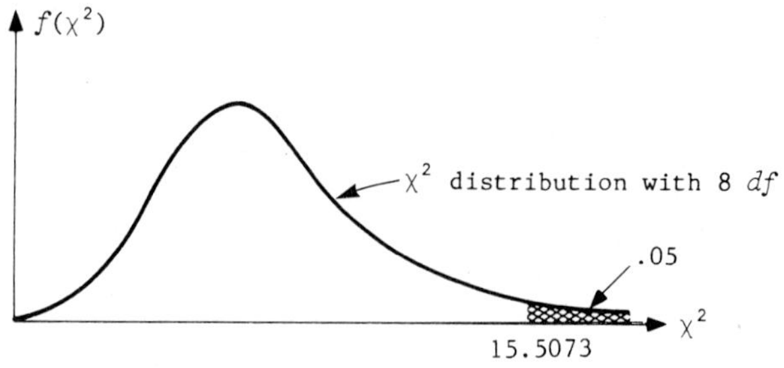

b. At the intersection of the $\chi^2_{.01}$ column and the row corresponding to 15 df, we locate the entry 30.5779. Thus, $P(\chi^2 > 30.5779) = .01$ when $df = 15$.

18.6 As part of an investigation of the cost of living indices in different areas of the country, random samples of recent college graduates in four cities were obtained. Their starting salaries (in thousands of dollars) are recorded below.

LOS ANGELES	CHICAGO	WASHINGTON, D.C.	BOSTON
18.2	15.9	14.8	17.1
16.8	16.2	16.1	15.9
15.9	16.9	17.1	17.2
19.3	15.8	16.8	17.0
17.9	16.8	15.9	16.5
17.0	17.1		

a. What type of experimental design is represented here? What assumptions are necessary for the analysis of these data using the methods of Chapter 17?

b. Use a nonparametric procedure to test for a difference in the probability distributions of starting salaries for recent college graduates in the four cities. Use $\alpha = .05$.

Solution

a. The data are from a completely randomized design, in which independent random samples were selected from each of the four populations of starting salaries to be compared. The analysis of variance F test of Chapter 17 requires the assumption that the four salary distributions are approximately normal, with equal variances. If we are unwilling to make these restrictive assumptions, then a nonparametric procedure may be preferred.

b. We will perform a Kruskal-Wallis test of

H_0: The probability distributions of the populations of starting salaries are identical for the four cities

against

H_a: At least two of the starting salary distributions differ.

At significance level α, the null hypothesis will be rejected if the value of the test statistic, H, exceeds χ^2_α with $(p - 1)$ degrees of freedom, where p is the number of independent samples upon which the test is based. Thus, in our example, with $\alpha = .05$ and $p - 1 = 3$ df, H_0 will be rejected if $H > 7.81473$.

To compute the value of H, it is necessary to obtain the rank sum for each of the four samples, where the rank of each observation is computed according to its relative magnitude when all four samples are combined. The rankings are shown in the following table.

LOS ANGELES		CHICAGO		WASHINGTON, D.C.		BOSTON	
Salary	Rank	Salary	Rank	Salary	Rank	Salary	Rank
18.2	21	15.9	4.5	14.8	1	17.1	17
16.8	11	16.2	8	16.1	7	15.9	4.5
15.9	4.5	16.9	13	17.1	17	17.2	19
19.3	22	15.8	2	16.8	11	17.0	14.5
17.9	20	16.8	11	15.9	4.5	16.5	9
17.0	14.5	17.1	17				
R_1 =	93.0	R_2 =	55.5	R_3 =	40.5	R_4 =	64.0

(Note that tied observations are handled in the usual manner, by assigning the average value of the ranks to each of the tied observations.)

The test statistic is

$$H = \frac{12}{n(n+1)} \sum_{j=1}^{p} \frac{R_j^2}{n_j} - 3(n+1),$$

where, for our example, $n_1 = 6$, $n_2 = 6$, $n_3 = 5$, $n_4 = 5$, $p = 4$, and $n = n_1 + n_2 + n_3 + n_4 = 22$. Substitution of these values and the rank sums computed in the table yields:

$$H = \frac{12}{22(23)}\left[\frac{(93.0)^2}{6} + \frac{(55.5)^2}{6} + \frac{(40.5)^2}{5} + \frac{(64.0)^2}{5}\right] - 3(23)$$

$$= 73.57 - 69 = 4.57$$

Since the computed value of H does not exceed the critical value of 7.81473, there is insufficient evidence to support the alternative hypothesis that the starting salary probability distributions differ in at least two of the four cities.

Exercises

18.4 Use the table of critical values of the χ^2 distribution to find the following values of χ^2_α:

a. $\chi^2_{.01}$ with 2 degrees of freedom.

b. $\chi^2_{.025}$ with 10 degrees of freedom.

18.5 A consumer testing agency has recorded the lifetimes (in complete months of service) before failure of the picture tubes for random samples of three name-brand television sets. The data are presented below:

BRAND A	BRAND B	BRAND C
32	41	48
25	39	44
40	36	43
31	47	51
35	45	41
29	34	52
37		
39		

a. Discuss the experimental design employed here. What assumptions are required for a parametric test of the hypothesis of equal means for the three lifetime distributions?

b. Use a nonparametric procedure to test for a difference in the probability distributions of the picture tube lifetimes for the three brands of television sets. Use a significance level of $\alpha = .10$.

18.5 THE FRIEDMAN F_r TEST FOR A RANDOMIZED BLOCK DESIGN

Example

18.7 The food editor of the newspaper in a large city wishes to compare the prices of meat for four local grocery stores. For six different types of meat, she recorded the price per pound at each of the four stores. The results are shown in the following table.

MEAT	PRICE PER POUND			
	Store 1	Store 2	Store 3	Store 4
Ground beef	\$2.29	\$2.09	\$2.15	\$2.09
Sirloin steak	4.09	3.79	3.89	3.69
Chuck roast	2.69	2.59	2.59	2.79
Pork chops	2.78	2.59	2.69	2.69
Chicken	1.69	1.55	1.59	1.59
Ham	2.69	2.49	2.59	2.49

a. Discuss the experimental design employed here.

b. Use a nonparametric test procedure to determine if there is a difference in the probability distributions of the meat prices among the four stores. Use $\alpha = .10$.

Solution

a. This represents a randomized block design with $b = 6$ blocks (types of meat), and $p = 4$ treatments (stores). The p population means may be compared using the analysis of variance techniques of Chapter 17. However, these parametric methods require the assumption that the four populations of meat prices have normal probability distributions and that their variances are all equal. In part b, we will perform the nonparametric counterpart, which requires no distributional assumptions.

b. The elements of the Friedman F_r test for this randomized block design are as follows:

H_0: The probability distributions of meat prices are identical for the four grocery stores

H_a: At least two of the four probability distributions of meat prices are different

At significance level α, the null hypothesis is rejected if the test statistic, F_r, exceeds the critical value χ^2_α with $(p - 1)$ degrees of freedom. For our example, we have $p - 1 = 4 - 1 = 3$ df and $\alpha = .10$; thus, H_0 will be rejected if $F_r > 6.25139$.

In order to compute the value of F_r, it is first required to rank the observations within each block (type of meat), and then obtain the rank sums for each of the four treatments (stores). The results are shown in the following table.

TYPE OF MEAT	STORE 1 Price	STORE 1 Rank	STORE 2 Price	STORE 2 Rank	STORE 3 Price	STORE 3 Rank	STORE 4 Price	STORE 4 Rank
Ground beef	\$2.29	4	\$2.09	1.5	\$2.15	3	\$2.09	1.5
Sirloin steak	4.09	4	3.79	2	3.89	3	3.69	1
Chuck roast	2.69	3	2.59	1.5	2.59	1.5	2.79	4
Pork chops	2.78	4	2.59	1	2.69	2.5	2.69	2.5
Chicken	1.69	4	1.55	1	1.59	2.5	1.59	2.5
Ham	2.69	4	2.49	1.5	2.59	3	2.49	1.5
	R_1 =	23	R_2 =	8.5	R_3 =	15.5	R_4 =	13.0

(Tied observations within blocks are assigned the average value of the ranks each tied observation would receive if they were unequal but successive measurements.)

The test statistic is computed as follows:

$$F_r = \frac{12}{bp(p+1)} \sum_{j=1}^{p} R_j^2 - 3b(p+1)$$

$$= \frac{12}{6(4)(5)}[(23)^2 + (8.5)^2 + (15.5)^2 + (13.0)^2] - 3(6)(5)$$

$$= 101.05 - 90 = 11.05$$

Since the calculated value of $F_r = 11.05$ exceeds the critical value of 6.25139, we conclude that the meat price distributions differ for at least two of the stores.

The food editor may now wish to compare meat price distributions for specific pairs of stores by performing the Wilcoxon signed rank test for paired difference designs.

Exercise

18.6 In the belief that most people are influenced by a product's price, label, and advertising, a local bar invited college students to participate in a beer taste test. Each rater was given three glasses of beer, in a randomized order. Glasses I and II contained the same, inexpensive local brand of beer, but students were told that Beer I was very expensive and that Beer II was not. Glass III contained a very expensive imported beer, but students were told nothing about it. Tasters were asked to rate each of the three beers on a scale from 1 to 20, with higher values indicating better taste. Ratings submitted by eight randomly selected students are shown in the following table.

STUDENT	RATINGS		
	Beer I	Beer II	Beer III
1	17	11	13
2	19	15	12
3	16	15	19
4	13	11	17
5	15	15	11
6	17	14	17
7	19	15	17
8	20	16	19

a. What type of experimental design is represented here?

b. Perform a nonparametric analysis to determine if there is a difference among the probability distributions of student ratings for the three beers. Use $\alpha = .05$.

18.6 SPEARMAN'S RANK CORRELATION COEFFICIENT

Examples

18.8 Most major universities offer a career placement service, which assists students in finding jobs upon graduation. A recruiter from a pharmaceutical company recently interviewed 12 graduating seniors interested in a sales position with his firm. He then ranked the candidates with respect to their performance on the interview (1 is the least favorable ranking, 12 is the most favorable), for comparison to their respective grade point averages. Results are shown below:

GRADE POINT AVERAGE	INTERVIEW RANK
3.91	10
3.73	8
3.52	12
3.41	9
3.27	11
3.03	4
2.97	5
2.91	7
2.70	6
2.53	2
2.35	3
2.21	1

a. Why would it be inappropriate to use the sample Pearson product moment correlation, r, to make an inference about the population correlation, ρ, between grade point average (GPA) and ranking on interview performance?

b. Compute a nonparametric measure of the correlation between GPA and ranking on interview performance for this sample data.

Solution

a. Inferences about the population correlation, ρ, based on the sample correlation, r, require the assumptions that the two random variables, GPA and ranking on interview performance, are normally distributed. This assumption is clearly violated for the variable which assigns ranks to the interview performances. Thus, a nonparametric measure of correlation is preferred.

b. The sample value of Spearman's rank correlation coefficient is computed as follows:

$$r_S = \frac{SS_{uv}}{\sqrt{SS_{uu}SS_{vv}}}$$

where the u's represent the ranks of the observations on the first variable (GPA, in our example) and the v's represent the ranks on the second variable (interview performance rating).

The rankings and preliminary computations are shown in the following table.

GPA	RANK ON GPA u_i	INTERVIEW RANK v_i	u_i^2	v_i^2	u_iv_i
3.91	12	10	144	100	120
3.73	11	8	121	64	88
3.52	10	12	100	144	120
3.41	9	9	81	81	81
3.27	8	11	64	121	88
3.03	7	4	49	16	28
2.97	6	5	36	25	30
2.91	5	7	25	49	35
2.70	4	6	16	36	24
2.53	3	2	9	4	6
2.35	2	3	4	9	6
2.21	1	1	1	1	1
	$\Sigma u_i = 78$	$\Sigma v_i = 78$	$\Sigma u_i^2 = 650$	$\Sigma v_i^2 = 650$	$\Sigma u_iv_i = 627$

(Note that the interview performances had already been ranked when we received the data.)

Now,

$$SS_{uv} = \Sigma u_i v_i - \frac{(\Sigma u_i)(\Sigma v_i)}{n} = 627 - \frac{(78)(78)}{12} = 120$$

$$SS_{uu} = \Sigma u_i^2 - \frac{(\Sigma u_i)^2}{n} = 650 - \frac{(78)^2}{12} = 143$$

$$SS_{vv} = \Sigma v_i^2 - \frac{(\Sigma v_i)^2}{n} = 650 - \frac{(78)^2}{12} = 143$$

Substitution yields:

$$r_S = \frac{SS_{uv}}{\sqrt{SS_{uu}SS_{vv}}} = \frac{120}{\sqrt{(143)(143)}} = \frac{120}{143} = .839$$

The positive value of r_S indicates a general tendency for the two variables to increase together; i.e., the higher a candidate's GPA, the higher his or her interview performance ranking tends to be.

18.9 Refer to Example 18.8. Use the shortcut formula to compute Spearman's rank correlation coefficient, r_S, for the GPA-interview ranking data.

Solution

The following shortcut formula can be used for computing r_S when there are no ties in the rankings of the observations:

$$r_S = 1 - \frac{6\Sigma d_i^2}{n(n^2 - 1)}$$

where $d_i = u_i - v_i$, the difference in rankings on GPA and interview performance for the ith individual.

The necessary computations are shown in the following table.

GPA	RANK ON GPA u_i	INTERVIEW RANK v_i	$d_i = u_i - v_i$	d_i^2
3.91	12	10	2	4
3.73	11	8	3	9
3.52	10	12	-2	4
3.41	9	9	0	0
3.27	8	11	-3	9
3.03	7	4	3	9
2.97	6	5	1	1
2.91	5	7	-2	4
2.70	4	6	-2	4
2.53	3	2	1	1
2.35	2	3	-1	1
2.21	1	1	0	0
				$\Sigma d_i^2 = 46$

Then we calculate

$$r_S = 1 - \frac{6\Sigma d_i^2}{n(n^2 - 1)} = 1 - \frac{6(46)}{12(12^2 - 1)} = 1 - .161$$

$$= .839, \text{ as obtained in Example 18.7.}$$

18.10 Refer to Examples 18.8-18.9. Perform a test (at significance level $\alpha = .01$) of the null hypothesis that the population Spearman rank correlation coefficient, ρ_S, between GPA and interview ranking is zero, against the alternative hypothesis that the two variables are positively correlated.

Solution

The elements of the test are the following:

H_0: $\rho_S = 0$
H_a: $\rho_S > 0$

For $\alpha = .01$, the rejection region (obtained by consulting Table XVI in the text) consists of all values of r_S such that $r_S > .703$. In Examples 18.8 and 18.9, we computed $r_S = .839$. This value is in the rejection region, and we conclude that GPA and interview ranking are positively correlated.

Exercises

18.7 It is a common belief among professional salesmen that their income tends to increase with experience. An industrial sales corporation has provided the following data for seven of its salesmen:

EXPERIENCE (Years)	ANNUAL INCOME (Thousands of Dollars)
11	42
9	37
5	51
1.5	21
3	19
7	28
1	30

a. Compute the value of Spearman's rank correlation coefficient, r_S, for these sample data.

b. Use the shortcut formula to calculate the value of r_S for the above data.

18.8 Refer to Exercise 18.7. Test the null hypothesis that the population Spearman rank correlation coefficient, ρ_S, is zero, against the alternative hypothesis that the random variables, years of experience and annual income, are positively correlated. Use $\alpha = .05$.

19
THE CHI-SQUARE TEST AND THE ANALYSIS OF CONTINGENCY TABLES

SUMMARY

This chapter presented methods of analyzing data from business experiments that give rise to *count* or *classificatory* data.

A χ^2 procedure may be applied to *one-dimensional* count data to test hypotheses that *multinomial probabilities* are equal to specified values. When count data are classified in a *two-dimensional contingency table*, the χ^2 statistic allows us to test the independence of the two methods of classifying the data.

The chapter concluded with some words of caution regarding common misuses of the χ^2 procedure.

19.1 ONE-DIMENSIONAL COUNT DATA: MULTINOMIAL DISTRIBUTION

Examples

19.1 Automotive manufacturers are now predicting that by 1995, 40% of all new cars purchased will be subcompacts, 35% will be compacts, 20% will be mid-sized, and the remaining 5% will be luxury models. A random sample of $n = 200$ auto purchases in June 1985 showed that 63 were subcompacts, 55 were compacts, 49 were mid-sized, and 33 were luxury. Does this sample evidence indicate a significant difference between the current and projected trends for the purchase of new automobiles? Use a significance level of $\alpha = .05$.

Solution

We define the following notation:

p_1 = true proportion of current new automobile purchases that are subcompacts,

p_2 = true proportion of current new car purchases that are compacts,

p_3 = true proportion of current new car purchases that are mid-sized,

p_4 = true proportion of current new car purchases that are luxury models.

The null hypothesis of interest is that the current purchasing trend is identical to that predicted for 1995; the alternative hypothesis is that there is a significant difference between current and projected trends. Thus, we have:

H_0: $p_1 = .40$, $p_2 = .35$, $p_3 = .20$, $p_4 = .05$
H_a: At least one of the proportions differs from its hypothesized value

Since our multinomial experiment consists of $k = 4$ possible outcomes, the test procedure will be based on a χ^2 distribution with $k - 1 = 4 - 1 = 3$ degrees of freedom. Thus, at $\alpha = .05$, the null hypothesis will be rejected for all values of the test statistic X^2 such that

$$X^2 > \chi^2_{.05} - 7.81473.$$

Now, if the null hypothesis were true (i.e., if $p_1 = .40$, $p_2 = .35$, $p_3 = .20$, and $p_4 = .05$), then we would expect to observe the following counts for each possible outcome of the experiment.

$$E(n_1) = np_{1,0} = 200(.40) = 80 \qquad E(n_2) = np_{2,0} = 200(.35) = 70$$

$$E(n_3) = np_{3,0} = 200(.20) = 40 \qquad E(n_4) = np_{4,0} = 200(.05) = 10$$

In order to measure the amount of disagreement between the sample data and the null hypothesis, we compute the test statistic:

$$X^2 = \frac{[n_1 - E(n_1)]^2}{E(n_1)} + \frac{[n_2 - E(n_2)]^2}{E(n_2)} + \frac{[n_3 - E(n_3)]^2}{E(n_3)} + \frac{[n_4 - E(n_4)]^2}{E(n_4)}$$

$$= \frac{(n_1 - 80)^2}{80} + \frac{(n_2 - 70)^2}{70} + \frac{(n_3 - 40)^2}{40} + \frac{(n_4 - 10)^2}{10}$$

$$= \frac{(63 - 80)^2}{80} + \frac{(55 - 70)^2}{70} + \frac{(49 - 40)^2}{40} + \frac{(33 - 10)^2}{10} = 61.75$$

The computed value of $X^2 = 61.75$ exceeds the critical value of $\chi^2 = 7.81473$. Thus, at significance level $\alpha = .05$, we reject the null hypothesis and conclude that the current trend in purchasing new automobiles differs significantly from that projected for 1995.

19.2 Refer to Example 19.1. Construct a 95% confidence interval for p_4, the proportion of current new car purchases that are for luxury models. Interpret the interval.

Solution

Recall from Chapter 8 that the general form of a 95% confidence interval for p_4 is given by

$$\hat{p}_4 \pm z_{.025}\sqrt{\frac{\hat{p}_4\hat{q}_4}{n}}$$

where, for this example,

$\hat{p}_4 = \dfrac{33}{200} = .165$, $\hat{q}_4 = 1 - \hat{p}_4 = 1 - .165 = .835$, $n = 200$, and

$z_{.025} = 1.96$.

Substitution yields the desired interval:

$$.165 \pm 1.96\sqrt{\frac{(.165)(.835)}{200}} = .165 \pm .051 \quad \text{or} \quad (.114, .216)$$

We estimate, with 95% confidence, that luxury models account for between 11.4% and 21.6% of current new car purchases. In other words, the projected proportion of .05 for 1995 is currently being exceeded.

19.3 A newspaper article in one metropolitan city stated that the top two auto rental companies accounted for 39% and 27%, respectively, of the total volume of car rentals in the city. A sample of 160 randomly selected incoming passengers at the city's airport provided the following information regarding their choice of a car rental agency:

CAR RENTAL AGENCY		
Company 1	Company 2	Other Auto Rental Company
50	39	71

Does the sample provide sufficient information to refute the percentages reported by the newspaper? Use $\alpha = .01$.

Solution

The relevant hypothesis test is composed of the following elements.

H_0: $p_1 = .39$, $p_2 = .27$, $p_3 = .34$
H_a: At least one proportion differs from its hypothesized value

where

p_1 = proportion of auto rentals in the city which are made with Company 1,

p_2 = proportion of auto rentals which are made with Company 2,

p_3 = proportion of auto rentals which are made with neither of the top two car rental agencies.

[Note that, since $p_1 + p_2 + p_3 = 1$, the hypothesized value of p_3 is given by

$$p_{3,0} = 1 - (p_{1,0} + p_{2,0}) = 1 - (.39 + .27) = 1 - .66 = .34.]$$

The multinomial experiment of selecting a car rental agency has $k = 3$ possible outcomes (Company 1, Company 2, Other). Thus, the test procedure is based on a χ^2 distribution with $k - 1 = 2$ df. At significance level $\alpha = .01$, the null hypothesis will be rejected if

$$X^2 > \chi^2_{.01} = 9.21034.$$

The expected counts that would be observed for each outcome, assuming the null hypothesis were true, are computed as follows:

$$E(n_1) = np_{1,0} = 160(.39) = 62.4$$
$$E(n_2) = np_{2,0} = 160(.27) = 43.2$$
$$E(n_3) = np_{3,0} = 160(.34) = 54.4$$

The test statistic is then given by

$$X^2 = \sum_{i=1}^{k} \frac{[n_i - E(n_i)]^2}{E(n_i)} = \frac{(50 - 62.4)^2}{62.4} + \frac{(39 - 43.2)^2}{43.2} + \frac{(71 - 54.4)^2}{54.4}$$
$$= 7.94$$

Since the value of X^2 does not lie in the rejection region, there is insufficient evidence (at significance level .01) to refute the newspaper's report.

Exercises

19.1 Before credit guidelines were tightened two years ago, it is known that 35% of the purchases at a large department store were paid for with a national credit card, 30% with the department store credit card, 15% with cash, and 20% by check. However, a recent survey, conducted to determine how shoppers at the department store prefer to pay for their purchases, produced the following results:

METHOD OF PAYMENT			
National Credit Card	Department Store Credit Card	Cash	Check
145	110	106	139

Do these survey results indicate (at α = .01) that the proportions of shoppers who prefer the various modes of payment have changed significantly from previous years?

19.2 A large food wholesaler has been experimenting with a new process to make "natural" peanut butter. They conducted a consumer survey which asked respondents to give their taste preference for one of the three types of peanut butter: standard "smooth" peanut butter; standard "crunchy" peanut butter; or new "natural" peanut butter. The results are shown below:

CONSUMER PREFERENCE		
Smooth	Crunchy	Natural
87	109	104

Is there sufficient evidence to indicate that a preference exists for one or more of the types of peanut butter? Use α = .05.

19.2 CONTINGENCY TABLES

Examples

19.4 A recent sample of 300 randomly selected purchases on the New York Stock Exchange were classified according to annual income of the buyer and the price of a single share of the purchased stock. The results are shown in the following table.

ANNUAL INCOME OF BUYER	PRICE PER SHARE: Less than $10	$10-$29.99	$30-$49.99	$50 or More	TOTALS
Less than $20,000	28	21	9	2	60
$20,000 - $50,000	29	43	45	24	141
More than $50,000	4	29	38	28	99
TOTALS	61	93	92	54	300

Test to see whether the buyer's annual income and price per share of stock are dependent. Use $\alpha = .05$.

Solution

We wish to conduct the following test for independence:

H_0: The price per share of a purchased stock is independent of the buyer's annual income

H_a: Price per share and annual income are dependent

The two-dimensional contingency table contains $r = 3$ rows and $c = 4$ columns. Thus, the χ^2 procedure will be based on $(r - 1)(c - 1) = (3 - 1)(4 - 1) = (2)(3) = 6$ df. At $\alpha = .05$, the rejection region consists of those values of the test statistic X^2 such that

$$X^2 > \chi^2_{.05} = 12.5916.$$

The next step is to compute the cell frequencies that we would expect to obtain if the null hypothesis were true, i.e., if the two classifications "price per share" and "annual income" were in fact independent. Thus, for example,

$$\hat{E}(n_{11}) = \frac{r_1c_1}{n} = \frac{(60)(61)}{300} = 12.20$$

$$\hat{E}(n_{12}) = \frac{r_1c_2}{n} = \frac{(60)(93)}{300} = 18.60$$

$$\vdots$$

$$\hat{E}(n_{33}) = \frac{r_3c_3}{n} = \frac{(99)(92)}{300} = 30.36$$

$$\hat{E}(n_{34}) = \frac{r_3c_4}{n} = \frac{(99)(54)}{300} = 17.82$$

All of the observed and estimated expected (in parentheses) cell counts are shown in the table below.

ANNUAL INCOME	PRICE PER SHARE			
	Less than $10	$10-$29.99	$30-$49.99	$50 or More
Less than $20,000	28 (12.20)	21 (18.60)	9 (18.40)	2 (10.80)
$20,000 - $50,000	29 (28.67)	43 (43.71)	45 (43.24)	24 (25.38)
More than $50,000	4 (20.13)	29 (30.69)	38 (30.36)	28 (17.82)

Then the value of the test statistic is calculated as follows:

$$X^2 = \sum_{i=1}^{3} \sum_{j=1}^{4} \frac{[n_{ij} - \hat{E}(n_{ij})]^2}{\hat{E}(n_{ij})}$$

$$= \frac{(28 - 12.20)^2}{12.20} + \frac{(21 - 18.60)^2}{18.60} + \frac{(9 - 18.40)^2}{18.40} + \cdots$$

$$+ \frac{(29 - 30.69)^2}{30.69} + \frac{(38 - 30.36)^2}{30.36} + \frac{(28 - 17.82)^2}{17.82}$$

$$= 53.66$$

Since $X^2 = 53.66$ exceeds the critical value of $\chi^2 = 12.5916$, there is sufficient evidence (at $\alpha = .05$) to conclude that the price per share of a purchased stock and the buyer's annual income are dependent.

19.5 An automobile supply and repair shop has compiled the following information from a random sample of 67 recent work orders:

TYPE OF CAR	TYPE OF WORK REQUIRED				
	Brakes	Cooling System	Engine Repair	Other	TOTALS
Foreign	6	8	12	6	32
Domestic	15	4	10	6	35
TOTALS	21	12	22	12	67

Is there evidence (at $\alpha = .01$) of a relationship between the type of car and the type of repair work required?

Solution

The relevant hypothesis test consists of the following elements.

H_0: Type of repair work required is independent of the type of car

H_a: Type of repair work and type of car are dependent

The test will be based on a χ^2 distribution with $(r - 1)(c - 1) = (2 - 1)(4 - 1) = 3$ df, since the contingency table has $r = 2$ rows and $c = 4$ columns. Thus, at $\alpha = .01$, H_0 will be rejected if

$X^2 > \chi^2_{.01} = 11.3449.$

Calculation of the estimated expected cell frequencies proceeds as follows:

$$\hat{E}(n_{11}) = \frac{r_1 c_1}{n} = \frac{(32)(21)}{67} = 10.03$$

$$\hat{E}(n_{12}) = \frac{r_1 c_2}{n} = \frac{(32)(12)}{67} = 5.73$$

$$\vdots$$

$$\hat{E}(n_{24}) = \frac{r_2 c_4}{n} = \frac{(35)(12)}{67} = 6.27$$

The observed estimated expected cell frequencies are shown in the following table.

TYPE OF CAR	TYPE OF WORK REQUIRED			
	Brakes	Cooling System	Engine Repair	Other
Foreign	6 (10.03)	8 (5.73)	12 (10.51)	6 (5.73)
Domestic	15 (10.97)	4 (6.27)	10 (11.49)	6 (6.27)

The test statistic is then computed as follows:

$$X^2 = \sum_{i=1}^{2} \sum_{j=1}^{4} \frac{[n_{ij} - \hat{E}(n_{ij})]^2}{\hat{E}(n_{ij})}$$

$$= \frac{(6 - 10.03)^2}{10.03} + \frac{(8 - 5.73)^2}{5.73} + \cdots + \frac{(10 - 11.49)^2}{11.49} + \frac{(6 - 6.27)^2}{6.27}$$

$$= 5.25$$

At significance level $\alpha = .01$, this value of the test statistic does not lie within the rejection region. We cannot conclude that the type of car and the type of repair work required are dependent.

Exercises

19.3 A banking institution in a large city has conducted a survey to investigate attitudes about borrowing money. Each of 300 randomly selected savings account customers in the 20-35 year age group was asked to classify his or her own attitude toward borrowing, and also the attitude of his or her parents toward borrowing, into one of the following categories:

1) Never borrow money.
2) Borrow money only in emergency situations or to make large purchases.
3) Borrow money to solve occasional, temporary cash-flow problems.
4) Borrow money as necessary to meet regular obligations.

The responses are classified in the following table.

ATTITUDE OF RESPONDENT	ATTITUDE OF PARENTS			
	1	2	3	4
1	50	5	5	5
2	30	40	10	5
3	25	10	30	20
4	15	15	10	25

Test to determine if there is a relationship (at $\alpha = .05$) between the attitudes of the respondents and the attitudes of parents toward borrowing money.

19.4 An automobile association in a particular state conducted a survey of gasoline stations to obtain information about the availability of weekend service. The results are presented in the following table.

Is there sufficient evidence to conclude that the availability of weekend service and type of station are related? Use a significance level of $\alpha = .01$.

TYPE OF STATION	WEEKEND SERVICE			
	Open Saturday Only	Open Sunday Only	Open Saturday and Sunday	Open Neither Day
Major Oil Companies	12	7	3	28
Independent Stations	11	3	10	10

20
DECISION ANALYSIS

SUMMARY

This chapter discussed decision-making methods which take into account the gains and losses associated with alternative actions, and the probabilities of the occurrences of these gains and losses.

Every decision-making problem can be classified into one of three categories:

1. decision making under certainty
2. decision making under uncertainty
3. decision making under conflict

This text emphasizes the basic concepts required for *decision making under uncertainty*; each problem in this category contains four common elements: *actions*, *states of nature*, *outcomes*, and the *objective variable*.

After summarizing the elements of a decision problem in a *payoff table* or an *opportunity loss table*, the decision maker may select a course of action based on one of four criteria. The *expected payoff* and *expected utility* criteria require that a probability distribution be assigned to the states of nature.

On the basis of available sample information, the *prior probabilities* of the states of nature can be revised using Bayes' rule to determine *posterior probabilities*. The expected payoff for each action can be computed using the posterior probabilities; the *expected payoff criterion using posterior probabilities* chooses the action with the maximum expected payoff. The *expected utility criterion* can be extended in the same manner to incorporate sample information. The *expected value of perfect information* is the maximum expected value of sample information and is an upper bound on the amount a decision maker is willing to pay for sample information. Since sample information is never perfect, a realistic assessment of the expected worth of sample information is needed. To be of use to the decision maker, the assessment must be made *before* the sample is taken; accordingly, the analysis is known as *preposterior analysis*. A better approach to some decision problems is to allow an infinite number of states of nature; a two-action decision problem with linear payoff functions is particularly amenable to such an approach.

20.1 THREE TYPES OF DECISION PROBLEMS

20.2 DECISION MAKING UNDER UNCERTAINTY: BASIC CONCEPTS

Examples

20.1 Term life insurance is an attractive option for young families, since it offers more coverage per premium dollar than whole life policies. A recently married man has an opportunity to purchase a \$10,000 one-year term life insurance policy for \$200. If he does not purchase the policy, he will deposit the \$200 in a savings account that yields 6% annual interest. Identify the elements of this decision problem.

Solution

1. The *actions*, or alternatives, which the man has chosen to consider are: buy the insurance policy for \$200, or deposit the \$200 in a savings account.
2. The *states of nature*, upon which the outcome of the action depends, are that the man is either alive or deceased at the end of one year.
3. The *outcomes*, or consequences, can be enumerated by considering the result of each possible action/state of nature combination. Thus, if the man buys the policy (action) and is alive at the end of one year (state of nature), the outcome is -\$200, the cost of the policy. If the \$200 is deposited in a savings account and the man is alive at the end of one year, the outcome is \$12 (i.e., 6% of \$200). The remaining two outcomes are determined in a similar manner.
4. In this example, the motive (or objective) is return on investment; thus, the *objective variable*, used to express the decision outcomes, is measured in terms of dollars.

20.2 Refer to Example 20.1. Determine the payoff table for the decision problem.

Solution

Each of the possible actions is associated with a row of the table; each state of nature is associated with a column. The values in the body of the table are the outcomes which result from each action/state of nature combination. For example, if the man purchases a policy and dies within the year, his beneficiaries receive $10,000; thus, the return on investment is $10,000 - $200 = $9,800. The complete payoff table is shown below.

		STATE OF NATURE	
		Man alive at end of year	Man deceased at end of year
ACTION	Purchase $10,000 policy	-$200	$9800
	Deposit $200 in savings account	$12	$12

20.3 Refer to Example 20.1. Construct a decision tree for the insurance policy decision problem.

Solution

The decision tree for this example is shown below:

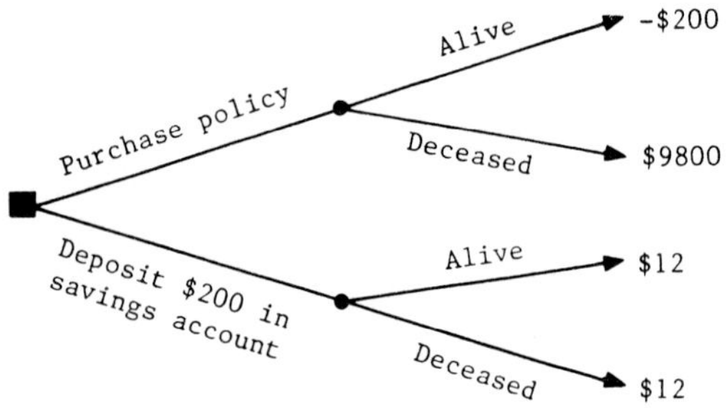

At the symbol ■, the man chooses between two possible actions, and then moves along the corresponding branch of the tree. The branch to be followed at a chance fork, denoted by ●, will be determined by the chance occurrence of one of the states of nature. The outcomes of each action/state of nature combination are depicted at the ends of the respective branches.

Note that the payoff table and the decision tree both convey the same information; only the manner of presentation differs.

Exercises

20.1 Give an example of a problem in your major area which involves decision making under uncertainty. Identify the actions, states of nature, outcomes, and the objective variable.

20.2 Identify the elements of the decision problems described below:

a. A floral shop has an opportunity to purchase a large shipment of injured or damaged plants at a much reduced price. Each plant that can be nursed to good health can be sold for a large profit; if a plant's condition does not improve, it cannot be sold.

b. Private ticket agencies often buy large quantities of tickets to special sporting events, concerts, etc., with the intention of selling them at higher prices. However, in order to acquire tickets for the best seats, the agency often must purchase them months in advance of the event, before the demand for the tickets can be determined. If the event is not as popular as anticipated, the agency may have to take losses on unsold tickets, or tickets sold at reduced prices.

20.3 Refer to Exercise 20.2(a). Suppose that the cost to the florist for a single injured plant is $3. If the condition of the plant improves, it can be sold for $12, yielding a profit of $12 - $3 = $9 to the florist. Otherwise, the plant cannot be sold and the florist makes a "profit" of -$3 (i.e., a loss).

a. Construct a payoff table for this decision problem.

b. Illustrate the decision problem by means of a decision tree.

20.3 TWO WAYS OF EXPRESSING OUTCOMES: PAYOFFS AND OPPORTUNITY LOSSES

Examples

20.4 Refer to Example 20.2. Convert the payoff table for the insurance decision problem to an opportunity loss table.

Solution

To find the opportunity loss for a particular action/state of nature combination, we subtract the payoff for that combination from the maximum payoff that could have occurred for the same state of nature. This implies that the opportunity loss associated with the maximum payoff in a column must be zero.

For the payoff table of Example 20.2, the maximum payoff for the state of nature "alive at end of year" occurs for the action "deposit \$200 in a savings account"; thus, the opportunity loss for this particular action/state of nature combination is \$0. Similarly, the opportunity loss for the combination "deceased/purchase policy" is \$0.

The remaining two opportunity losses are obtained by subtraction as described previously:

For "alive/purchase policy" combination,

opportunity loss = \$12 - (-\$200) = \$212;

For "deceased/deposit \$200 in savings account" combination,

opportunity loss = \$9800 - \$12 = \$9788.

The completed opportunity loss table is as follows:

		STATE OF NATURE	
		Man alive at end of year	Man deceased at end of year
ACTION	Purchase \$10,000 policy	\$212	\$0
	Deposit \$200 in savings account	\$0	\$9788

20.5 The operator of a news stand has the option of buying as many as fifteen newspapers for resale at the stand. Papers cost him ten cents each, and he sells them for twenty-five cents each; newspapers that are unsold during the day are worthless. Past experience indicates that he always sells at least ten newspapers per day. Set up the payoff table for this decision problem.

Solution

The actions to be considered by the operator represent the possible numbers of newspapers he may purchase: 10, 11, 12, 13, 14, or 15. The states of nature correspond to the numbers of newspapers he would be able to sell (i.e., the demand): 10, 11, 12, 13, 14, or 15. (Note that we have incorporated the information that he will always be able to buy and sell at least 10 newspapers.)

Now, if the operator buys 10 papers and sells all of them, his net profit is:

Amount received in sales - Cost of papers to operator

$$= 10(\$.25) - 10(\$.10)$$
$$= \$2.50 - \$1.00$$
$$= \$1.50$$

In addition, if the operator buys 10 papers and the demand is for more than 10 papers, his profit is still only \$1.50, since he cannot sell more papers than he has on hand.

As another example, assume that the operator buys 14 papers and sells only 12; his net profit is then:

$$12(\$.25) - 14(\$.10) = \$3.00 - \$1.40 = \$1.60$$

The payoff table showing the outcome (in dollars) for each action/ state of nature combination is shown below:

		STATE OF NATURE (DEMAND)					
		10	11	12	13	14	15
ACTION (BUY)	10	1.50	1.50	1.50	1.50	1.50	1.50
	11	1.40	1.65	1.65	1.65	1.65	1.65
	12	1.30	1.55	1.80	1.80	1.80	1.80
	13	1.20	1.45	1.70	1.95	1.95	1.95
	14	1.10	1.35	1.60	1.85	2.10	2.10
	15	1.00	1.25	1.50	1.75	2.00	2.25

20.6 Refer to Example 20.5. Convert the payoff table for the news stand example to an opportunity loss table.

Solution

The opportunity loss associated with the maximum payoff in each column is zero. For any other payoff, the corresponding opportunity loss is computed by subtracting that particular payoff from the maximum payoff within the column in which it is located. The resulting opportunity loss table is shown below:

		STATE OF NATURE (DEMAND)					
		10	11	12	13	14	15
ACTION (BUY)	10	0	.15	.30	.45	.60	.75
	11	.10	0	.15	.30	.45	.60
	12	.20	.10	0	.15	.30	.45
	13	.30	.20	.10	0	.15	.30
	14	.40	.30	.20	.10	0	.15
	15	.50	.40	.30	.20	.10	0

Observe, for example, that if the demand on a particular day is for 13 newspapers, and the news stand operator has decided to purchase 11 papers, then he has lost the opportunity to make an additional \$.30 profit.

20.7 Refer to Examples 20.1 and 20.2. Suppose that the following third alternative is also available to the man: He can buy a \$200 government bond that pays 4½% annual interest.

a. Expand the payoff table of Example 20.2 to include this possible action.

b. Explain why the action of buying the government bond is inadmissible.

Solution

a. If the man buys the government bond and is still alive at the end of the year, his return on investment is 4½% of \$200, or \$9. Similarly, his heirs will receive a return of \$9 if he purchases the bond and dies during the year. Hence, the expanded payoff table is as shown below.

		STATE OF NATURE	
		Man alive at end of year	Man deceased at end of year
ACTION	Purchase \$10,000 policy	-\$200	\$9800
	Deposit \$200 in savings account	\$12	\$12
	Purchase \$200 government bond	\$9	\$9

b. Note that the action "deposit \$200 in savings account (a_2)" *dominates* the action "purchase \$200 government bond (a_3)," because, for both possible states of nature the payoff for action a_2 is greater than the payoff for action a_3. Thus, action a_3 is *inadmissible* and should be eliminated from consideration.

Exercises

20.4 Refer to Exercise 20.3. Convert the payoff table for this decision problem to an opportunity loss table.

20.5 Consider the following payoff table:

		STATE OF NATURE			
		S_1	S_2	S_3	S_4
ACTION	a_1	10	8	6	4
	a_2	9	7	6	0
	a_3	12	-1	0	2
	a_4	6	6	6	6

a. Are there any inadmissible actions? Explain your reasoning.

b. Construct an opportunity loss table for the problem.

20.4 CHARACTERIZING THE UNCERTAINTY IN DECISION PROBLEMS

20.5 SOLVING THE DECISION PROBLEM USING THE EXPECTED PAYOFF CRITERION

Examples

20.8 Refer to Example 20.2. Historical evidence accumulated by actuaries has shown that only 1½% of all married men in this man's age group do not live through the next year. Use this information to determine which action produces the maximum expected payoff.

Solution

We will use the available relative frequency information to assign a probability of .015 to the state of nature "Man is deceased at end of year" and a probability of 1 - .015 = .985 to the state of nature

"Man is alive at end of year." Our assessment of the probability distribution for the states of nature is reflected in the payoff table:

		STATE OF NATURE	
		Man is alive at end of year (.985)	Man is deceased at end of year (.015)
ACTION	a_1: Purchase \$10,000 policy	-\$200	\$9800
	a_2: Deposit \$200 in savings account	\$12	\$12

The expected payoff for action a_1 is given by

$$EP(a_1) = \Sigma xp(x),$$

where x is the payoff and $p(x)$ is the probability associated with the corresponding state of nature. Thus,

$$EP(a_1) = (-\$200)(.985) + (\$9800)(.015) = -\$50.$$

Similarly, the expected payoff for action a_2 is

$$EP(a_2) = (\$12)(.985) + (\$12)(.015) = \$12.$$

Now, using the expected payoff criterion, the man should choose action a_2 (i.e., deposit \$200 in a savings account at 6% interest), because this choice will produce the largest expected payoff.

20.9 Refer to Example 20.5. Past records kept by the news stand operator indicate the following probability distribution for the daily demand for newspapers:

STATE (Demand)	10	11	12	13	14	15
P(State will occur)	.1	.2	.2	.2	.2	.1

Which action would you recommend to the operator, on the basis of the expected payoff criterion?

Solution

For convenience, we reproduce the payoff table computed in Example 20.5, and show in parentheses the probabilities of occurrence of each state of nature:

			STATE OF NATURE (DEMAND)					
			10 (.1)	11 (.2)	12 (.2)	13 (.2)	14 (.2)	15 (.1)
ACTION (BUY)	a_1:	10	1.50	1.50	1.50	1.50	1.50	1.50
	a_2:	11	1.40	1.65	1.65	1.65	1.65	1.65
	a_3:	12	1.30	1.55	1.80	1.80	1.80	1.80
	a_4:	13	1.20	1.45	1.70	1.95	1.95	1.95
	a_5:	14	1.10	1.35	1.60	1.85	2.10	2.10
	a_6:	15	1.00	1.25	1.50	1.75	2.00	2.25

The expected payoffs can then be computed as follows:

$$EP(a_1) = 1.50(.1) + 1.50(.2) + 1.50(.2) + 1.50(.2) + (1.50(.2) + 1.50(.1)$$
$$= 1.50$$

$$EP(a_2) = 1.40(.1) + 1.65(.2) + \cdots + 1.65(.2) + 1.65(.1)$$
$$= 1.625$$

$$EP(a_3) = 1.30(.1) + 1.55(.2) + \cdots + 1.80(.2) + 1.80(.1)$$
$$= 1.70$$

In a similar manner, you can show that the expected payoffs associated with the remaining three actions are:

$EP(a_4) = 1.725$, $EP(a_5) = 1.70$, $EP(a_6) = 1.625$.

Since action a_4 leads to the largest expected payoff, \$1.725, the news stand operator would be advised to purchase 13 papers daily, according to the expected payoff criterion.

Exercises

20.6 Refer to Example 20.4. Use the opportunity loss table for the insurance decision problem to find the expected loss for each action. (Assume that the probability is only .015 that the man will die during the next year.) Then select the action that produces the minimum expected opportunity loss. Compare your result with the decision obtained using the expected payoff criterion.

20.7 Refer to Example 20.9. Suppose that the news stand operator's records indicate the following probability distribution for the daily demand for newspapers:

STATE (Demand)	10	11	12	13	14	15
P(State will occur)	.3	.3	.1	.1	.1	.1

a. Use the expected payoff criterion to determine the best action.

b. Compare the result obtained in part a with that obtained in Example 20.9. Comment on the importance of an accurate assessment of the probability distribution for the possible states of nature.

20.8 Consider the following payoff table:

		STATE OF NATURE		
		S_1	S_2	S_3
	a_1	10,000	-1000	3500
ACTION	a_2	6000	5000	4000
	a_3	6000	6000	3000

For each of the following probability distributions for the states of nature, determine the action that produces the largest expected payoff:

a. $P(S_1) = .4$, $P(S_2) = .2$, $P(S_3) = .4$.

b. $P(S_1) = .5$, $P(S_2) = .4$, $P(S_3) = .1$.

20.6 THE EXPECTED UTILITY CRITERION

20.7 CLASSIFYING DECISION MAKERS BY THEIR UTILITY FUNCTIONS

Examples

20.10 The following is the payoff table for the insurance decision problem described in Example 20.2:

		STATE OF NATURE	
		Man alive at end of year	Man deceased at end of year
ACTION	a_1: Purchase \$10,000 policy	-\$200	\$9800
	a_2: Deposit \$200 in savings account	\$12	\$12

We now assign the following utility values as outcomes for this example (the probabilities assigned to the states of nature are shown in parentheses):

		STATE OF NATURE	
		Man alive at end of year (.985)	Man deceased at end of year (.015)
ACTION	a_1: Purchase \$10,000 policy	0	1
	a_2: Deposit \$200 in savings account	.02	.02

a. Interpret the utility values shown in the table.

b. Determine which action should be taken, based on the expected utility criterion.

Solution

a. The minimum payoff in the table (-\$200) receives a utility value of 0; the maximum payoff (\$9800) receives a utility value of 1.

The utility value .02 assigned to the payoff of \$12 represents the probability that causes us to have no preference between

1) receiving \$12 with certainty, and

2) participating in a gamble in which we can win \$9800 (i.e., receive the maximum payoff) with probability .02, or lose \$200 (i.e., receive the minimum payoff) with probability .98.

b. The expected utilities are computed as follows:

$$EU(a_i) = \sum_{\substack{\text{all states}\\ \text{of nature}}} \begin{pmatrix}\text{Utility of}\\ \text{action } a_i\text{/state of}\\ \text{nature combination}\end{pmatrix}\begin{pmatrix}\text{Probability of}\\ \text{the state}\\ \text{of nature}\end{pmatrix}$$

Thus,

$$EU(a_1) = 0(.985) + 1(.015) = .015$$

and

$$EU(a_2) = .02(.985) + .02(.015) = .02.$$

The expected utility criterion tells us to select action a_2, which has the higher expected utility.

20.11 Refer to Example 20.5. Suppose the news stand operator uses the following function:

$$U(x) = \frac{\sqrt{x + .5}}{1.7}, \quad -.5 < x < 2.5$$

Which action will the operator choose, on the basis of the expected utility criterion? (The payoff table for this decision problem is reproduced below for convenience. The probability distribution for the states of nature is shown in parentheses.)

		STATE OF NATURE (DEMAND)					
		10 (.1)	11 (.2)	12 (.2)	13 (.2)	14 (.2)	15 (.1)
ACTION (BUY)	a_1: 10	1.50	1.50	1.50	1.50	1.50	1.50
	a_2: 11	1.40	1.65	1.65	1.65	1.65	1.65
	a_3: 12	1.30	1.55	1.80	1.80	1.80	1.80
	a_4: 13	1.20	1.45	1.70	1.95	1.95	1.95
	a_5: 14	1.10	1.35	1.60	1.85	2.10	2.10
	a_6: 15	1.00	1.25	1.50	1.75	2.00	2.25

Solution

The first step is to convert the payoff table from monetary units (dollars, x) to utility units by means of the utility function. Thus, for example,

$$U(1.50) = \frac{\sqrt{1.50 + .5}}{1.7} = .83,$$

$$U(1.40) = \frac{\sqrt{1.40 + .5}}{1.7} = .81,$$

$$U(1.65) = \frac{\sqrt{1.65 + .5}}{1.7} = .86.$$

The entire utility value table is shown below:

		STATE OF NATURE (DEMAND)					
		10 (.1)	11 (.2)	12 (.2)	13 (.2)	14 (.2)	15 (.1)
ACTION (BUY)	a_1: 10	.83	.83	.83	.83	.83	.83
	a_2: 11	.81	.86	.86	.86	.86	.86
	a_3: 12	.79	.84	.89	.89	.89	.89
	a_4: 13	.77	.82	.87	.92	.92	.92
	a_5: 14	.74	.80	.85	.90	.95	.95
	a_6: 15	0	.78	.83	.88	.93	1

(Recall that the minimum and maximum payoffs are assigned utility values of 0 and 1, respectively.)

It is now required to compute the expected utility for each action, using the formula presented in the previous example. Thus, for example,

$$EU(a_1) = .83(.1) + .83(.2) + .83(.2) + .83(.2) + .83(.2) + .83(.1) = .83,$$

$$EU(a_2) = .81(.1) + .86(.2) + .86(.2) + .86(.2) + .86(.2) + .86(.1) = .855,$$

$$EU(a_3) = .79(.1) + .84(.2) + .89(.2) + .89(.2) + .89(.2) + .89(.1) = .87.$$

Similarly, you can verify that

$$EU(a_4) = .875, \quad EU(a_5) = .869, \quad EU(a_6) = .784.$$

According to the expected utility criterion, the news stand operator should choose action a_4 (i.e., buy 13 newspapers), because it has the highest expected utility.

20.12 Graph each of the following utility functions and classify the decision maker's attitude toward risk.

a. $U(x) = \dfrac{.5x^2 + .1x}{13}, \quad 0 \leqslant x \leqslant 5$

b. $U(x) = \dfrac{x}{10}, \quad 0 \leqslant x \leqslant 10$

c. $U(x) = \dfrac{\sqrt{x + 50}}{20}, \quad -50 \leqslant x \leqslant 350$

Solution

a.

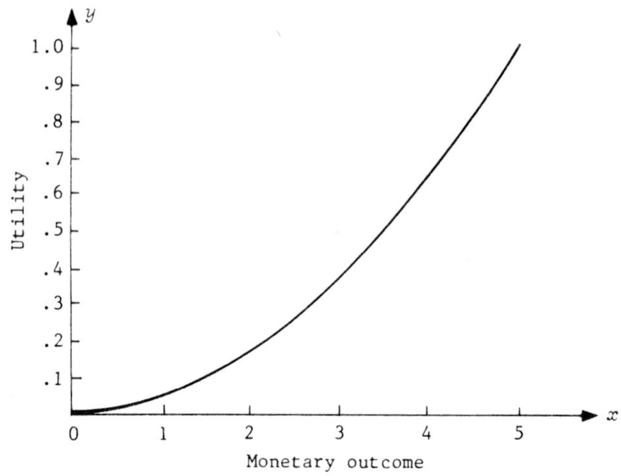

The shape of the utility function is convex, and thus represents a risk-taking attitude of the decision maker.

b.

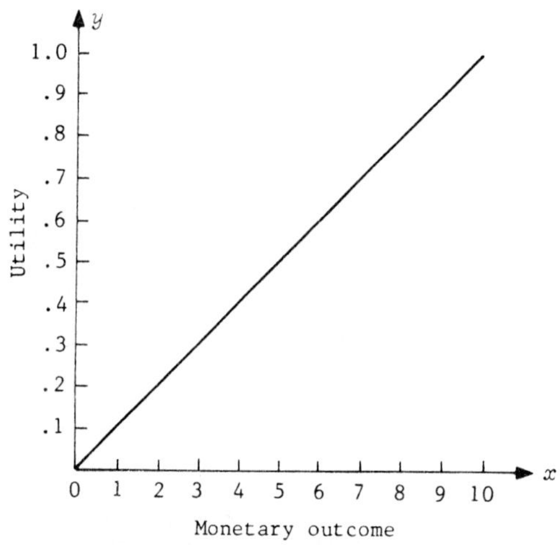

This utility function graphs as a straight line, which characterizes a risk-neutral decision maker.

c.

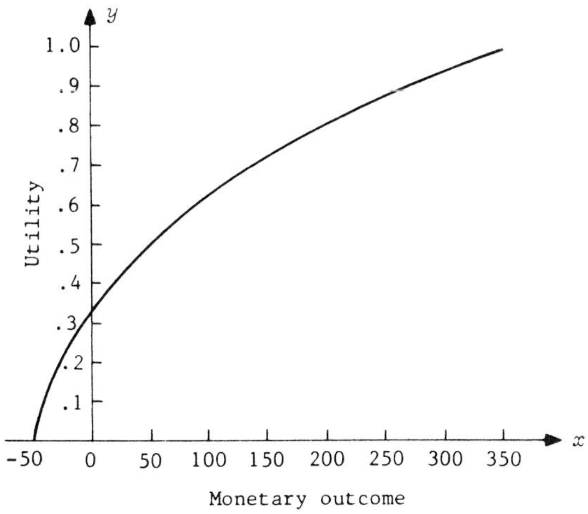

This utility function is concave, and the decision maker would thus be classified as a risk avoider.

Exercises

20.9 Consider the following payoff table and corresponding utility table:

		STATE OF NATURE	
		S_1	S_2
ACTION	a_1	190	190
	a_2	120	310

Payoff Table

		STATE OF NATURE	
		S_1	S_2
ACTION	a_1	.6	.6
	a_2	0	1

Utility Table

If the probability that state of nature S_1 occurs is .6, determine the optimal action under the expected utility criterion.

20.10 Refer to Exercise 20.9. Graph the utility function and classify the decision maker's attitude toward risk.

20.8 REVISING STATE OF NATURE PROBABILITIES: BAYES' RULE

Examples

20.13 An assembly machine in a factory production line is known to operate at either a 1% or a 5% defective rate. If the defective rate is determined to be 5%, the machine is shut down and readjusted. The 5% defective rate is known to occur 20% of the time. A random sample of 10 parts from the past hour's production results in two defectives. Find the posterior probability that the machine is operating at a 5% defective rate, given two defectives in a random sample of ten.

Solution

Define the following events:

S_1: the defective rate is .01;
S_2: the defective rate is .05;
I: two defectives are observed in a sample of ten.

We wish to find $P(S_2|I)$.

Let x = the number of defectives in a sample of ten; x is a binomial random variable with

$$P(x = 2) = \binom{10}{2}p^2(1 - p)^8,$$

where p is the defective rate. Therefore,

$$P(I|S_1) = \binom{10}{2}(.01)^2(.99)^8 = .003$$

and

$$P(I|S_2) = \binom{10}{2}(.05)^2(.95)^8 = .06.$$

Note also that

$$P(S_1) = .8 \quad \text{and} \quad P(S_2) = .2.$$

We now apply Bayes' rule to find

$$P(S_2|I) = \frac{P(I|S_2)P(S_2)}{P(I|S_1)P(S_1) + P(I|S_2)P(S_2)} = \frac{(.06)(.2)}{(.003)(.8) + (.06)(.2)} = .833.$$

The sample information indicates that the posterior probability is .833 that the machine is operating at a 5% defective rate.

20.14 The marketing director of a major department store chain plans future sales strategy based partly on the actions of the major competition. In the past, the major competition has run a major sale 10% of the time, a minor sale 70% of the time, and no sale 20% of the time. An informant forwards information to the marketing director concerning the major competition's future plans; the informant accurately predicts a major sale 90% of the time, a minor sale 70% of the time, and no sale 60% of the time. In each case, the probabilities of incorrect predictions are equally divided between the other two choices; e.g., the probability the informant predicts a minor sale, given that the competition will have a major sale, is equal to the probability the informant predicts no sale, given that the competition will have a major sale; namely,

$$\frac{(1 - .90)}{2} = \frac{.10}{2} = .05.$$

Suppose the informant predicts that the major competition will not have a sale next month. Based on this information, what are the posterior probabilities of no sale, a minor sale, and a major sale next month by the major competition?

Solution

The calculations involved in using Bayes' rule to compute posterior probabilities are summarized in the following *probability revision table*.

(1) STATE OF NATURE	(2) PRIOR PROBABILITY	(3) CONDITIONAL PROBABILITY OF SAMPLE INFORMATION	(4) PROBABILITY OF INTERSECTION OF STATE AND SAMPLE INFORMATION	(5) POSTERIOR PROBABILITY
S_1: Major Sale	.10	.05	.005	.022
S_2: Minor Sale	.70	.15	.105	.457
S_3: No Sale	.20	.60	.120	.521
			.230	1.000

The decision problem has three states of nature, for which prior probabilities are known (columns 1 and 2). In column (3) we calculate the conditional probability of the sample information, given each state of nature; e.g., the probability the informant predicts no sale, given that the competition will have a minor sale, is .30/2 = .15. In column (4), the probability of the intersection of the state of nature and the sample information is determined by multiplying the results in columns (2) and (3). Each entry in column (4) is divided by the sum of the column (4) entries to determine the posterior probabilities in column (5). Note that the sample information revised the probabilities of Major Sale and Minor Sale downward and the probability of No Sale upward. Thus, the marketing director can be more confident that the competition will not have a sale than he was prior to obtaining the sample information.

Exercises

20.11 Complete the following probability revision table.

(1) STATE OF NATURE	(2) PRIOR PROBABILITY	(3) CONDITIONAL PROBABILITY OF SAMPLE INFORMATION	(4) PROBABILITY OF INTERSECTION OF STATE AND SAMPLE INFORMATION	(5) POSTERIOR PROBABILITY
S_1	.1	.7		
S_2	.2	.6		
S_3	.3	.3		
S_4	.4	.4		

20.12 Refer to Example 20.13. Find the posterior probabilities of S_1 and S_2 if:

a. one defective out of 10 is observed;
b. no defectives are observed.

20.13 Refer to Example 20.14. Find the posterior probabilities for Major Sale, Minor Sale, and No Sale if:

a. the informant predicts a Minor Sale;
b. the informant predicts a Major Sale.

20.14 Eighty percent of all television sets produced by an electronics firm contain no major defects. Before the sets can be shipped to retail outlets for sale, they must pass a final inspection; 98% of the sets with no major defects pass final inspection, while 10% of the sets with at least one major defect pass final inspection. If you purchase a television set manufactured by this firm, what is the probability that it contains no major defects?

20.15 The three major appliance outlets in a city sell two (and only two) brands, Brand A and Brand B, of refrigerators. Brand A comprises 60% of the total number of refrigerators sold in the first store, 30% in the second store, and 50% in the third store. The first store makes 50% of all refrigerator sales in the city, while the second and third stores make 20% and 30%, respectively, of all refrigerator sales. If your neighbor has just purchased a Brand A refrigerator, what is the probability that it was purchased at the first store?

20.9 SOLVING DECISION PROBLEMS USING POSTERIOR PROBABILITIES

Example

20.15 Refer to Example 20.13. If the assembly machine is shut down and readjusted, a monetary cost is incurred because of lost production. However, this cost is justified by the difference in profit between a 1% and a 5% defective rate. The payoff table for hourly production is shown below:

		STATE OF NATURE (Defective Rate)	
		1%	5%
ACTION	a_1: Shut Down and Readjust	\$200	\$200
	a_2: No Shut Down or Readjustment	\$250	\$50

a. Use the prior probabilities to determine which action should be taken under the expected payoff criterion.

b. Use the posterior probabilities to determine which action should be taken under the expected payoff criterion.

Solution

a. We first compute the expected payoff for each action, using the prior probabilities of .8 for a 1% defective rate and .2 for a 5% defective rate:

$$EP(a_1) = \$200(.8) + \$200(.2) = \$200$$

and

$$EP(a_2) = \$250(.8) + \$50(.2) = \$210.$$

Since the expected payoff for a_2 is larger than that for a_1, the assembly machine should not be shut down and readjusted.

b. Recall from Example 20.13 that the posterior probability for the 5% defective rate is

$$P(S_2|I) = .833.$$

Similarly, we use Bayes' rule to calculate the posterior probability for the 1% defective rate:

$$P(S_1|I) = \frac{P(I|S_1)P(S_1)}{P(I|S_1)P(S_1) + P(I|S_2)P(S_2)} = \frac{(.003)(.8)}{(.003)(.8) + (.06)(.2)} = .167$$

The expected payoff for each action, using the posterior probabilities, is now computed:

$$EP(a_1) = \$200(.167) + \$200(.833) = \$200$$

and

$$EP(a_2) = \$250(.167) + \$50(.833) = \$83.40.$$

The expected payoff criterion chooses action a_1. This selection incorporates both prior and sample information, and differs from the action selected in part **a**, where only prior information is used.

Exercises

20.16 Refer to Exercise 20.11. Suppose the payoff table is as shown below:

		STATE OF NATURE			
		S_1	S_2	S_3	S_4
	a_1	100	-50	125	200
ACTION	a_2	-50	0	100	200
	a_3	100	100	100	100

Select the action with the maximum expected payoff, using:

a. the prior probabilities for the states of nature;
b. the posterior probabilities for the states of nature.

20.17 Refer to Exercise 20.12. In each case, use the posterior probabilities to determine which action yields the maximum expected payoff. Use the payoff table in Example 20.15.

20.18 Refer to Example 20.12. If the payoff table is as given below (payoffs are given in thousands of dollars), use the posterior probabilities to determine which action has the maximum expected payoff.

		STATE OF NATURE (Posterior Probabilities in Parentheses)		
		Major Sale (.022)	Minor Sale (.457)	No Sale (.521)
ACTION	a_1: Major Sale	1	2	7
	a_2: Minor Sale	-2	3	5
	a_3: No Sale	-7	1	2

20.19 a. Repeat Exercise 20.18, if the informant predicts a minor sale by the competition.

b. Repeat Exercise 20.18, if the informant predicts a major sale by the competition.

(HINT: The required posterior probabilities were computed in Exercise 20.13.)

20.10 THE EXPECTED VALUE OF PERFECT INFORMATION

Example

20.16 Refer to Example 20.13 and the corresponding payoff table, presented in Example 20.15. What is the maximum amount we should be willing to pay for sample information, i.e., what is the expected value of perfect information?

Solution

The expected value of perfect information (*EVPI*) is the expected opportunity loss for the action selected by the expected opportunity loss (*EOL*) criterion. Recall that the *EOL* criterion selects the action that minimizes the expected opportunity loss.

We convert the payoff table to an opportunity loss table by subtracting the payoff for each action/state of nature combination from the maximum payoff for that state of nature. The results are shown in the following table:

		STATE OF NATURE (Defective Rate) 1%	5%
ACTION	a_1: Shut Down and Readjust	\$50	\$0
	a_2: No Shut Down or Readjustment	\$0	\$150

We use the prior probabilities of .8 and .2 for the 1% and 5% defective rates, respectively, to calculate the expected opportunity loss for each action:

$EOL(a_1) = \$50(.8) + \$0(.2) = \$40$

and

$EOL(a_2) = \$0(.8) + \$150(.2) = \$30.$

The EOL criterion thus selects action a_2 and the expected value of perfect information is given by

$EVPI = EOL(a_2) = \$30.$

We are willing to pay no more than \$30 for sample information concerning the defective rate of the assembly machine.

Exercises

20.20 Refer to Exercises 20.11 and 20.16. Find the expected value of perfect information.

20.21 Find the expected value of perfect information for Exercise 20.18.

20.22 Consider the following payoff table:

		STATE OF NATURE (Prior Probabilities in Parentheses) S_1 (.6)	S_2 (.3)	S_3 (.1)
ACTION	a_1	-100	200	400
	a_2	50	100	150
	a_3	75	75	75

a. Find the action with the maximum expected payoff.

b. Find the *EVPI*.

20.11 THE EXPECTED VALUE OF SAMPLE INFORMATION: PREPOSTERIOR ANALYSIS (Optional)

Examples

20.17 Refer to Example 20.14 and the associated payoff table given in Exercise 20.18. The informant currently is paid \$300 per month for the information he forwards to the marketing director; the informant asks for a raise to \$450 per month. Should the marketing director raise the informant's salary?

Solution

To determine whether the marketing director should give the informant the requested raise, we must calculate the expected value of sample information (*EVSI*).

The first step in calculating the *EVSI* is to determine the expected payoff of sampling (*EPS*). Thus, we use the following probability revision table to determine the posterior probabilities for each of the three possible sample outcomes.

(1) STATE OF NATURE	(2) PRIOR PROBABILITY	(3) CONDITIONAL PROBABILITY OF SAMPLE INFORMATION	(4) PROBABILITY OF INTERSECTION OF STATE AND SAMPLE INFORMATION	(5) POSTERIOR PROBABILITY
	Informant's Prediction: Major Sale			
S_1 Major Sale	.10	.90	.090	.383
S_2 Minor Sale	.70	.15	.105	.447
S_3 No Sale	.20	.20	.040	.170
	1.00		.235	1.000
	Informant's Prediction: Minor Sale			
S_1 Major Sale	.10	.05	.005	.009
S_2 Minor Sale	.70	.70	.490	.916
S_3 No Sale	.20	.20	.040	.075
	1.00		.535	1.000

(continued)

(1) STATE OF NATURE	(2) PRIOR PROBABILITY	(3) CONDITIONAL PROBABILITY OF SAMPLE INFORMATION	(4) PROBABILITY OF INTERSECTION OF STATE AND SAMPLE INFORMATION	(5) POSTERIOR PROBABILITY
		Informant's Prediction: No Sale		
S_1 Major Sale	.10	.05	.005	.022
S_2 Minor Sale	.70	.15	.105	.457
S_3 No Sale	.20	.60	.120	.521
	1.00		.230	1.000

The first two columns show the states of nature and the associated prior probabilities. Column (3) gives the conditional probability of the sample information, given a particular state of nature. Thus, the second entry in column (3) is the conditional probability that the informant predicts a major sale, given that the competition will have a minor sale; from the information given in Example 20.2, this conditional probability is .30/2 = .15. Column (4) determines the probability of the intersection of the state and the sample outcome using the formula

$$P(S_i \cap I) = P(S_i)P(I|S_i).$$

The posterior probabilities in column (5) are calculated using Bayes' rule:

$$P(S_i|I) = \frac{P(I|S_i)P(S_i)}{\sum_{j=1}^{3} P(I|S_j)P(S_j)}$$

We use the expected payoff criterion with the posterior probabilities to determine which action is dictated by each sample outcome. Thus, if the informant predicts a major sale, we have, from the payoff table of Exercise 20.18:

$$EP\left(a_1 \middle| \begin{matrix}\text{Informant predicts}\\ \text{major sale}\end{matrix}\right) = \sum_{\text{all states}} (\text{payoff})\begin{pmatrix}\text{posterior probability}\\ \text{of state when informant}\\ \text{predicts major sale}\end{pmatrix}$$

$$= 1(.383) + 2(.447) + 7(.170) = 2.467$$

$$EP\left(a_2 \middle| \begin{matrix}\text{Informant predicts}\\ \text{major sale}\end{matrix}\right) = (-2)(.383) + 3(.447) + 5(.170) = 1.425$$

$$EP\left(a_3 \middle| \begin{array}{l}\text{Informant predicts}\\ \text{major sale}\end{array}\right) = -7(.383) + 1(.447) + 2(.170) = -1.894.$$

Thus, the expected payoff criterion selects a_1: Conduct a major sale when the informant predicts the competition will have a major sale.

Similarly, when the informant predicts a minor sale, we have the following expected payoffs:

$$EP\left(a_1 \middle| \begin{array}{l}\text{Informant predicts}\\ \text{minor sale}\end{array}\right) = 1(.009) + 2(.916) + 7(.075) = 2.366$$

$$EP\left(a_2 \middle| \begin{array}{l}\text{Informant predicts}\\ \text{minor sale}\end{array}\right) = -2(.009) + 3(.916) + 5(.075) = 3.105$$

$$EP\left(a_3 \middle| \begin{array}{l}\text{Informant predicts}\\ \text{minor sale}\end{array}\right) = -7(.009) + 1(.916) + 2(.075) = 1.003$$

Thus, the expected payoff criterion chooses a_2: Conduct a minor sale when the informant predicts a minor sale.

Finally:

$$EP\left(a_1 \middle| \begin{array}{l}\text{Informant predicts}\\ \text{no sale}\end{array}\right) = 1(.002) + 2(.457) + 7(.521) = 4.583$$

$$EP\left(a_2 \middle| \begin{array}{l}\text{Informant predicts}\\ \text{no sale}\end{array}\right) = -2(.022) + 3(.457) + 5(.521) = 3.932$$

$$EP\left(a_3 \middle| \begin{array}{l}\text{Informant predicts}\\ \text{no sale}\end{array}\right) = -7(.022) + 1(.457) + 2(.521) = 1.345$$

So the expected payoff criterion selects action a_1: Conduct a major sale when the informant predicts no sale.

The expected payoff of sampling (*EPS*) can now be calculated using the marginal probability distribution for the sample outcomes. The probabilities are the sums of the column (4) entries for each sample outcome. Thus,

$$P\begin{pmatrix}\text{Informant predicts}\\ \text{major sale}\end{pmatrix} = \sum_{\text{all states}} P\left(\begin{pmatrix}\text{Informant predicts}\\ \text{major sale}\end{pmatrix} \cap S_i\right)$$

$$= .090 + .105 + .040 = .235;$$

P(Informant predicts minor sale) and *P*(Informant predicts no sale) are computed in the same manner. The marginal probability of each sample outcome enables us to calculate

$$EPS = \sum_{\substack{\text{all sample} \\ \text{outcomes}}} \begin{pmatrix}\text{maximum expected} \\ \text{payoff for each} \\ \text{sample outcome}\end{pmatrix}\begin{pmatrix}\text{marginal probability} \\ \text{of each sample outcome}\end{pmatrix}$$

$$= (2.467)(.235) + (3.105)(.535) + (4.583)(.230) = 3.295.$$

Since the payoffs were given in thousands of dollars, we conclude that the expected payoff of sampling is \$3295.

To determine the expected gain attributed to sampling, we compare the *EPS* to the expected payoff of no sampling (*EPNS*); but the *EPNS* is just the expected payoff of the action selected by the expected payoff criterion using prior probabilities. Using the payoff table of Exercise 20.18, it can be shown that a_1 and a_2 have the same maximum expected payoff, namely \$2900; thus,

$EPNS$ = \$2900.

Finally, the expected value of sample information (*EVSI*) is the expected payoff of sampling minus the expected payoff with no sampling:

$EVSI = EPS - EPNS$ = \$3295 - \$2900 = \$395.

This figure is the mean dollar amount the department store will gain from sampling; the marketing director should be hesitant to exceed this amount for the purpose of acquiring sample information. Since the informant's request for \$450 exceeds the *EVSI*, the marketing director should refuse to raise the informant's salary to this figure.

20.18 Construct a decision tree to summarize the results of the preposterior analysis in Example 20.17.

Solution

The decision tree for Example 20.15 is shown on the following page. Reading from left to right, the first decision fork represents the decision whether to sample. The first decision fork along the upper branch (Do Not Sample) represents the three possible actions in the decision problem. The value \$2900 at this fork is the expected payoff of no sampling (*EPNS*). At the end of each action fork, we indicate the expected payoff for that action and place chance forks which branch into the three possible states of nature. On the state branches we write the prior probabilities and at the end of the branches we write the payoff corresponding to that action/state of nature combination.

The Sample branch of the decision tree has an extra chance fork due to the three possible sample outcomes; the expected payoff of sampling, \$3295 is written beside the sampling chance fork. On the branch for each sample outcome, we indicate the corresponding marginal

21
SURVEY SAMPLING

SUMMARY

This chapter introduced three sampling designs for conducting a sample survey: *simple random sampling*, *stratified random sampling*, and *cluster sampling*; the advantages and disadvantages of each design were discussed. For each design, the associated methods of estimating a population mean, a population total, and a population proportion were presented.

21.3 ESTIMATION IN SURVEY SAMPLING—BOUNDS ON THE ERROR OF ESTIMATION

21.4 ESTIMATION FOR SIMPLE RANDOM SAMPLING

Examples

21.1 A city's utilities department wishes to estimate the average number of kilowatts of electricity consumed daily per household. The daily electricity consumption was monitored for a simple random sample of 150 of the community's 8000 households, with the following results:

$\bar{x}$ = 20.25 kilowatts
s = 4.85 kilowatts

Construct an approximate 95% confidence interval for μ, the true mean daily consumption of electricity per household in this community.

Solution

The general form of an approximate 95% confidence interval for a population mean, based on simple random sampling, is

$$\bar{x} \pm 2 \frac{s}{\sqrt{n}}\sqrt{\frac{N - n}{N}}.$$

Substitution of the sample statistics, with $N = 8000$ and $n = 150$ yields:

$$20.25 \pm 2\left(\frac{4.85}{\sqrt{150}}\right)\sqrt{\frac{8000 - 150}{8000}} = 20.25 \pm .78 \quad \text{or} \quad (19.47,\ 21.03)$$

We estimate that the average daily consumption of electricity per household in this community is between 19.47 and 21.03 kilowatts, with approximately 95% confidence.

21.2 Refer to Example 21.1. Construct an estimate of the total amount of electricity consumed daily by households in the community and place a bound on the error of estimation.

Solution

The estimate of τ, the population total, is

$$\hat{\tau} = N\bar{x} = 8000(20.25) = 162{,}000 \text{ kilowatts.}$$

The estimated bound on the error of estimation is

$$2\sqrt{N^2\left(\frac{s^2}{n}\right)\left(\frac{N - n}{N}\right)} = 2\sqrt{(8000)^2\ \frac{(4.85)^2}{150}\left(\frac{8000 - 150}{8000}\right)}$$

$$= 2(3138.17) = 6276.34 \text{ kilowatts.}$$

21.3 A state comptroller is interested in estimating the proportion of vouchers for official state travel submitted last year that contain at least one illegal expense. In a simple random sample of 250 of the 4125 travel vouchers submitted last year, it was found that 68 contained at least one illegal expense. Construct an approximate 95% confidence interval for the true proportion of the state's official travel vouchers that contain at least one irregularity.

Solution

The general form of an approximate 95% confidence interval for a population proportion p, based on simple random sampling, is given by

$$\hat{p} \pm 2\sqrt{\frac{\hat{p}(1 - \hat{p})}{n}}\sqrt{\frac{N - n}{N}}.$$

In this example, $N = 4125$, $n = 250$, and $\hat{p} = 68/250 \approx .27$. The desired interval is now obtained by substitution:

$$.27 \pm 2\sqrt{\frac{.27(1 - .27)}{250}}\sqrt{\frac{4125 - 250}{4125}} = .27 \pm .05 \quad \text{or} \quad (.22,\ .32)$$

We are approximately 95% confident that between 22% and 32% of the vouchers submitted for official state travel last year contained at least one illegal expense.

Exercises

21.1 A private four-year university is considering a proposal to assess each student \$4 per semester to support an athletic scholarship fund. In a random sample of 400 of the university's 6780 students, only 125 were in favor of the proposal. Construct an approximate 95% confidence interval for the true proportion of all students at this university who favor the proposal.

21.2 A printing company employs 65 people in the bindery. The bindery foreman wishes to estimate the mean time required by a bindery employee to assemble eight sections of a magazine for stitching. Six bindery employees were randomly selected and timed on this task; the results are summarized below:

$\bar{x}$ = 4.51 seconds
s = 1.04 seconds

Estimate the average time required by all bindery workers to assemble a magazine for stitching; place a bound on the error of estimation.

21.3 Refer to Exercise 21.2. The bindery foreman is also interested in estimating the total number of magazines ruined (per job) in production by the bindery workers (e.g., wrinkled or torn pages, stitching or folding errors, stains, etc.). On a particular job, the foreman monitored the work of ten randomly selected bindery employees and observed the number of magazines ruined by each. He then computed the following statistics:

$\bar{x}$ = 72.18
s = 11.09

Estimate the total number of magazines ruined in the production of this job by all bindery employees and place a bound on the error of estimation.

21.6 STRATIFIED RANDOM SAMPLING

Examples

21.4 A realtor wished to estimate the average appraised value of residential condominium units in a city. She treated the four quadrants of the city (which correspond to the city's political zoning districts) as strata, and selected a random sample of residential condominium units from each. The results on appraised values are summarized in the following table:

QUADRANT	N_i	n_i	$\bar{x}_i$	s_i
1	1412	50	\$62,750	\$6420
2	760	30	56,490	4370
3	3528	100	51,830	3830
4	506	20	66,210	4050

Calculate an approximate 95% confidence interval for the mean appraised value of all residential condominium units in the city.

Solution

The general form of an approximate 95% confidence interval for a population mean, based on stratified sampling, is

$$\bar{x}_{st} \pm 2\sqrt{\frac{1}{N^2}\sum_{i=1}^{k} N_i^2\left(\frac{N_i - n_i}{N_i}\right)\frac{s_i^2}{n_i}},$$

where $\bar{x}_{st} = \frac{1}{N}\sum_{i=1}^{k} N_i\bar{x}_i$. For our example,

$$N = N_1 + N_2 + N_3 + N_4 = 1412 + 760 + 3528 + 506 = 6206$$

and

$$\bar{x}_{st} = \frac{1}{6206}[(1412)(62,750) + (760)(56,490) + (3528)(51,830) + (506)(66,210)]$$

$$= 56,058.$$

Substitution yields the desired confidence interval:

$$56,058 \pm 2\sqrt{\frac{1}{(6206)^2}\left[(1412)^2\left(\frac{1412 - 50}{1412}\right)\frac{(6420)^2}{50} + (760)^2\left(\frac{760 - 30}{760}\right)\frac{(4370)^2}{30} + (3528)^2\left(\frac{3528 - 100}{3528}\right)\frac{(3830)^2}{100} + (506)^2\left(\frac{506 - 20}{506}\right)\frac{(4050)^2}{20}\right]}$$

or

56.058 ± 638 or (\$55,420, \$56,696)

With approximately 95% confidence, we state that the mean appraised value of a residential condominium unit in this city is between \$55,420 and \$56,696.

21.5 Refer to Example 21.4. Estimate the total appraised value of all residential condominium units in the city and place a bound on the error of estimation.

Solution

The estimate of the population total appraised value is

$$\hat{\tau} = N\bar{x}_{st} = (6206)(\$56{,}058) = \$347{,}895{,}950.$$

The estimated bound on the error of estimation is:

$$2\sqrt{\sum_{i=1}^{4} N_i^2\left(\frac{N_i - n_i}{N_i}\right)\frac{s_i^2}{n_i}}$$

$$= 2\sqrt{\left[(1412)^2\left(\frac{1412 - 50}{1412}\right)\frac{(6420)^2}{50} + (760)^2\left(\frac{760 - 30}{760}\right)\frac{(4370)^2}{30} + (3528)^2\left(\frac{3528 - 100}{3528}\right)\frac{(3830)^2}{100} + (506)^2\left(\frac{506 - 20}{506}\right)\frac{(4050)^2}{20}\right]}$$

$= \$3{,}956{,}869$

21.6 A nationwide chain of audio equipment stores wishes to estimate the overall proportion of its accounts receivable that are delinquent. The chain's auditors select a random sample of 100 accounts receivable from each of the three sales regions (East, Central, and West) and observe the number that are delinquent. The data are summarized in the table below:

REGION	NUMBER OF ACCOUNTS RECEIVABLE N_i	PROPORTION OF SAMPLED ACCOUNTS THAT ARE DELINQUENT $\hat{p}_i$
East	745	.13
Central	630	.18
West	820	.11

Construct an approximate 95% confidence interval for the population proportion of the chain's accounts receivable that are delinquent.

Solution

The chain's auditors have treated the sales regions as strata; the appropriate confidence interval formula is then

$$\hat{p}_{st} \pm 2\sqrt{\frac{1}{N^2}\sum_{i=1}^{3} N_i^2\left(\frac{N_i - n_i}{N_i}\right)\frac{\hat{p}_i(1-\hat{p}_i)}{n_i - 1}}$$

where $n_1 = n_2 = n_3 = 100$, $N = 745 + 630 + 820 = 2195$, and

$$\hat{p}_{st} = \frac{1}{N}(N_1\hat{p}_1 + N_2\hat{p}_2 + N_3\hat{p}_3)$$

$$= \frac{1}{2195}[(745)(.13) + (630)(.18) + (820)(.11)] = .14.$$

We now obtain the approximate 95% confidence interval by substitution:

$$.14 \pm 2\sqrt{\frac{1}{(2195)^2}\left[(745)^2\left(\frac{745 - 100}{745}\right)\frac{(.13)(.87)}{99} + (630)^2\left(\frac{630 - 100}{630}\right)\frac{(.18)(.82)}{99} + (820)^2\left(\frac{820 - 100}{820}\right)\frac{(.11)(.89)}{99}\right]}$$

or

$.14 \pm .04$ or $(.10, .18)$

We estimate, with approximately 95% confidence, that between 10% and 18% of the audio equipment chain's accounts receivable are delinquent.

Exercises

21.4 An aerospace corporation would like to estimate the average number of worker-days lost per year due to sickness. Random samples of the four different types of employees yielded the following summary information on worker-days lost due to sickness last year.

EMPLOYEE GROUP	N_i	n_i	$\bar{x}_i$	s_i
Laborers	540	75	6.8	2.4
Supervisors	90	12	5.1	2.1
Researchers	125	20	3.9	1.8
Administrators	40	8	3.5	1.5

Construct an approximate 95% confidence interval for the mean number of worker-days lost per year due to sickness in the corporation.

21.5 Refer to Exercise 21.4. Estimate the total number of worker-days lost per year due to sickness by employees of the aerospace corporation. Place a bound on the error of estimation.

21.6 The police department in a mid-sized Florida city is interested in expanding a citizens' crime alert program. Under the program, member households undertake crime prevention measures (such as identification of household goods, patrolling of neighborhoods, etc.), with the assistance and supervision of the police department. Because expansion of the program would require an increase in local taxes, the city government wishes to determine the proportion of households in favor of the proposal. The city's households are divided into those who currently are members of the crime alert program and those who are not. Random samples of households are selected from each group, and their opinions toward the proposal are noted. The results are summarized below:

GROUP	N_i	n_i	SAMPLE PROPORTION OF HOUSEHOLDS IN FAVOR OF PROPOSAL
Nonmembers	24,240	1500	.44
Members	12,850	700	.73

Construct an approximate 95% confidence interval for the true proportion of households in the city that favor expansion of the crime alert program.

21.7 CLUSTER SAMPLING

Examples

21.7 A manufacturer of minicomputers wishes to estimate the mean number of service calls per year for equipment sold to universities. The following data on total number of service calls last year are based on a random sample of 6 of the 30 universities that purchased minicomputers from this manufacturer last year.

UNIVERSITY	NUMBER OF MINICOMPUTERS m_i	TOTAL NUMBER OF SERVICE CALLS LAST YEAR x_i
1	10	4
2	5	4
3	6	2
4	12	6
5	8	2
6	5	3

It is also known that the manufacturer sold 250 minicomputers to universities last year. Estimate the mean number of yearly service calls for a minicomputer sold by this manufacturer and place a bound on the error of estimation.

Solution

We will treat each university as a cluster and make the following identifications:

$N = 30, \quad n = 6, \quad M = 250.$

The following preliminary calculations are required:

$$\sum_{i=1}^{6} x_i = 21 \qquad \sum_{i=1}^{6} x_i^2 = 85 \qquad \sum_{i=1}^{6} m_i = 46$$

$$\sum_{i=1}^{6} m_i^2 = 394 \qquad \sum_{i=1}^{6} x_i m_i = 175$$

$$\bar{x} = \frac{21}{46} = .46 \qquad \bar{M} = \frac{250}{30} = 8.33$$

$$\sum_{i=1}^{6} (x_i - \bar{x}m_i)^2 = \sum_{i=1}^{6} x_i^2 - 2\bar{x}\sum_{i=1}^{6} x_i m_i + \bar{x}^2 \sum_{i=1}^{6} m_i^2$$

$$= 85 - 2(.46)(175) + (.46)^2(394) = 7.37$$

The estimate of the mean number of yearly service calls per minicomputer is then given by

$\bar{x} = .46,$

and the estimated bound on the error of estimation is:

$$2\sqrt{\left(\frac{N-n}{NnM^2}\right)\frac{\sum_{i=1}^{6}(x_i - \bar{x}m_i)^2}{n-1}}$$

$$= 2\sqrt{\left(\frac{30-6}{(30)(6)(8.33)^2}\right)\left(\frac{7.37}{5}\right)}$$

$= .11$

21.8 Refer to Example 21.7. Construct an approximate 95% confidence interval for the total number of service calls per year to universities that have purchased minicomputers from this manufacturer.

Solution

The general form of an approximate 95% confidence interval for a population total, based on cluster sampling, is as follows:

$$\hat{\tau} \pm 2\sqrt{N^2\left(\frac{N-n}{Nn}\right)\frac{\sum_{i=1}^{6}(x_i - \bar{x}m_i)^2}{n-1}}$$

where $\hat{\tau} = M\bar{x}$.

We now substitute the values obtained in Example 20.7:

$$250(.46) \pm 2\sqrt{(30)^2\left(\frac{30-6}{(30)(6)}\right)\left(\frac{7.37}{5}\right)} = 115 \pm 26.6 \quad \text{or} \quad (88.4,\ 141.6)$$

21.9 A regional association of nurses is interested in estimating the proportion of graduating nurses who plan to specialize in geriatric nursing. A simple random sample of 4 of the 25 nursing schools in the region is selected, and each graduating student nurse is asked to complete a questionnaire regarding his or her plans for specialization. The results are summarized below:

NURSING SCHOOL	NUMBER OF GRADUATING STUDENT NURSES m_i	NUMBER WHO PLAN TO SPECIALIZE IN GERIATRIC NURSING a_i
1	150	10
2	200	15
3	100	12
4	50	4

Estimate the proportion of graduating student nurses in this region who plan to specialize in geriatric nursing. Place a bound on the error of estimation.

Solution

For the estimation of a population proportion, based on cluster sampling, the following preliminary calculations are required:

$N = 25,\ n = 4$

$$\sum_{i=1}^{4} a_i = 41 \qquad \sum_{i=1}^{4} a_i^2 = 485 \qquad \sum_{i=1}^{4} m_i = 500$$

$$\sum_{i=1}^{4} m_i^2 = 75{,}000 \qquad \sum_{i=1}^{4} a_i m_i = 5900$$

$$\hat{p} = \frac{\sum_{i=1}^{4} a_i}{\sum_{i=1}^{4} m_i} = \frac{41}{500} = .082$$

$$\sum_{i=1}^{4} (a_i - \hat{p}m_i)^2 = \sum_{i=1}^{4} a_i^2 - 2\hat{p}\sum_{i=1}^{4} a_i m_i + \hat{p}^2 \sum_{i=1}^{4} m_i^2$$

$$= 485 - 2(.082)(5900) + (.082)^2(75{,}000) = 21.7$$

Also, since M and $\bar{M}$ are unknown, we will compute the average cluster size for the sample:

$$\bar{m} = \frac{\sum_{i=1}^{4} m_i}{4} = \frac{500}{4} = 125$$

Now, our estimate of the proportion of graduating student nurses who intend to specialize in geriatric nursing is $\hat{p} = .082$, and the estimated bound on the error of estimation is:

$$2\sqrt{\left(\frac{N - n}{Nn\bar{m}^2}\right)\frac{\sum_{i=1}^{4} (a_i - \hat{p}m_i)^2}{n - 1}} = 2\sqrt{\left(\frac{25 - 4}{(25)(4)(125)^2}\right)\left(\frac{21.7}{3}\right)} = .020$$

Exercises

21.7 A marketing survey is being undertaken to estimate the average amount of money spent per month on snack food items by households in a particular suburban community. A cluster sampling design is to be implemented, with residential blocks forming the clusters. A marketing researcher selected a simple random sample of 8 of the 200 residential blocks in the community. Each household within the selected blocks was asked to report the amount of money it spends monthly on snack food items. The data are summarized below:

BLOCK	NUMBER OF HOUSEHOLDS	TOTAL AMOUNT SPENT MONTHLY ON SNACK FOOD ITEMS
1	25	\$504
2	22	490
3	35	685
4	28	547
5	32	629
6	27	507
7	38	723
8	35	644

Construct an approximate 95% confidence interval for the mean monthly expenditure for snack food items by households in this community.

21.8 A state university system is studying a proposal for expansion of its upper division facilities to accommodate junior college transfer students from within the state. The governing board of the university system would like to obtain an estimate of the proportion of current junior college students who intend to pursue upper division studies at an in-state university. Six of the 24 junior colleges within the state were randomly selected and each student at the selected institutions was asked to complete a questionnaire regarding his or her educational plans. The results of the survey are shown below:

JUNIOR COLLEGE	NUMBER OF STUDENTS	NUMBER OF STUDENTS WHO PLAN TO ATTEND AN IN-STATE UNIVERSITY
1	2843	1240
2	4197	2635
3	2639	1124
4	3850	2837
5	4276	2944
6	3712	2108

Construct an approximate 95% confidence interval for the true proportion of current junior college students in the state who plan to further their education at an in-state university.

21.8 DETERMINING THE SAMPLE SIZE

Examples

21.10 Refer to Example 21.3. Suppose the state comptroller wishes to estimate the proportion of vouchers that contain at least one illegal expense to within .03 with approximately 95% confidence. In order to obtain this accuracy, how many of last year's 4125 travel vouchers should be sampled?

Solution

It is necessary to solve the following equation for n:

$$2\hat{\sigma}_{\hat{p}} = 2\sqrt{\frac{\hat{p}(1 - \hat{p})}{n}}\sqrt{\frac{N - n}{N}} = .03$$

where $N = 4125$ and $\hat{p}$ will be set equal to .5 as a conservative measure in the sample size calculation. For a first approximation to n, we will assume that

$$\left(\frac{N - n}{N}\right) \approx 1.$$

Thus,

$$2\sqrt{\frac{(.5)(.5)}{n}} = .03 \quad \text{or} \quad n = 1112.$$

This solution will be larger than the actual sample size needed to achieve the desired accuracy, because the value of $(N - n)/N$ will not equal 1. We now substitute $n = 1112$ into the finite population correction and re-solve for n:

$$2\sqrt{\frac{(.5)(.5)}{n}}\sqrt{\frac{4125 - 1112}{4125}} = .03 \quad \text{or} \quad n = 812.$$

This solution will be too small because we used $n = 1112$ in the finite population correction factor. As a final iteration, we substitute $n = 812$ into the finite population correction and solve for n:

$$2\sqrt{\frac{(.5)(.5)}{n}}\sqrt{\frac{4125 - 812}{4125}} = .03 \quad \text{or} \quad n = 893.$$

Thus, the state comptroller should examine 893 of last year's travel vouchers in order to reduce the bound on the error of estimation to .03.

21.11 Refer to Example 21.4. Suppose the realtor wishes to estimate the average appraised value of residential condominium units to within \$500 with approximately 95% confidence. If equal sample sizes are to be used, approximately how many condominium units should be sampled from each quadrant in order to achieve the desired accuracy in estimating the population mean?

Solution

It is necessary to solve the following equation for n_s:

$$2\sqrt{\frac{1}{N^2}\sum_{i=1}^{4} N_i^2\left(\frac{N_i - n_s}{N_i}\right)\frac{s_i^2}{n_s}} = 500$$

At the first stage, we will substitute the sample variances obtained in Example 21.4 and assume that

$$\left(\frac{N_i - n_s}{N_i}\right) \approx 1:$$

$$2\sqrt{\frac{1}{(6206)^2}\left[(1412)^2\frac{(6420)^2}{n_s}+(760)^2\frac{(4370)^2}{n_s}+(3528)^2\frac{(3830)^2}{n_s}+(506)^2\frac{(4050)^2}{n_s}\right]}$$

$= 500$ or $n_s = 117.$

At the next stage, we substitute $n_s = 117$ into the finite population correction and re-solve for n_s:

$$2\sqrt{\frac{1}{(6206)^2}\left[(1412)^2\left(\frac{1412-117}{1412}\right)\frac{(6420)^2}{n_s}+(760)^2\left(\frac{760-117}{760}\right)\frac{(4370)^2}{n_s}+(3528)^2\left(\frac{3528-117}{3528}\right)\frac{(3830)^2}{n_s}+(506)^2\left(\frac{506-117}{506}\right)\frac{(4050)^2}{n_s}\right]}$$

$= 500$ or $n_s = 110.$

Finally, we substitute $n_s = 110$ into the finite population correction and re-solve the original equation for n_s:

$$2\sqrt{\frac{1}{(6206)^2}\left[(1412)^2\left(\frac{1412-110}{1412}\right)\frac{(6420)^2}{n_s}+(760)^2\left(\frac{760-110}{760}\right)\frac{(4370)^2}{n_s}+(3528)^2\left(\frac{3528-110}{3528}\right)\frac{(3830)^2}{n}+(506)^2\left(\frac{506-110}{506}\right)\frac{(4050)^2}{n_s}\right]}$$

$= 500$ or $n_s = 111.$

The realtor should sample 111 residential condominium units from each quadrant in order to estimate their mean appraised value to within $500 with approximately 95% confidence.

Exercises

21.9 Refer to Exercise 21.2. How many bindery employees should be sampled if the foreman wishes to estimate the mean assembly time for a magazine to within .60 second with approximately 95% confidence?

21.10 Refer to Example 21.6. How many accounts receivable should be sampled from each sales region if it is desired to reduce the bound on the error of estimation of the proportion of delinquent accounts to .03? (Assume equal sample sizes are to be selected from each stratum.)

ANSWERS TO SELECTED EXERCISES

CHAPTER 1

1.1 a. values of monthly starting salary for all 1990 college graduates with degrees in accounting
    b. measure of reliability

1.2 Almost one-fourth of the homes tune in to Monday Night Football.

1.3 b. the set of percentages of no-shows for all past and future realizations of this particular flight

1.4 set of closing prices for all 1500 NYSE stocks (i.e., the population)

CHAPTER 2

2.1 a. ratio b. ratio c. nominal

2.2 a. ratio b. ordinal c. nominal
    d. ratio e. nominal f. ratio

2.5 b. reconsider the price structure, perhaps begin an advertising campaign

2.8 a. client expenses, 136.8°; company salaries, 86.4°; rent and equipment, 50.4°; profit, 28.8°; miscellaneous, 57.6°

    b. client expenses, \$76,000; company salaries, \$48,000; rent and equipment, \$28,000; profit, \$16,000; miscellaneous, \$32,000

2.14 a. 70

CHAPTER 3

3.1 3 3.2 69.5 3.4 15 3.5 7.08% 3.6 24.228

3.7 566.25 3.8 5.95 3.9 8 3.10 12

3.11 a. \$29,800 b. median 3.14 \$275,000,000

3.15 \$265 3.16 33.5, 5.79 3.17 11.95, 3.46

3.18 a. 8, 66, 64 b. 213, 9269, 45369

3.19 370.11, 19.24   3.20 11.95   3.21 3066.67, 55.38

3.22 a. possible that no marketing texts have first-year sales between 700 and 1700; at least 3/4
b. approximately 68%; approximately 95%
c. approximately 2.5%; approximately 16%

3.23 a. approximately 16%   b. approximately 81.5%

3.24 26 seconds   3.25 \$475, \$92   3.26 23.77, 16.36

3.27 63.9, 369.38, 19.22   3.28 a. 2   b. −1   c. 50th

3.29 a. −1.33   b. −.67   c. 0   d. 1.5   e. 2

3.30 a. −.5   b. \$17,360

3.31 z = 3.6; unlikely event if Department of Transportation results are valid

3.32 z = 3.35; very unlikely

3.33 Q_L = 228; median = 266.5; Q_U = 291

3.34 Q_L = 171; median = 301.5; Q_U = 427

3.35 a. 63   3.36 a. 256

CHAPTER 4

4.1 a. Choose two cities from among the five specified: (Boston, Atlanta); (Boston, Dallas); (Boston, Cleveland); (Boston, Los Angeles); (Atlanta, Dallas); (Atlanta, Cleveland); (Atlanta, Los Angeles); (Dallas, Cleveland); (Dallas, Los Angeles); (Cleveland, Los Angeles)
b. 3/10

4.2 P(A) = .992; P(B) = .096; P(C) = .008

4.3 b. Selected worker's breakfast is adequate and his efficiency is unsatisfactory.
c. Selected worker's efficiency is satisfactory.
e. Selected worker's efficiency is satisfactory, or his breakfast is adequate, or both.

4.4 a. .80   b. .32   c. .48   d. .29   e. .71

4.5 a. Head of household is at least 25 years old, or has an annual income over \$30,000, or both; $P(G \cup H)$ = .74.
b. .30   c. .46   d. .24   e. .54

4.6 .45, .55   4.7 a. .87   b. .77

4.8 .5, .87   4.9 .80

4.10 a. 1/12; 2/3   b. no   c. no

4.11 a. yes   b. no   c. no

4.12 no   4.13 .24   4.14 b, d, e

4.15 a. 3/10 b. 2/9 c. 28/45 d. 14/45

4.16 c. 3/5 4.17 .64

CHAPTER 5

5.1 a. discrete; x = 0, 1, 2, ...
b. discrete; x = 0, 1, 2, ...
c. continuous; $x \geqslant 0$ hours (days, etc.)
d. continuous; $x \geqslant 0$ inches
e. continuous; $x \geqslant 0$
f. discrete; x = 0, 1, 2, ...

5.3 .015

5.4

x	\$0	\$10,000
$p(x)$	.999	.001

5.5

x	0	1	2
$p(x)$	.81	.18	.01

5.6 a. .80 b. .20 c. .92 d. .05

5.7 a. 2.38, 1.5756, 1.255 b. .98

5.9 a. not binomial b. binomial

5.10 a.

x	0	1	2	3
$p(x)$	.343	.441	.189	.027

b. .216

5.11 a. .787 b. .595 c. .783 d. 6, 3.6 e. .939

5.12 a. .350 b. .9933 5.13 a. .135 b. $(.595)^3 = .211$

CHAPTER 6

6.1 a. 1/3 b. 2/9 6.2 a. 3/4 b. 50 minutes, 11.55 minutes

6.3 a. .0401 b. .0532 c. .0838 d. .7791

6.4 a. 2.58 b. −1.96 c. −.75

6.5 a. .0401 b. .5987

6.6 a. .0985 b. .3745 c. .0262

6.7 a. .0032 b. 10.3265

6.8 a. .329680 b. .450852

6.9 .368 6.10 .8365 6.11 .9599

CHAPTER 7

7.1 a.

m	2	3	4
$p(m)$	.3	.4	.3

b. $E(m) = 2(.3) + 3(.4) + 4(.3) = 3 = \mu$

7.2 a.

m	3	4	5
$p(m)$	.3	.4	.3

b. $E(m) = 4$, $\mu = 4.6$

7.3 a. approximately normal with mean $\mu_{\bar{x}}$ = \$8000 and standard deviation $\sigma_{\bar{x}}$ = \$237.17
b. .0174 c. .9652

7.4 $P(z \leqslant -2.13) = .0166$

7.5 a. approximately normal with mean $\mu_{\bar{x}}$ = \$31,000 and standard deviation $\sigma_{\bar{x}}$ = \$3000
b. 100 c. .8484, .9953

CHAPTER 8

8.1 a. 1.645 b. 2.33 c. 2.58

8.2 b. \$329.00 ± \$14.13

8.3 \$19.80 ± \$.67

8.4 105

8.5 a. −2.552 b. 1.895 c. 1.717

8.6 a. (399.37, 440.63)

8.7 a. 1712 ± 110.9

8.8 .64 ± .124

8.9 Since .60 is in the interval, do not cease home deliveries

8.10 4157

CHAPTER 9

9.1 $z = -3$; yes

9.2 $z = 1.44$; no

9.3 a. p-value = .0013

9.4 p-value = .1498

9.5 $t = 2.86$; yes

9.6 a. $t = -1.65$; no

9.7 $z = .83$, do not cease home deliveries

9.8 $z = 5.96$; yes

9.9 $\beta = .1492$ for $\alpha = .05$;
$\beta = .3372$ for $\alpha = .01$

CHAPTER 10

10.1 $z = -4.60$; yes

10.2 $-\$7 \pm \$2.99$

10.3 $t = -.49$; do not reject H_0

10.4 -8.2 ± 37.30

10.5 a. 4.94 b. 1.65 c. 2.90

10.6 $F = 1.59$; no

10.7 $z = 1.21$; no

10.8 a. $\$1.18 \pm \$.55$

10.10 $z = -1.90$; no

10.11 $-.06 \pm .062$

10.12 314, 314

10.13 77, 77

CHAPTER 11

11.1 b. -2, 1.5

11.2 b. $\hat{y} = -15.20 + 191.34x$ c. 16465.4 d. 616.22

11.3 2058.175

11.4 16465.4

11.5 $t = 5.86$; reject H_0

11.6 191.34 ± 75.324

11.7 $t = 1.50$; no

11.8 a. .90 b. .81

11.9 $t = 5.86$; yes

11.10 .219

11.11 673.62 ± 35.69

11.12 673.62 ± 91.62

11.14 a. $y = \beta_0 + \beta_1 x + \varepsilon$ b. $\hat{y} = 10.88 + .236x$
c. $t = 5.33$; reject H_0 d. .936; .876 e. 15.596 ± 1.835

CHAPTER 12

12.1 a. $\hat{y} = 1.2093 + .3710x_1 + .0021x_2$ b. 3.91

12.2 a. .126 b. .021

12.3 a. $t = 2.82$; no

12.4 a. $y = \beta_0 + \beta_1 x_1 + \beta_2 x_2 + \varepsilon$
b. $t = 2.67$; at $\alpha = .05$, reject H_0: $\beta_2 = 0$

12.5 .7194

12.6 $F = 7.68$; reject H_0: $\beta_1 = \beta_2 = 0$

12.8 Yes

12.9 Errors appear normally distributed

CHAPTER 13

13.1 a. quantitative b. qualitative c. quantitative
d. quantitative e. qualitative

13.2 a. $E(y) = \beta_0 + \beta_1 x + \beta_2 x^2$

13.3 a. $E(y) = \beta_0 + \beta_1 x_1 + \beta_2 x_2$

b. yes; $E(y) = \beta_0 + \beta_1 x_1 + \beta_2 x_2 + \beta_3 x_1 x_2$

c. $E(y) = \beta_0 + \beta_1 x_1 + \beta_2 x_2 + \beta_3 x_1 x_2 + \beta_4 x_1^2 + \beta_5 x_2^2$

13.4 $F = 38.61$; yes

13.5 $F = 98.13$; yes

13.6 a. $x_1 = \begin{cases} 1 & \text{if fair performance} \\ 0 & \text{otherwise} \end{cases}$

$x_2 = \begin{cases} 1 & \text{if poor performance} \\ 0 & \text{otherwise} \end{cases}$

b. $E(y) = \beta_0 + \beta_1 x_1 + \beta_2 x_2$

c. β_0

d. β_2

13.7 $E(y) = \beta_0 + \beta_1 x_1$, where x_1 = annual gross income

13.8 $E(y) = \beta_0 + \beta_1 x_1 + \beta_2 x_2$, where $x_2 = \begin{cases} 1 & \text{if short form} \\ 0 & \text{otherwise} \end{cases}$

13.9 $E(y) = \beta_0 + \beta_1 x_1 + \beta_2 x_2 + \beta_3 x_1 x_2$

13.10 $E(y) = \beta_0 + \beta_1 x_1 + \beta_2 x_1^2$

13.11 $E(y) = \beta_0 + \beta_1 x_1 + \beta_2 x_1^2 + \beta_3 x_2$, where $x_2 = \begin{cases} 1 & \text{if short form} \\ 0 & \text{otherwise} \end{cases}$

13.12 $E(y) = \beta_0 + \beta_1 x_1 + \beta_2 x_1^2 + \beta_3 x_2 + \beta_4 x_1 x_2 + \beta_5 x_1^2 x_2$

13.13 $E(y) = \beta_0 + \beta_1 x_1 + \beta_2 x_1^2$

13.14 H_0: $\beta_3 = \beta_4 = \beta_5 = 0$

13.15 H_0: $\beta_2 = \beta_5 = 0$

13.17 a. 99.99, -29.29; 60.75, -8.05; 139.15, -51.55; 43.04, .16; 80.11, 23.69; 46.19, -1.09; 116.48, -29.68; 85.13, -11.83; 102.93, 41.37; 64.87, -3.57; 109.74, 38.26; 66.92, 18.08; 149.29, 21.91; 97.04, .46; 126.96, 31.14; 88.12, -13.92; 40.93, 6.07; 63.84, -9.14; 77.08, -9.08; 89.12, -13.92.

CHAPTER 14

14.1 a. center line = $\bar{\bar{x}}$ = .996

b. UCL = 1.039, LCL = .953

d. Yes

14.2 a. center line = $\bar{R}$ = .074

b. UCL = $\bar{R}D_4$ = (.074)(2.114) = .1564
LCL = 0

d. Yes

14.3 b. $\bar{p} = \frac{93}{2,500} = .0372$

c. UCL = .094, LCL = 0; No

CHAPTER 15

15.1

	1970	1971	1972	1973	1974	1975	1976
a.	37.62	32.84	35.77	54.33	100.00	93.86	92.46
b.	100.00	87.30	95.09	144.44	265.84	249.52	245.79

	1977	1978	1979	1980	1981	1982
a.	98.19	114.72	235.96	438.25	222.62	168.86
b.	261.04	304.97	627.27	1165.05	591.81	448.90

15.2

Jan.	Feb.	Mar.	Apr.	May	June
102.44	101.05	99.30	99.30	100.00	101.05

July	Aug.	Sept.	Oct.	Nov.	Dec.
101.39	101.05	100.70	100.00	99.30	98.95

15.3

1983, QI	1983, QII	1983, QIII	1983, QIV
100.00	95.76	136.20	135.28

1984, QI	1984, QII	1984, QIII	1984, QIV
143.70	154.03	149.13	187.61

15.4

1972	1973	1974	1975	1976	1977	1978	1979
100.00	109.08	120.92	130.44	142.46	156.54	173.28	194.17

1980	1981	1982
215.42	246.90	274.07

15.5

1970	1975	1985
100.00	361.69	383.89

15.6

1970	1971	1972	1973	1974	1975	1976	1977	1978
-	45.42	65.89	105.37	139.64	148.63	144.83	155.53	216.53

1979	1980	1981	1982	1983
369.10	454.81	476.94	424.61	-

15.7

1970	1971	1972	1973	1974	1975	1976	1977	1978
-	-	73.93	104.36	127.65	142.24	152.78	175.30	253.75

1979	1980	1981	1982	1983
351.69	412.07	452.31	-	-

15.8

1973	1974	1975	1976	1977	1978	1979
148.60	150.88	153.80	156.77	160.89	166.35	171.71

1980	1981	1982
178.42	183.01	186.96

15.9

1973	1974	1975	1976	1977	1978	1979
148.60	153.92	158.60	162.17	168.00	175.77	181.67

1980	1981	1982
190.37	192.70	195.15

CHAPTER 16

16.1 a. Forecast for year 11: F_{11} = 140.47
Forecast for year 12: F_{12} = 140.47

b. F_{11} = 139.75; F_{12} = 139.75

16.2 a.

Year	1	2	3	4	5
E_t	–	115.20	124.80	128.40	124.56
T_t	–	8.40	9.00	6.30	1.23

Year	6	7	8	9	10
E_t	128.20	135.18	143.62	151.40	146.71
T_t	2.44	4.71	6.58	7.18	1.25

b. $F_{11} = 147.96$; $F_{12} = 149.21$

16.3 $E(Y_t) = \beta_0 + \beta_1 t$, where Y_t is the value of the index in year t.

16.4 a. $\hat{Y}_t = 94.8214 + 6.2702t$

b. For year 9: (131.96, 170.54)
For year 10: (136.85, 178.19)

16.5 $d = 0.56$; reject H_0

CHAPTER 17

17.1 a. completely randomized
b. $F = 10.00$; yes
c. 18.375 ± 6.404
d. −15.33 ± 12.68

17.2 The mean number of tires sold daily by method 2 is significantly greater than the mean daily number sold by method 3.

17.3 a. $t = -1.05$; do not reject H_0 b. $F = 1.10$; do not reject H_0

c. $t^2 = 1.10 = F$; $t_{.025}$ (8 df) = 2.306,
$F_{.05}$ (1 df, 8 df) = 5.32 = $(2.306)^2$

17.4 a. randomized block

b.

SOURCE	df	SS	MS	F
Restaurant (Treatments)	2	32.452	16.226	1.57
Day (Blocks)	4	54.307	13.577	1.31
Error	8	82.741	10.343	
Totals	14	169.500		

c. $F = 1.57$; no d. $F = 1.31$; no e. 3.46 ± 3.78

17.5 a.

SOURCE	df	SS	MS	F
Brand (Treatments)	2	38	19	9.5
Type (Blocks)	2	1022	511	255.5
Error	4	8	2	
Totals	8	1068		

b. $F = 9.5$; yes c. 3.00 ± 3.21

17.6 a.

SOURCE	df	SS	MS	F
Union	1	7168.444	7168.444	26.34
Plan	2	5425.167	2712.584	9.97
Union-Plan Interaction	2	159.389	79.695	0.29
Error	30	8165.000	272.167	
Totals	35	20918.000		

b. $F = .29$; no

17.7 a. (343.59, 365.75) (Note: $t_{.025}$ with 30 df is approximately 1.645.)

b. (-40.67, -9.33)

17.8 a.

SOURCE	df	SS	MS	F
Rate, x_1	3	95.62	31.873	94.79
Temperature, x_2	3	38.83	12.943	38.49
x_1x_2	9	15.51	1.723	5.124
Error	16	5.38	.336	
Total	31	155.34		

b. $E(y) = \beta_0 + \beta_1x_1 + \beta_2x_2 + \beta_3x_1^2 + \beta_4x_2^2 + \beta_5x_1x_2 + \beta_6x_1^2x_2 + \beta_7x_1x_2^2 + \beta_8x_1^3 + \beta_9x_2^3 + \beta_{10}x_1x_2^3 + \beta_{11}x_1^3x_2 + \beta_{12}x_1^2x_2^2 + \beta_{13}x_1^2x_2^3 + \beta_{14}x_1^3x_2^2 + \beta_{15}x_1^3x_2^3$

c. Yes; $F = 29.7318$ d. Yes; $F = 5.125$ e. $R^2 = .96537$

17.9 a. $E(y) = \beta_0 + \beta_1x_1 + \beta_2x_2 + \beta_3x_1x_2 + \beta_4x_1^2 + \beta_5x_2^2$

b. $\hat{y} = 29.85625 + .56x_1 - .1625x_2 - .1135x_1x_2 - .275x_1^2 - .23125x_2^2$

c. The two models are different d. $R^2 = .842068$ e. Yes; $F = 5.70$

CHAPTER 18

18.1 $S = 14$; reject H_0 ($p = .0577$)

18.2 b. $T_B = 47.5$; do not reject H_0

18.3 $T_- = 1.5$; reject H_0

18.4 a. 9.21034 b. 20.4831

18.5 b. $H = 11.65$; reject H_0

18.6 b. $F_r = 6.94$; reject H_0

18.7 a. .50 b. .50

18.8 Do not reject H_0

CHAPTER 19

19.1 $X^2 = 43.83$; yes

19.2 $X^2 = 2.66$; no

19.3 $X^2 = 108.35$; reject H_0

19.4 $X^2 = 11.31$; no

CHAPTER 20

20.3 a.

		STATE OF NATURE	
		Condition of plant improves	Condition of plant does not improve
ACTION	Florist buys plant	\$9	-\$3
	Florist does not buy plant	\$0	\$0

20.4

		STATE OF NATURE	
		Condition of plant improves	Condition of plant does not improve
ACTION	Florist buys plant	\$0	\$3
	Florist does not buy plant	\$9	\$0

20.5 a. Action a_2 is inadmissible.

b.

		STATE OF NATURE			
		S_1	S_2	S_3	S_4
ACTION	a_1	2	0	0	2
	a_2	3	1	0	6
	a_3	0	9	6	4
	a_4	6	2	0	0

20.6 Choose action a_2.

20.7 a. Choose action a_2 or a_3.

20.8 a. Choose action a_1. b. Choose action a_3.

20.9 Choose action a_1.

20.10 Risk-avoider

20.12 a. $P(S_1|I) = .536$, $P(S_2|I) = .464$ b. $P(S_1|I) = .858$, $P(S_2|I) = .142$

20.13 a. $P(S_1|I) = .009$, $P(S_2|I) = .916$, $P(S_3|I) = .075$

b. $P(S_1|I) = .383$, $P(S_2|I) = .447$, $P(S_3|I) = .170$

20.14 .975

20.15 .588

20.16 a. a_1 b. a_1

20.17 a. a_1 b. a_2

20.18 $EP(a_1) = 4.583$

20.19 a. $EP(a_2) = 3.105$ b. $EP(a_1) = 2.467$

20.20 30

20.21 .70

20.22 a. $EP(a_2) = 75$ b. 70

20.23 a. \$218.21 b. \$3.21 c. \$1.84

20.24 \$6.85

CHAPTER 21

21.1 .3125 ± .0450

21.2 4.51; .81

21.3 4691.7; 419.4

21.4 5.99 ± .39

21.5 4762.05; 312.09

21.6 .54 ± .02

21.7 \$19.54 ± \$.69

21.8 .60 ± .08

21.9 11

21.10 142